THE INDEPENDENT CONSULTANT'S Q&A BOOK

Other Books by The Author

Cutting-edge Consultants:
Succeeding in Today's Exploding Growth Markets

Going Global: New Opportunities for
Growing Companies to Compete in Emerging Markets

The McGraw-Hill Handbook of
Global Trade and Investment Financing

Financing The Small Business

When The Bank Says No! Creating Financing
for Closely Held Businesses

Recession-proof Your Business

Tap The Hidden Wealth In Your Business

Buying In: A Guide to Acquiring
a Business or Professional Practice

Getting Out: A Step-by-Step Guide
to Selling a Business or Professional Practice

The Battle-Weary Executive: A Blueprint for New Beginnings

ADAMS

THE INDEPENDENT CONSULTANT'S Q&A BOOK

Lawrence W. Tuller

Adams Media Corporation
Holbrook, Massachusetts

Published by
Adams Media Corporation
260 Center Street, Holbrook, MA 02343

ISBN: 1-58062-105-8

Printed in the United States of America.

J I H G F E D C B A

Library of Congress Cataloging-in-Publication Data

Tuller, Lawrence, W.
    The independent consultant's Q&A book / Lawrence W. Tuller.
        p.   cm.
    Includes index.
    ISBN 1-58062-105-8
    1. Business consultants. 2. New business enterprises. I. Title. II. Title: Independent consultant's question and answer book.
    HD69.C6T854   1999
    001'.068—dc21   98-29180
                                                                         CIP

This publication is designed to provide accurate and authoritative information with regard to the subject matter covered. It is sold with the understanding that the publisher is not engaged in rendering legal, accounting, or other professional advice. If legal advice or other expert assistance is required, the services of a competent professional person should be sought.
    — From a *Declaration of Principles* jointly adopted by a Committee of the American Bar Association and a Committee of Publishers and Associations

This book is available at quantity discounts for bulk purchases.
For information, call 1-800-872-5627 (in Massachusetts, 781-767-8100).

Visit our home page at http://www.adamsmedia.com

Contents

Chapter 1

Getting Ready
How to Prepare to Start a Consulting Business

Q. Let's begin at the beginning. What is a consultant?

A. A consultant is anyone offering expert advice or opinions to another. Most people who hold themselves out as consultants charge a fee for this advice. In other cases, they contribute their advice without charging. Anyone who tries to earn a living as a consultant cannot afford to give away advice too many times.

Q. I have heard doctors, lawyers, accountants, engineers, architects, actuaries, psychologists, and many other so-called professionals call themselves consultants. Is it necessary to obtain a license to become a consultant?

A. That depends on what type of consulting you want to do. Theoretically, based on the common definition of a consultant, anyone selling "expert" advice is a consultant. State regulatory agencies control certain types of advice-sellers. Most of the "professionals" you mention must have licenses to be in the business.

Doctors, lawyers, dentists, psychologists, architects, and so on must be licensed to hold themselves out as experts. Public accountants, persons specializing in marriage, sex, or dating counseling, driving instructors, financial, estates, or tax planners, astrologers, spiritual healers, computer science consultants, human relations counselors, and those in a multitude of other personal service specialities may have the option of becoming certified by their peers or not, as they choose.

Q. What about management consultants? Are they licensed?

A. No. Management consultants may add some letters after their names, indicating certification by one of the management consulting trade associations, but this is not the same as state licensing. No state-issued exams are required. No controls over credentials exist. Anyone can hang up a management consulting shingle.

Q. What is a management consultant?

A. A management consultant sells business (management) advice to private- and public-sector companies and employees. Such advice ranges from how to run a company more efficiently to more specialized areas such as recruiting management personnel, arranging new financing, performing market studies, designing manufacturing systems, locating acquisition candidates, selling a company, developing an export program, performing engineering studies, managing tax planning, and conducting business start-ups.

Q. Why would a company hire a consultant?

A. Companies hire management consultants to solve management problems. They do this for any or all of these three reasons: company personnel do not have the expertise to solve the problem; company personnel have the expertise but do not have the time to devote to solving the problem; or company personnel have already come up with a solution to the problem and top management wants a second opinion to verify their findings.

A QUESTION OF COMPETENCY

Q. You said a consultant is anyone who sells "expert" advice or opinions. Does that mean you have to be an expert in a certain specialty to get into consulting?

A. If you mean by "expert" someone who ranks at the top of his or her field, such as the chief surgeon at John Hopkins Hospital, the commander of a space flight, or a five-star general, the answer is unequivocally no. Hubert Bermont states in his book, *The Complete Consultant* that "one of the 'secrets' of successful consulting is knowing more about your field than anyone else." This is simply not the case.

How many doctors pulling in $1 million a year are at the top of their field? One in one thousand? How many lawyers charging millions of dollars in fees are the top in their field? One in ten thousand? Conversely, how many practicing lawyers, doctors, and accountants are merely skillful at what they do and still make a very good living? The vast majority.

Contrary to what many practicing consultants would like us to believe, a person does not have to be an expert in anything to be successful in management consulting. But we do have to be competent and skillful at what we do. We must have enough training and knowledge gained through experience to know the difference between the right way to accomplish a management task and the wrong way. In other words, clients won't pay for advice unless they believe we know something about solving business problems *that they don't know.*

Q. What do you mean by training and knowledge? Do I have to go back to college to get some specialized degree?
A. Absolutely not. Training for management consulting has nothing to do with college or graduate school. Too many new graduates—business majors and MBAs—think textbooks and case studies train them to be management consultants. Nothing could be further from the truth. Yes, many take jobs with national consulting firms—A.T. Kearny, Booz-Allen & Hamilton, Arthur Andersen— and command high starting salaries, but they often don't have the vaguest idea what management consulting is all about.

When I speak of training I'm talking about specific, technical training in such areas as computers, biochemistry, accounting, mechanical engineering, and so on. If you intend to provide management consulting advice in these technical areas, you'd better have credentials to prove your ability to handle the job.

Excluding technical fields, no formal training is necessary. On-the-job experience, however, is essential.

On-the-job experience is probably the best way to gain knowledge in most management consulting specialties. Working in an overseas position with a company, learning a second language, and mastering a new culture, for example, are invaluable training for entering the international consulting field.

What qualifies a person to be a consultant to financially troubled companies? Perhaps the best qualification would be working as an executive for several companies in financial difficulty and being instrumental in turning them around. This type of experience will give you an accumulation of basic knowledge about specific management problems.

For twenty years before I began my consulting business, I held executive positions in troubled companies—first in divisions of some very large corporations (ITT, TRW, General Mills) and later as owner and manager of companies I acquired through LBOs. Not all were successfully turned around, but enough were to qualify me as a turnaround specialist, which became one of the specialties in my consulting firm.

Q. If I don't have to be "expert" in anything, what skills and talents *are* necessary to be a success in management consulting?

A. Years of training and a storehouse of knowledge do not necessarily lead to success as a management consultant. The secret is to be able to communicate and translate this knowledge into solving a client's problem. All successful management consultants have outstanding communication skills—both oral and written. One without the other isn't enough. We need the skills to explain things to clients and to translate recommendations into written reports.

Good communication skills are also the cornerstone of selling. And selling is the primary talent necessary in virtually any consulting specialty. If you can't sell, don't get into consulting. Do something else. Without outstanding selling skills you will bang your head against a stone wall trying to compete, and never come out a winner.

I can't emphasize enough the selling aspects of consulting. We constantly sell: first to establish a reputation, then to get clients. Later, we must sell to convince client personnel to implement recommendations. Still later, we must sell to bill and collect fees without angering the client. And finally, during the follow-up to an engagement, we use our selling skills to land additional work.

A good friend of mine was a vice president of engineering for a food processing company. After twenty years, he left to form a consulting business specializing in production scheduling, control, and efficiency in the food processing industry. Although technically qualified, he was a terrible salesman, preferring to let his credentials speak for him.

Despite his lack of sales acumen, he quickly landed two fairly large clients and thought he had it made. In two years, he lost both clients when they merged with larger companies. Try as he might, he couldn't land another client. He never did understand that he had to get out and sell, that his credentials only carried him so far, and that clients would not come to him. He had to go out and get them. My friend no longer has a management consulting business and has never understood why he failed.

Q. What skills other than communications and selling are necessary?
A. Persuasion is also critical. Consultants always play a comparatively passive role. We recommend, advise, suggest, and cajole. We do not make management decisions: that's left to client personnel.

To get anything accomplished in such a position, a person must have a high level of persuasive skill. Consultants should be convincing without being dogmatic, authoritative without being abrasive, tenacious without being obstinate, firm without being obnoxious, flexible without being indecisive, and likable without fraternizing.

The key is to get client personnel to implement our recommendations while believing that they originated them. Make them the heroes. Keep your ego to yourself.

BUSINESS OR PROFESSION—IT MAKES A BIG DIFFERENCE

Q. I have read other consulting books and spoken with consultants that consider management consulting a profession. Do you agree?

A. A profession is a vocation or occupation requiring advanced education and training, and involving intellectual skills. Professionals are accredited by some authoritative body—such as a state, the federal government, or a national trade organization that represents all members of the profession (the American Bar Association, the American Medical Association, and the like).

By these standards, consulting is a far cry from a profession. It is simply a business, like any other service business, and should be treated the same. Management consulting does not require advanced education. (In fact, it doesn't *require* any education.) It would be ludicrous to consider management consulting an intellectual pursuit. Consultants deal in hard, cold facts, solving problems for clients. They are not out to win Nobel Prizes.

Management consulting does not yet have a national organization representing all consultants. Several consulting organizations have tried to get started in this area, but none have progressed very far. There is no requirement to belong to one of these organizations, and in fact no need, except as an ego-builder. Membership won't buy you one client.

Q. How long does it take to become established in a management consulting business?
A. That depends on a variety of circumstances: the current and near-term projected state of the national economy; the choice of specialized market niches; competition; and most important, how aggressively a person goes after potential clients.

It's surprising to many people contemplating a consulting business that in economic downturns, whether in the whole economy or in a specialized industry, consulting falls off. One would think that during tough times consultants could do more good for clients than during good times. And that is true. The problem is that clients don't see it that way. When sales drop, and cash dries up, regardless of how much they may need consulting help, they tend to procrastinate until an upturn is in sight.

Of course, there are exceptions. Some industries seem to be immune to the economy—waste management, water purification, certain pharmaceuticals, and a few niches in the defense industry, for example. Other businesses tend to thrive when the economy is down: home remodeling, auto and equipment repair businesses, bankruptcy lawyers, and so on.

By and large, however, you should be prepared for downturns.

The choice of specific market niches, together with competition, either hastens business growth or hinders it. For example, certain consulting markets are booming and will be for the foreseeable future: international consulting, troubled company consulting, government contracting, and financing specialists.

An aggressive marketing campaign always shortens the time it takes to get established. Those who are willing to spend the money to advertise and promote, those who are capable of employing active selling techniques, will get clients a lot faster than others.

As a general rule of thumb, new consultants or those changing market niches should plan on three years as a reasonable start-up period. Not three years to get clients. Three years before you earn a living wage.

Q. If I am a management consultant, doesn't that mean my main focus should be on offering general management advice on how to run a company?

A. Most consultants think that they can run a company better than existing management. That's fine as long as they keep their opinions to themselves. Those who try to sell such advice to owners or managers don't get very far.

Every manager thinks he can run the company, or department, better than an outside consultant. The last thing they want is to hear a consultant say he can do a better job.

Nobody hires a consulting generalist anymore. That *was* done forty years ago, and it's still done to some extent in lesser-developed countries. But in the United States, Europe, and Japan, generalist consultants are either retired or on their way out the nearest door.

To sell consulting services, one has to be a specialist in something. The whole idea behind management consulting is to solve problems that client personnel either cannot or do not want to handle. These problems are always specific. And specific problems call for specific answers, from a specialist.

7

A good friend of mine who started a consulting business held himself out as an expert in "operations." I asked him what he meant by "operations." "Well, you know. Operations is running a company. I'm an expert in running companies." When no clients came running, it didn't take very long for him to change his tune.

CHOOSING THE RIGHT MARKETS

Q. What are the main types of management consulting, and which is the best field to get into?
A. There is no best consulting field to get into. What turns out to be the best for one person will be the worst for someone else. The choice depends on your experience, knowledge, personal lifestyle, and sales ability.

When looking for the right market, it helps to view management consulting in terms of the type of work clients typically demand.

I like to think that management consulting consists of two types of engagements: project work and general management work. Obviously they overlap each other, but most consultants are generally stronger in one or the other of these two areas.

Q. What do you mean by "project work" and "general management work"?
A. Project work includes such engagements as designing and installing a computer system, refinancing debt, restructuring a client's balance sheet, and overseeing business acquisitions and divestitures. Each project has a beginning and an end. It's easy for both the consultant and the client to determine the success or failure of the engagement. Additional engagements may or may not follow; generally they do not.

General management work is more nebulous. It might involve assisting clients to develop a strategic planning process, originate an export program, turn a troubled company around, start up a small business, or research and evaluate new markets, products, and customers. These assignments continue for relatively long periods, usually developing into new work over time. Engagements are open-ended: they extend into additional work.

When fitting market niches to your abilities, it's important to recognize whether they are project-oriented or general management-oriented and then judge your own likes, dislikes, and ability to handle each type of workload.

Q. What are the hottest markets now and for the next decade?

A. I believe management consultants who are willing to take a hard look at where they have been, why their business is faltering, and where they should turn will see enormous opportunities in a number of market niches that cry out for consulting specialists. Here is a look at some of the most exciting.

The most promising market today and for the foreseeable future is international consulting. Nearly all international business requires the use of consultants: sourcing joint venture partners, arranging countertrade deals, performing country surveys, identifying market and product demand, negotiating with foreign officials, and so on.

Within this broad market, sourcing and arranging trade finance, raising foreign direct investment capital, and setting up the administrative machinery of a foreign plant, project, or office is the highest-paid work and that which is most in demand—especially by American companies.

With an accelerating number of small and mid-size companies unable to meet high debt service payments, with banks drawing in their credit lines, and with the number of bankruptcies increasing annually, advising troubled companies is one niche that I predict will grow by leaps and bounds over the next few years. Since very few capable consultants have chosen this market, the demand for consultants far exceeds the supply.

More and more small and mid-size companies are taking on government contract work, and this trend will continue indefinitely as Washington searches for less expensive and more reliable contractors. However, most of these companies have never handled government contracts before and stumble repeatedly, losing substantial revenues, before they learn how to cope with the particulars of government work. Consultants willing and able to step into this niche will find more business than they can handle.

Environmental cleanup and protection has blossomed in recent years. Green business is in vogue and companies are beginning to feel consumer pressure to clean up their act. Once again, consultants with the know-how to help companies stay clear of the Environmental Protection Agency (EPA) and state regulators and make necessary changes voluntarily stand to gain substantial business.

Small businesses are starting up every day in every nook and cranny of the country. Nine out of ten entrepreneurs have no idea how to set up a company, raise working capital, plan tax strategies, manage the myriad of government regulations and reports, and handle all the other administrative details. Most entrepreneurs are either salespeople or inventory-producers. Very few know how to set up and run a company successfully. Small company consulting is an ideal place for new consultants to begin building a fruitful business.

Business acquisition and divestiture work (also called mergers and acquisitions, or M&A) is beginning to return, especially for smaller companies. Innovative financing instruments, creative merger or joint venture structures, and a variety of other changes, call for M&A consultants to lend a hand.

Designing and installing micro-computer network systems; strategic planning; research and development, market research, evaluation, and new product introductions; organization planning and employee motivation; and company refinancing and restructuring; all are booming consulting markets that will be around for many years.

RESEARCH AND EVALUATE

Q. How should I conduct my research activities to learn more about these hot consulting markets and the qualifications that are required to get in?

A. Broadly speaking, there are five different ways to research a new consulting market, all of which I have used successfully:

1. *Subscribe to trade periodicals in a specialty.* At least 20 high quality magazines and journals are available for international trade. Half-a-dozen monthly magazines are published dealing with troubled companies. Several M&A periodicals are currently on the market. In addition, the Small Business Administration (SBA) has shelves full of booklets for small businesses. Government contracting, strategic planning, and environmental periodicals seem to be everywhere. With a little digging, you'll find out which ones fit your specialty.

2. *Set up meetings* with bankers, lawyers, public accountants, local development agencies, state and federal trade agencies, and anyone else you can think of that could bring you up to speed about their views of changes in the marketplace.

3. *Meet other management consultants.* Ask for their perspective on the future of management consulting, what changes they see in their own markets, and what ideas or recommendations they might have for you. Some will refuse to answer, afraid you'll steal a client. But many will talk, as long as they know you just want their advice—nothing more.

4. *Join as many business organizations in your area as possible.* Learn what problems local companies are experiencing, how new government regulations and tax laws affect their business, and what economic changes they see in the future.

5. *Use local libraries* to research conditions in your chosen field. Public libraries are a good start. Department of Commerce libraries, found in many major cities, are better. University business school libraries are the best.

Q. I'm not sure my skills are current. Where can I get additional training to beef up my technical and consulting skills?

A. The same periodicals used for market research are excellent sources for learning about current developments in your specialty. Most people who have been around the business world for what seems like a lifetime tend to forget skills learned years earlier. Now is the time to stretch back, resurrect information from those first jobs or assignments, and dust off the old manuals, workbooks, and textbooks. (Reading trade periodicals is an excellent way to jog one's memory.)

The SBA is also a good place to take refresher courses. Most are free or very inexpensive. The teaching isn't all that great, but the subject matter is usually current. Community college and other adult evening school courses serve the same purpose but take longer.

I had held several corporate executive titles and operating general management positions when I started my consulting business. Although a practicing CPA in my younger days, I hadn't given accounting a thought for many years. I also had completely forgotten that in the early days most of my work was with small businesses. I took an adult evening school course in small business tax planning and had a few working sessions with a CPA friend, and I was soon ready to tackle both small business clients and accounting and tax assignments.

PUBLIC IMAGE

Q. I have heard from other consultants that the best way to establish credentials as an expert is to develop a public image. Is it a good idea to make the effort to do this before trying to penetrate new markets?

A. In over fifteen years as a management consultant, I have learned the hard way that without a favorable public image it is virtually impossible to develop new market niches, much less to start a consulting business from scratch. Most new clients enter the fold as a result of hearing about your reputation. I don't know of a better or faster way to develop a reputation than through image-building.

What is a public image? It's the perception that people have of your capabilities, honesty, and point of view. In consulting, the latter two seem to count as much as the first.

In addition to references from satisfied clients, the most effective public imaging techniques are those that identify you as an authority.

The key to becoming a public authority on a specific topic is to *tell people you are an authority*. To do this you need an audience— the bigger the better. Consultants have three favorite means of reaching public audiences: by writing, either books or trade journal articles; by speaking at public gatherings, dinners, seminars, classrooms, conferences, rallies, and so on; and by teaching courses at educational institutions (not necessarily famous ones).

I have used all three methods: writing (hardly a week passes without a letter or phone call from a reader), countless speeches at every conceivable type of professional gathering, and teaching.

Q. Other than becoming a public authority, how can I develop a good public image?
A. By taking a stand. Taking a stand is a little trickier than becoming an authority. By taking a positive position on a public issue—tax reform, deficit spending, abortion, environmental safety, the topic is immaterial as long as it relates to the specialty you are trying to sell—we also take a stand *against* something. Each controversy always has two sides.

By voicing an opinion on one side or the other, we inevitably alienate the other side. As long as the side we choose represents more potential clients than the one we don't, we are safe from a marketing standpoint. Obviously, it pays to research positions before barging ahead.

A person can take a public stand in several ways: run for an elected office (school board, planning commission, zoning board, etc.), write letters to the editor of a local newspaper, parade with activists, buy TV or radio time for a brief pronouncement of your views, and so on.

Q. Are there any other ways to build a good public image?
A. Yes. Become a supporter.

Becoming a supporter is a very safe way to go, although it is not as effective as becoming an authority or taking a stand.

Most people end up supporting some type of charitable cause inadvertently, simply because they believe in it. That's all well and good, but to establish a public image such support has to be made public. You might be a great Boy or Girl Scout leader, a marvelous Habitat for Humanity worker, or a great fundraiser for the United

Way or for your alma mater, but if that's as far as it goes, it won't help a bit in building your image.

For that you need publicity: local radio or TV coverage, commendation awards, public acknowledgments in a local newspaper, or trade journal, publicity shots. If you don't know how to arrange this, you might consider hiring a publicity agent. Publicity agents are relatively inexpensive and usually effective. When the publicity occurs, be certain the media mentions your consulting experience.

PLANNING THE BUSINESS

Q. What type of game plan should I put together to ensure success?

A. Management consultants are notoriously lax in planning the development of their own businesses. One reason is that they often really don't believe what they preach to clients. This is a deadly course. Smart clients always see through insincerity.

Some consultants get by without a game plan, but the successful ones won't take the gamble. Whether starting a new consulting business or changing to new markets, it only makes sense to lay out the steps that will lead us there, including the cost and the time it should take.

A game plan doesn't have to be any more formal than that designed by a football coach for next week's game. It should, however, be on paper so that it can be referred to from time to time to check on our progress. Key elements include:

1. A one-sentence description of market niches to focus on.
2. A one- or two-sentence description of the type of clients to go after.
3. A brief outline of advertising, promotion, and marketing approaches to attract clients.
4. Additional personnel, partners, or consortium members that will be needed.
5. A detailed marketing budget, including advertising and promotion expenses, travel expenses, research costs, and additional office expenses.

6. A projected series of milestone dates. Missing two or more dates probably indicates a need to revise the plan.

Q. Let's assume I make the effort to lay out such a game plan including dated milestones and projected costs. How much cash should I have on reserve to start a new consulting business or to develop new markets?

A. Using the three-year rule of thumb I mentioned earlier, the ideal situation is to have enough cash to live on for three years without generating any fee income. For most people, however, this is unreasonable.

It will be easy enough for you to determine personal living expenses. (If you can't do that, you're probably in the wrong business.)

When I consult to other consultants (which has become an increasing share of my business), and especially newcomers, I suggest budgeting on a sliding scale over a three-year period. Start with an estimate of annual hours available for consulting, normally 1,936 hours figured on a 40-hour week after deducting two weeks vacation and eight holidays. Next, break annual hours into six-month segments of 968 hours each.

When developing a new business (or a new market) nearly all hours are devoted to marketing of one form or another, which means no billable hours. This stage also requires a fair amount of administrative time in the beginning. Therefore, the first six months of a game plan could read:

	Available Hours	Marketing Hours	Administrative Hours	Billable Hours
First six months	968	726	242	-0-

By the second six-month period, marketing efforts should begin to pay off and a few clients should be on board, requiring a modest amount of productive time. The second six-month period projection might read:

	Available Hours	Marketing Hours	Administrative Hours	Billable Hours
Second six months	968	726	146	96

If the average billing rate is $100 per hour, this yields income of $9,600 during this period.

By the third six-month segment, billable hours should approximate 25 percent of the total, or 242 hours, which, at $100 per hour, generates income of $24,200. Administrative hours usually remain at about 15 percent, so the excess must come out of marketing time.

Billable hours during the fourth six-month segment frequently drop off, mainly because extra hours have been devoted to production work during the third segment with less time dedicated to marketing. Also, original marketing efforts have now been exhausted and new approaches are needed. Billable hours during this period might come in at 15 percent, yielding $14,500 in billings.

Billable hours during the fifth and sixth segments (the third year) should begin leveling out at a normal workload. In most market niches, a good rule of thumb for a sustaining client base is that marketing should account for about 35 to 40 percent of available time, administration 10 percent, and production 50 to 55 percent. At $100 per hour, a one-person consulting business should generate between $55,000 and $65,000 in fee income per year.

Obviously, if this isn't enough to live on, you should either increase the hourly rate or find another line of work.

Q. What about start-up expenses?
A. Projecting start-up expenses gets a little trickier. A lot depends on how much travel is involved in marketing, the content and extent of an advertising campaign, and what type of office you set up. Those are the biggest expenses, assuming you don't begin hiring unbillable people—a mistake during the start-up stage.

The amount of travel and advertising are directly dependent on market niches. Developing an international consulting business, for example, requires a much greater amount of travel, including overseas trips, than focusing on local small business work.

Project work such as systems design and implementation or environmental cleanup can easily require higher advertising and promotion expenses than government contract jobs.

Focusing on mergers and acquisitions work requires extensive telephone expense, computer equipment, and a high-tech office.

Marketing, travel, and office expenses should be budgeted for the same six-month intervals as available hours. It's obviously important to live within these budgets to avoid running out of cash. I usually recommend that, with the exception of extraordinary travel expenses, single consultants should estimate an expense budget of between $10,000 and $20,000 for the first and second years and about $10,000 to $12,000 for the third year, exclusive of cash paid for office furniture, office equipment, and salaries.

After the third year, marketing expenses usually decrease markedly as a larger client base develops and more out-of-pocket expenses are billed to clients.

Q. I can't believe that the hundreds of people beginning consulting businesses every year have $25,000 to $50,000 as a cash reserve! Are you sure it takes this much?

A. I'll answer that question from personal experience. I actually started a consulting business twice. The first time my wife devoted all her time to raising our two kids. We had $10,000 in the bank that we were willing to put into the business. Being a neophyte, I believed that all I had to do was hang out my shingle, join a few social clubs, run a couple of ads in the local paper, and clients would stream in. Not so. Nine months later I had billed a total of $1,500 to one small client. The $10,000 had evaporated. I returned to work as an employee for a large corporation.

Years later I started again. This time my wife had a good job and we had $60,000 to put into the business. While I concentrated on developing an international clientele, my wife went after part-time work with small business start-ups in the immediate area. After the first year I had spent $20,000 on travel, promotion, advertising, and entertaining—with two potential clients but no billable hours. My wife spent less than $1,000 on office expenses and billed out $5,000.

By the end of the second year, and another $10,000 in expenses, the international business caught on. By the third year, I had easily recouped my investment and was off to the races with more business than I could handle. The fourth year, we dropped the small business market.

Can you start a consulting business for less than $50,000? Yes. But it takes luck and the right choice of markets. Can you change market niches at less expense? Certainly.

A good friend of mine recently switched his consulting focus in this way. The change required expenses of less than $10,000 for two years. Two years and one month into his new specialty, my friend closed his first acquisition. With a single fee he recouped his investment and reported taxable income of over $165,000 the third year.

Q. It seems that a second source of income is probably the best insurance for staying in business. Is this a good way to go?

A. I always advise consultants, newcomers or established, as well as all other business start-up clients, that a second source of income is practically a necessity. Many consultants find that a spouse's income is enough to pay the rent and buy the groceries, at least for a while, even though it means lowering their standard of living temporarily.

Put off buying that new car, delay remodeling your home, put the new swimming pool on hold, and skimp on entertainment expenses. No one likes to cut back, but starting any business requires sacrifices. Consulting can provide a respectable income eventually, but it's a tough business to get started.

A second source of income relieves at least some anxiety and frees a person to devote full time and energy to building the business. I found this freedom gave me an extremely important psychological edge. Knowing that the family would survive, the rent would get paid, and the groceries would keep coming in, it was a lot easier to pick and choose the right clients and the right engagements.

Q. What about borrowing money to start the business? Isn't that another alternative?

A. If you find a bank willing to make loans to a start-up consulting business without collateral, let me know. I have been in the finance game for over thirty years and have never found one. Of course, if you don't mind taking a second mortgage on your home, or pledging pension entitlements, securities investments, or rental real estate, borrowing money is easy.

In the consulting business, however, this can be extremely risky. There is no fallback position. If the business doesn't build by the time borrowed money runs out, then what? And what about making debt service payments while trying to get started?

If management consulting was a "sure thing" business, with a very short start-up period, it would be a good idea to go ahead and risk a loan. But it isn't a sure thing and it does not have a short start-up period (unless you hit it lucky, like playing the slots at Atlantic City). Therefore, prudent financial management dictates that you stay away from the banks. Naturally, if a rich uncle wants to lend a hand, terrific.

Q. What type of brochure should I have? What type of business card format works best? And how should my letterhead look?

A. Brochures, business cards and letterhead are our primary, and least expensive, advertising tools.

Some consultants spend thousands of dollars on fancy three- and four-color brochures filled with photos and testimonials. This is usually a big mistake. Clients already know us and don't need a brochure. Potential clients look at a brochure once, and either file it away or toss it out. Most consultants eventually learn that spending a lot of money on a fancy brochure doesn't bring in clients and that the money could be better used for other, more effective advertising.

On the other hand, a modest brochure is essential. I recommend a simple black print, colored stock, one page, three-fold brochure.

A printer will charge $300 to $500 for 1,000 copies. You can design it yourself with desktop publishing software.

The content should be simple, and should spell out precisely what specialties are offered. It should also include a brief profile of your background and credentials.

An associate in my consortium decided to skip a formally printed brochure. He typed up a simple, three-fold page on his word processor and printed it on white resumé stock. When he hands it out he explains that the reason for its simplicity is that he is in the process of developing a new brochure that isn't quite ready. Potential clients love it. Several have told him they appreciate his not wasting money (and, indirectly, increasing fees) for the sake of a fancy brochure.

Use black, raised print on a flat white background for business cards. Nothing fancy. Just the name of the firm, your name, consulting specialty, phone number, and address. You should also include a fax number and e-mail address if available.

The same principle applies to letterhead: nothing fancy. Most prospective clients see expensive letterhead, business cards, and brochures as an extravagance, adding nothing to the consultant's ability. Use black print on 20-lb. white paper. Include the same information as on your business card. That's all.

During the fifteen years in my current consulting business, I have tried about everything to get clients, including fancy, expensive brochures, business cards, and letterhead. To my knowledge I have never landed a new client or kept an old client because of fancy logos, wording, or paper. Why spend money when you don't get anything for it? Better to focus your resources elsewhere.

Chapter 2

DON'T TRY TO FOOL THE CLIENT
How to Get Good Clients Quickly

Q. Why is it that many consultants try to fool clients about their abilities?

A. Without formal testing, licensing, or national certification, any fly-by-nighter can hang up a consulting shingle, and many do.

A good example occurred in the mergers and acquisitions field. In the late seventies and early eighties, reputable, competent mergers and acquisitions consultants performed a valuable service for entrepreneurs and smaller companies wishing to buy or sell businesses. They assisted them in locating buyers and sellers, they sourced appropriate financing, and they helped with company valuations and buy/sell negotiations. They performed a valuable service by helping clients get their companies ready for sale, and by following up with both buyers and sellers during the transition period.

Word got out about the high fees charged by M&A experts. Real estate agents, securities brokers, insurance salespeople, and the unskilled unemployed decided to join the feast. Business brokerages sprang up all over the country. Several franchises blossomed. People who otherwise couldn't make it in consulting chose the business brokerage route.

But without performance standards, most of these telephone brokers acted like unlicensed real estate agents, listing both companies for sale and buyers looking to purchase; *they never performed consulting services*. Many charged high fees, providing little if any service in return. Some ran off with retainers.

This gave the business a bad reputation. Many qualified consultants dropped out, chose other markets, and left the smaller acquisitions and divestitures to brokers. As a result, legitimate clients—both buyers and sellers—suffered.

Q. But what about consultants in other markets? Don't they also have a tendency to try to fool clients?
A. Unfortunately, yes. This is a disservice to clients and hurts the public image of management consulting.

The worst offenders are frequently new consultants trying to build a business. Panicked by a lack of clients, they try to sell any service a prospective client desires, without regard to capabilities. They get the job, bill monthly, stumble through the engagement, and leave a disappointed and disillusioned client.

Q. Don't established consultants do the same thing?
A. Yes, some do, especially when they see their business declining. Instead of conscientiously evaluating new, growing market niches to shift into, they try to milk existing clients for whatever fees they can get. Then they complain that management consulting is going to hell.

A much better way for both new and established consultants to increase their client base is to follow the direction of those who have already met and conquered the obstacles to getting new clients.

PRODUCTS AND MARKETS

Q. How do I get new clients?
A. The first step is to define clearly what you are selling, what specialty you are in, what work you can and cannot do, and what type of clients you want to attract. As we learned earlier, there is no such thing as "general management" in the consulting world. Generalists soon join the ranks of the unemployed, just like their cousins in industry.

Also, it doesn't take long to learn that we can't be all things to all people. Whether we are just beginning or already established, it's imperative to clearly and succinctly identify which product line or lines we want to sell. Clients want help solving specific problems. They don't want to be told how to run their business.

So what are we selling? First off, we sell ourselves. A person can be the greatest financier in the world, with thousands of solid contacts in financial institutions, but if a prospective client doesn't like the way you look or talk, you won't get hired to refinance the company. So the starting point is to dress up your appearance and polish our manners.

Next, we need to figure out what type of work we can do well and then develop appropriate credentials to convince clients of our competency. Maybe it's market research or personnel evaluations, engineering design or Environmental Protection Agency regulations, tax laws or strategic planning. Perhaps heavy experience in international finance or personal contacts in foreign government bureaus leads to international consulting. The strongest skills, talents, experience, technical qualifications, or personality quirks in your repertoire define what services you can sell.

And remember, the service being sold is advice: advice about correcting problems arising in one or more of these areas. Advice is the only service we have to sell. Management consultants sell business advice, engineering consultants sell engineering advice, and so on. And the only time clients will pay for advice is when they have a problem they can't solve themselves.

Q. So what makes consulting any different from other businesses selling advice, such as medicine and law?
A. Most business managers, engineers, salespeople, controllers, and so on already consider themselves proficient in their field. The techniques for selling problem-solving advice to these experts is entirely different from a doctor selling advice for curing appendicitis, or a lawyer selling advice for managing a bankruptcy proceeding.

Doctors and lawyers sell advice about matters we know little about. Consultants sell advice about matters we should know a lot about. Therefore, consultants must provide special knowledge: they must prove that they can solve a specific type of problem faster and cheaper than the client, even though the client knows a great deal already.

When all is said and done, we really sell intelligence. Intelligence about strategic planning procedures, intelligence about developing an export program, intelligence about staying clear of the EPA, intelligence about buying a company.

Q. Do I have to pick only one specialty or can I claim expertise in several areas?
A. If you have the skills it's always better to focus on more than one specialty. One narrows the market too much. But don't get too broad or a prospective client will never believe you. The "jack of all trades, master of none" syndrome can kill any sales pitch. Three seems to be a good number in clients' eyes.

Most management personnel have difficulty defining the problem they want solved. The higher they are in the organization, the more difficulty they have focusing. They can't see the trees for the forest. Offering three interrelated services that are broad enough to include problems that client personnel don't even know exist opens additional doors.

Q. I have heard consultants say that within ten minutes of an initial interview they can identify the client's major problem. If that's so, why not settle the issue right there, bill the client, and go on to the next job?
A. Because client executives won't believe you. They are having difficulty deciding how to achieve a specific result in their business. They expect you to analyze the situation thoroughly to come up with the right answer. Remember the law of cause and effect. Most clients become confused and identify the effect as the problem rather than facing up to resolving the cause.

Never divulge your opinion of the problem or its solution to a prospective client. They won't agree until you build a level of confidence. Let your spectrum of three skills bring the results.

When I go to a doctor with an ache in my side, she can probably immediately identify it as appendicitis, but I won't believe I need an operation until she examines me and runs a series of tests. Then I feel confident that she has analyzed the problem correctly. The same principle holds in consulting.

Q. What about the types of clients I want to attract. Isn't that important to define also?

A. It's crucial. The type of client you target defines what markets to go after.

Let's assume, for example, that your background includes many years in the publishing business and that you want to sell your skills in strategic planning. Publishing may not be the best industry to concentrate in forever, but it could be a good place to start. You probably already know most of the companies and have good contacts in some of them.

Or, with your linguistic ability and several years of business exposure in Europe recruiting management personnel, it may be logical to sell this type of service to clients that have foreign branches.

Or maybe you have managed divisions in financial difficulty and turned them around. This experience could be put to good use consulting to troubled companies, say in the health care, pharmaceutical, or medical equipment industries—or some other rapidly growing industry. (Just don't go after troubled company clients in a dying industry.)

The last point I want to make, and probably the most important, brings us back to trying to fool the client. Inexperienced, unhappy, or failing management consultants frequently make the mistake of not only misleading prospective clients about what type of work they are capable of doing, but also what industry experience they have had.

Don't get me wrong. I don't mean to imply that a person must have years of experience in the publishing industry to take on a publishing client. Nor do you need eighteen years as a production control manager in a manufacturing company to be able to service manufacturing companies. However, all of us have experience in one or more industries or types of businesses. We know that solving problems in manufacturing companies, for instance, takes a different twist than that required in retail establishments.

When trying to start a consulting business, or when branching out into new market niches, it's a good idea to stick with industries and types of companies we are familiar with.

If you have concentrated in manufacturing, don't try to fool prospective clients about being a retailing genius. If you have heavy experience in strategic planning or organizational development for Fortune 500 companies, don't try to convince entrepreneurs that you can handle small business engagements.

You may be able to do all these things, but your credentials don't prove it.

Q. So how do I go about getting clients?
A. If there were a simple answer to that question all consultants would be overworked millionaires. The facts are, however, that selling consulting services is a very tough job. Different marketing approaches work for different consultants, depending on a person's sales abilities, resources, and geographic location.

Furthermore, different selling tactics work for different types of clients. Different techniques apply for selling different types of services. Any consultant who advocates a "best" way to get clients doesn't understand the business.

Personal networking, cold calls, professional contacts, government bureaus, direct mail, trade groups, industry trade associations, and sub-contracting work are all viable avenues for landing new clients. Your specialty and background will help determine which path is right for you.

PERSONAL NETWORKING

Q. What is personal networking?
A. We all have friends, business associates, former employers or employees, or know people through social or civic organizations. Personal networking means letting each of these people know that

we are in management consulting, seeking work in a specific specialty, from particular types of clients. Asking these contacts for specific leads to individuals or companies is personal networking.

All of us have a cadre of people we either know well, know casually, or have barely met. Friends, relatives, ex-employers, people we have worked with, bankers we have known, and professionals (lawyers, accountants, engineers, architects) all make good referral contacts. Old Christmas card lists are a good starting place. So is that old file of business cards. College alumni rosters or yearbooks provide valuable names. We all have some means, formal or informal, of keeping track of those we have known over the years.

Personal contacts don't have to be in the business world. Doctors and dentists usually know a lot of people. So do college professors. Anyone who knows or remembers you well enough not to be embarrassed by your call is worth calling. The main idea is to let as many people as possible know what you do for a living and that you could use their help.

To be effective, personal networking must be a dedicated, well-planned effort. Networking takes many hours of telephoning, letters, and meetings, most of which produce nothing but renewed friendship. Still, on the chance that one person can help get a client, its usually worth the effort.

Q. How should I approach these people?

A. The primary rule in personal networking is *never ask the contact for work*. Your aim is a referral from your friend. Chances are very high that even if a contact has a need for a consultant with our qualifications we won't get the job, simply because of the prior association. This is especially true with close friends and relatives.

Here are a few other tips:

1. Ask for help, for advice about how to get leads. Everyone loves to give advice. Its boosts egos.
2. Don't spend too much time talking. If they can help they will tell you quickly. If they can't, ask them to think about it for a while and call back in a couple of weeks.

3. Follow up. Let the network know how you are doing. Schedule a regular series of calls, just to keep in touch. Chances are good that eventually leads will spring up.
4. Don't become discouraged. Networking is difficult, time-consuming, and, for many people, demeaning work. None of us likes to ask for favors. Experienced consultants usually find that the best they can do through networking is a 5 percent success rate. But that's 5 percent we wouldn't have without networking.

COLD CALLING

Q. Some people say cold calling is a waste of time. Is it?
A. People who say cold calling doesn't work either specialize in market niches where cold calls are inappropriate or doesn't have much sales ability. Many consultants find cold calling the best way to get clients. Others disdain the technique as below their "professional" status.

My philosophy has always been that I do what I have to do to get business. If that means cold sales calls, so be it.

Usually cold calling works best through a third party, such as bankers or lawyers when going after troubled company clients. These people generally have clients in deep financial trouble and welcome a competent consultant's help to preserve their own fees.

On the other hand, cold calling has never worked for me with international or mergers and acquisitions prospects. That's not to say it wouldn't work for you—but I have not been successful in these markets.

Q. What strategy should I use for cold calling?
A. The first step is research. The second step is more research. The third step is still more research.

The worst mistake is to make a cold call without sufficient background information about who is being called and what his personal needs are. When I get calls from securities or insurance salespeople, or other pushers, unless they have something interesting to say about my background and/or needs, I hang up in ten seconds.

I don't have the time to chat with strangers, and I suspect most other people don't either, although you'd never know it with all the frivolous calls being made.

In the beginning, like so many other new consultants, I thought that all I needed was a calling list of machine tool manufacturers with the names of the CEOs (which I purchased from a database service company). I started calling the "A's" on my list of 500 companies with sales over $50 million, asking to speak with Mr. so-and-so, the CEO. I reached several cordial telephone operators and secretaries, and on the forty-second call a company controller, but never a CEO.

That's when I decided to do some research.

Q. What type of research or preparation should I do for cold calls?

A. You should know the answers to three questions before picking up a phone:

1. What companies, or divisions, appear to need your expertise?
2. Who (that is, the name) in each company, or division, has the functional responsibility for solving the types of problems you handle?
3. What sales pitch will you make?

The last point needs some clarification. Cold call recipients want to know immediately who you are and what you are selling. One sentence describing yourself and a one sentence sales pitch is all the time you can expect to be allotted. If the conversation continues, then you can elaborate.

This means preparing a precise definition of your talents and product. If the conversation continues, you need another convincing sentence stating why the company needs your service.

Q. What is the next step?

A. If you don't get cut off, ask to whom you should speak in the organization to arrange a meeting to describe your services in detail. *Do not try to close an order on the phone.* I have never heard of it working, and it makes a person sound like a fast-buck artist.

Once a meeting is lined up, preferably with someone in authority, plenty of time should be available to make a formal presentation. Keep the presentation short and simple. Nothing elaborate. Just a simple, straightforward explanation of how you can help solve the company's problem, why you can do this better than anyone else, and how your credentials prove your expertise.

Unless the prospect demands an immediate explanation of how long the job will take and what the cost will be, leave these matters until the next meeting. If you are forced to the wall, give only a broad fee range, explaining that only by understanding the details of the problem more fully can you come up with a more specific price.

GETTING REFERRALS

Q. What sales techniques other than cold calls work best?

A. Most new clients in practically every market niche come through referrals. This means establishing contacts with third parties that work with the types of clients you want.

Q. What types of third parties?

A. Who they are depends entirely on the market niches you go after. In general, lawyers specializing in corporate law and those dealing with creditor/debtor matters are a good starting point. They often have clients who need help solving business problems. Since lawyers are notoriously poor businesspeople, they usually can't do much for clients in these areas. If their egos don't get in the way, and they frequently do, lawyers can be a good source of referrals.

Smaller and mid-size local public accounting firms nearly always have clients in need of consulting help. Unfortunately, public accountants often forget their primary mission and are tempted to offer consulting advice—often very bad advice. However, as with lawyers, if their egos don't interfere, public accountants can be excellent referral candidates.

Also, with increasing public attention drawn to potential conflict of interest audits, such as happened to two major accounting firms on the BCCI engagement, public accountants may be more anxious to pass off consulting jobs in the future.

Some of the best consulting referrals come through banks and other financial services institutions, such as finance companies, small investment banks, leasing companies, and venture capital firms. These sources, however, value confidentiality. Before turning over prospective client leads they will want to verify your references carefully.

Q. How important are references?
A. Without references it's nearly impossible to get referrals, unless they come from friends or former business associates. No one believes we can do a job simply because we tell them we can.

The best references come from former clients. Of course, when you're just starting out, such resources don't exist.

The second best references come from business professionals: public accountants, corporate lawyers, and/or other management consultants (but only if they have a recognized name).

Bank references help but are not always enough, unless of course your friendly banker happens to be the president or a very high official in a large regional or money center bank. Such a reference can earn many points.

Some consultants use references from executives in operating companies. I have found this effective only if the executive sports a well-known public image.

For government contract work, references from high officials in procurement offices, the Department of Defense, or other related government agencies carry a lot of weight.

References from senators and congressional representatives also carry weight when you are soliciting government jobs, especially if you are trying to attract government agencies as clients.

References from state and local elected officials and federal judges can be influential in some circles.

For markets in a tightly knit circle of companies, such as the aerospace industry, knowing industry trade association officers or Department of Defense bureaucrats often knocks down hurdles.

Smaller local firms lean heavily on references from officials in city or county trade groups or local development commissions.

Q. What is the best way to approach third parties to solicit referrals?
A. If you know the individual personally, just call and ask for help.

Strangers take a bit more tact. I have had excellent success using this script:

1. Call a high-ranking official of the company, bank, or professional firm from which you hope to get referrals and ask for a brief meeting, just to introduce yourself. Bear in mind that these people get bombarded with requests from consultants looking for client leads. It may take many calls to finally get an appointment.
2. At the first meeting don't ask for direct leads. Keep it light and airy. Find out about their business and position first. Ask what is bothering them.
3. Keep the meeting short, not more than ten minutes.
4. Tell them about yourself just before the meeting ends. Ask if you can leave your brochure.
5. As you walk out the door—*then* ask for leads. The response is nearly always that nothing pops into mind, but that they will keep your brochure for future reference. Make sure you include a business card with the brochure—clipped to the *outside*. This should be in addition to the card you handed out at the beginning.
6. Follow up with a letter—the next day—thanking the person for taking time for the meeting.
7. Follow up with a phone call in two weeks. In another two weeks. And in another two weeks. If leads don't materialize after a follow-up letter and three follow-up phone calls, forget about it. Go on to another potential source.

DIRECT MAIL SOLICITATION

Q. How about using direct mail solicitation? Does this work for consultants as well as it does for selling other products and services?

A. Yes and no. We have to separate direct mail solicitation, which is a direct, positive request for work, and direct mail advertising, which is indirect and passive. Solicitations can be further segregated between mailings to prospective clients—the most positive, direct approach—and mailings to third-party intermediaries. Both can be very effective if done properly. Both can also fail miserably without careful preparation. The effectiveness of direct mail solicitations depends directly on the market niches.

Q. How should I prepare a mailing to prospective clients?

A. Start by preparing a very definitive prospect list of company names and addresses along with the names of the key executives. This list may include as few as fifteen or twenty names, or it may extend to several hundred.

The criteria for inclusion should be only those companies located in the geographic area you want to serve, of the size you can handle, and in your industry or market. This is not the time to shotgun a direct mailing to every business regardless of size, location, or industry.

One example of how to focus a mail solicitation was employed successfully by a consultant in my consortium who wanted to focus on start-up businesses. Every week the local newspaper listed names and addresses of start-up businesses derived from state registration files, including a brief description of the business.

Every week the consultant mailed a solicitation to each of these businesses located within an easy commute of his office. His one-page letter described his services, fee structure, and credentials. He also enclosed a brochure. Over a six-month period, inquiries averaged 10 percent per week. He landed about half of these as clients.

This is an excellent success ratio for mail solicitations. Most consultants figure that a 6 to 7 percent inquiry return and a subsequent 15 percent capture rate represents a successful campaign.

Q. How long should I keep at direct mailings to determine if the approach works for me?

A. This type of pin-pointing solicitation takes at least six to nine months to prove its worth. The more definitive the mailing list, the more must be mailed out, and the longer the time frame. The first five or six mailings might bring no results, but the seventh might produce several inquiries. You never know which will hit.

Q. What type of letter should I use to solicit clients directly?

A. That depends on a person's background, consulting specialty, market audience, and writing ability. I have used several different types of letters, each geared specifically to the audience I was trying to reach. They all consisted of the same information, but the format and writing style varied.

Here is a sample of the type I used to solicit export work. The prospect listing was derived from the roster of attendees at an export management conference sponsored by one of the Big 6 accounting firms.

Fig. 2-1

Dear Mr._____:

I hope you benefited as much as I did from the Latin America Export Opportunities Conference on May 6-7. It certainly substantiated that the door to Latin markets is beginning to open wide.

One critical element for financing exports to these markets was only briefly acknowledged: countertrade.

While many companies have taken years to develop expertise for arranging and managing countertrade contracts, other new-to-countertrade exporters suffer huge losses. Unfortunately, Latin markets are nearly impossible to reach without using countertrade techniques.

The enclosed brochure highlights the experience of our firm in helping exporters through the countertrade maze. In addition, with access to a network of local Latin American consultants, attorneys, and government bureaucrats standing ready to help American exporters identify customers and assist in distribution and government licensing, our firm is a valuable adjunct to your export management staff.

Return the enclosed postcard or give me a call and I will personally meet with you or your export managers to provide further information on how we can help.

Thank you for your interest.

Sincerely,

I continued mailing this solicitation to attendees at four other export conferences/seminars during the course of a year. The success rate was so high I added two countertrade specialists to my network.

Q. What about using direct mail solicitations to third-party intermediaries?

A. Results from intermediary solicitations are not as dramatic as the direct approach, although under certain circumstances can be effective. The idea is to look for referrals, as we discussed earlier, not clients.

Some bankers, lawyers, public accountants, and so on, prefer mail solicitation to interrupting phone calls. For my part, I flatly refuse to talk with anyone using telemarketing. On the other hand, many mail solicitations receive at least one glance. If it looks like something I'm interested in, I'll sit down and read the whole pitch, and maybe even respond.

A good consulting friend takes the opposite approach. He seldom reads mail, but enjoys fencing on the phone. He has been very successful in using third-party cold calls to round up referrals. He also tried direct mailings, with zero success.

Intermediary mail solicitation is a hit-or-miss proposition, just like cold calls. You'll never know whether it works unless you try.

I suggest the same non-pushy approach you'd use for cold calls. Don't ask for leads, just an appointment.

SUBCONTRACTING

Q. Other than cold calls, referrals, and mail solicitations, are there any other ways to get started in a new market?

A. One of the fastest ways to start a consulting business or to branch out into new markets is to subcontract work from other consultants. You don't make as much money as on your own, but at least it helps pay the rent until your own client base gets developed.

Other benefits also accrue.

1. A cadre of consultants can be developed to use as a consortium or network in the future.

2. The ins and outs of a new market can be learned from on-the-job training.
3. Leads can develop from the client's external advisors—bankers, lawyers, accountants—and from the client's suppliers and customers.

Q. Doesn't the fear of losing clients prohibit consultants from sub-contracting work to other consultants?
A. In some cases. If a consultant isn't sure of client loyalty or is scratching for new clients, he will never subcontract work—even if it means losing billable hours.

Most consultants with an established client base, however, know their own limitations. It's less risky to subcontract a job out and make a smaller incremental fee than to lose the client completely. More work may be forthcoming in the future.

Also, the specific assignment might not be in one's repertoire of abilities. As a manufacturing and service industry specialist I seldom take on retail clients. Yet, if I can get work refinancing a retail business I'll take it. If later on, another assignment develops from the same client—one that calls for revising the store's inventory system, for example—I wouldn't hesitate to subcontract the work to a consultant in my network.

Q. How do I get subcontracting work?
A. The best way is to network with local consultants, preferably those with complementary, not competitive, talents or specialties.

Low-key mail solicitations introducing yourself and letting them know your background usually brings results. So do cold calls. Meeting other consultants at trade conferences, seminars and shows is another good way to make introductions and exchange business cards.

Here are four tips for getting subcontract work:

1. Let other consultants know you are available for work but don't ask for it directly.
2. Let them know that when jobs arise that you can't handle, they will be brought in. Tit for tat, as it were.

3. Push hard to remain an independent consultant when taking a subcontract assignment. Don't go to work for another consultant as an employee. That trap is hard to get out of.
4. Strive for ongoing relationships within a network or a consortium.

Q. How do I get paid as a subcontractor?
A. Negotiate an hourly rate with the consultant. Remember, he has to make a profit on the job, so the rate might have to be lower than normal.

Although some consultants allow subcontractors to bill clients directly, most do not. The hiring consultant does the billing and collection, then pays subcontractors.

Q. Is there any value in taking non-consulting jobs from professionals such as public accountants, lawyers, engineers, or financial planners as fill-in work?
A. When you are beginning a new business, or when your existing business base is low, it only makes sense to earn income any way you can, without jeopardizing a long-range strategy. If this means taking on non-consulting assignments, so be it.

When I began my first consulting business I had a terrible time getting clients. My savings shrunk. Bills piled up. Panic set in. As an ex-practicing CPA it wasn't difficult to get tax return work from two public accounting firms in the area. For four months I gritted my teeth and filled in 1040s, at slave wages.

Should you take non-consulting, off-load work? When you're fighting for survival, any income is better than none.

Q. Does this ever result in getting new clients?
A. Surprisingly enough, the answer is sometimes yes. When I lowered my sights and prepared tax returns, three small businesses—a gas station, a jewelry store, and a co-op farm elevator—engaged me to do small consulting jobs. It wasn't much, but it was a start.

Don't expect to get clients this way, though. The odds are against it.

Before starting my second consulting business I worked with a manager at ITT who left the company before I did. He was a highly qualified mechanical engineer who had decided to start a consulting business. Running into the same brick wall that I did years earlier, he took some off-load drafting work from a local environmental engineering firm. Six months later the work ran out, and he solicited consulting work from the environmental firm's clients. Not one came with him. Several of his clients complained about this unethical practice. Be sure you do not diminish your long-term income potential by earning a reputation as an unethical person.

FOLLOW-UP

Q. I have several clients I don't want to lose. There is a good possibility for additional work from all of them. I've been following up with phone calls and letters; one finally called me back and asked me to stop pestering him. When there was more work he'd let me know—maybe. How do I get around this problem?

A. Staying in touch with prior clients is one of the best ways to get additional work, assuming prior jobs were satisfactorily completed. Once clients become comfortable with a consultant they are apt to request additional advice, perhaps in areas unrelated to the first engagement. Some consultants try to ensure this by negotiating a monthly retainer, but without an immediate need this wastes a client's money.

A much better way is to stay in touch informally, by phone or letter or both. Social events play a major role in developing sound client relations: keep in contact by inviting them to a ballgame, cruise, golf game, concert, or occasional breakfast, lunch, or dinner.

A similar principle holds for following up leads to new clients. A single call or mail solicitation generally does not bring a client into the fold. They want to be romanced a bit, made to feel important. This can be done periodically, and very gracefully, with a short phone call to ask how the business is doing, a Christmas card with a brief message, or a newsletter or other communique.

I have found that prospective clients, as well as those already signed up, like to receive my periodic mailing of a one-page newsletter providing current news in international markets. Other techniques work equally well.

By the same token, consultants who make pests of themselves don't stay in business long. If the client was satisfied in the past and another engagement comes up, you will likely be called upon. If not, you won't be. The same holds true for getting new clients. Once the contact has been made, obnoxious follow-up calls or letters won't get the job done.

While sustaining regular contacts is a critical part of client relations, such follow-up should be done gracefully and tactfully. The worst follow-up approach is to ask for work. Follow-up should be cordial. It should be short and to the point. And it should be regular. Bluntly asking for work hardly ever works. If it does, the client probably isn't worth having in the first place.

Chapter 3

BLOW YOUR OWN HORN
How to Structure Advertising and Promotion Programs that Work

Q. For decades, lawyers, public accountants, doctors, dentists, architects, and other professionals were afraid to advertise. Now they spend millions on it every year. Why haven't consultants picked up the ball and joined in?

A. Since the beginning, national organizations—such as the American Bar Association, the American Medical Association, and the American Institute of Certified Public Accountants, to mention only a few—preached that advertising was "unprofessional." If lawyers, doctors, public accountants, and so on, were caught advertising, their licenses could be revoked.

As competition increased and the fees of giant law firms, accounting firms, and medical clinics plummeted, the various professional associations suddenly decided that advertising wasn't unprofessional after all, and the bonanza began.

Management consultants, meanwhile, without representation from a national trade association, without a standard-setting body, without licensing of any kind, and in fact without any consensus on the definition of consulting, continue to think of themselves as "professionals," obeying long-outmoded rules that stamped advertising as unprofessional behavior.

On the other hand, since no laws or regulations prohibit advertising, a few (mostly local) firms have begun to blow their own horn. Lo and behold—many find a marked increase in their business!

If you are not worried about being called "unprofessional," advertising, along with its twin sisters, publicity and public relations, are excellent ways to develop a public image and thus increase a client base. On the other hand, you should bear in mind that an advertisement is not a magic wand that will automatically produce clients for you.

Q. How should I combine advertising, publicity, and public relations to get the biggest bang for my buck?
A. The best combination depends on two factors: (1) how much money you have to spend, and even more important, (2) what market niche you are going after.

You have to decide the first. I can provide some guidelines for the second. Let's begin with advertising.

In the consulting business, advertising is normally used to broadcast the services offered and why you can perform them better than competitors. Various media forms are used.

To be effective, advertising must target a specific, definable market and then choose the media that provides the broadest possible coverage of that market.

Some consulting markets respond well to direct advertising, providing it is tastefully presented. Prospective small business clients react well to local advertising. It has to be local because these companies are local.

Prospective clients for certain segments of international consulting such as countertrade assistance, FSC management, transport brokerage consulting, and joint venture coordination, frequently have no idea where to locate specialized talent. They may turn to national advertisements for ideas.

On the flip side, advertising in other consulting markets seldom produces *any* concrete leads. Strategic planning, organizational development, systems analysis, refinancing, and restructuring are a few examples.

Q. What are publicity and public relations?

A. Publicity and public relations really go hand-in-hand for consultants. The intent of both is to create a public image of the firm as a reputable company and consultants as knowledgeable and capable. This type of public imaging is similar to that described earlier for establishing personal credentials.

Publicity and public relations extend beyond a narrow market and attempt to favorably influence the attitude of broad public segments. The two are often lumped together as "promotion."

Promotion in one form or another is necessary for all management consultants regardless of their specialty. Keeping one's name in the public eye is vitally important to broadening a client base. The more visible you are, the better. It's equally important to build a public reputation that emphasizes strict adherence to honesty, confidentiality, and high work standards.

Some consultants abhor promotion of any type. They don't even carry business cards. Their rationale is that by staying out of the limelight their reputation for confidentiality will be improved. I disagree with this as a general principle, but it does work for some people in some markets.

Q. What type of advertising do you recommend?

A. It depends on the market niche and on your monetary resources. There is no "best" combination for everyone. However, we can take a look at several advertising methods that have proven helpful to consultants over the years.

One cardinal principle in consulting advertising is that it must be tasteful, low-key, and create the image of high-class work. Loud, brassy advertisements are a no-no. Cute, sexy ads are *verboten*. Hard-sell advertising, such as that used by automobile dealerships, should be avoided at all costs.

It's important to remember that your audience is comprised of business executives and professionals. Most are intelligent, well-educated, and like to think of themselves as first-class citizens. They do not respond well to sleazy ads using hard-sell tactics. And, as we discussed in the previous chapter, they do not appreciate being misled.

Make the ad upbeat. Make it concise. And above all, make it truthful.

Q. What type of information should be included in an advertisement?

A. The first steps are to identify the specific audience you are trying to reach, the precise message you want to convey, and the nature of the response you hope to get.

As we discussed earlier, advertising defines services offered for sale and persuades the audience to buy from you rather than competitors.

Two approaches can be used. The positive approach employs a variety of display methods that illustrate one or more services. It also employs persuasive techniques to convince audiences that they need these services.

The negative approach emphasizes price, convenience, and your unique expertise compared to the competition. The idea is to persuade the audience to shun competitors and buy from you.

Consultants seem to shy away from the negative approach, once again deeming it "unprofessional." But lawyers use it, public accountants use it, and health care professionals use it. Why shouldn't consultants?

Politicians have learned that although issue positions are certainly important reasons for choosing one candidate over another, the public responds much more strongly to advertising that documents the shortcomings of the opposition.

When you are trying to get established in a highly competitive market niche, negative ads might be the only feasible way to attract attention. When choosing this route, don't be afraid to name competitors. Explain why you can do a better job, at a more reasonable price, in a more efficient manner. This is a dog-eat-dog business. Given a chance, your competitors would cut you down to size as well.

Whether positive or negative advertising seems more appropriate, the content of the ad should be similar. Include the firm name, address, phone number; your name and credentials; and a brief description of the services. Beyond that, technique takes over. The audience determines which persuasive tactics get the message across best.

USING AN ADVERTISING AGENCY

Q. Should I hire an advertising agency to handle the work for me?

A. First-time advertisers using various media or attempting to get a particularly complex point across may benefit from utilizing a small advertising agency. Such experts usually do the job faster, less expensively, and more effectively than amateurs. I say small, because I see no need to pay three and four times the price for big city agencies. (Most big agencies won't take small clients anyway.)

The size of the agency isn't as important as the talent and experience of its principals. One item to watch for, however, is the extent to which the agency uses sub-contractors. Advertising involves several skills: design and layout, written copy, typesetting and/or graphics, media coordination, and perhaps printing and assembling. A quality agency should do everything except full-color printing on its own. Subcontracting increases the cost and frequently lowers the quality.

It's also important to feel comfortable working with an agency every step along the way. Allowing the agency to take any of the above steps without your approval inevitably increases costs. It's also a sure way to get an unsatisfactory product. Regardless of the agency chosen, it's important to stay on top of every step and let the principals know that it's your ad, not theirs.

After running a few ads, you will find that it doesn't take long to catch on to what works and what doesn't. From that point forward, most advertising can be done less expensively, faster, and better *internally*. A strong desktop publishing software package and a first-rate copier are essential.

MEDIA

Q. I know that companies use a variety of media to get their message across. Which ones work the best for consultants?

A. Media can generally be grouped into four categories: broadcasting (radio and TV), newspapers and magazines, trade shows, and direct mail.

The choice of media relates to the location and breadth of the audience (local, regional, national, international), the amount of money available, and a person's communicative talents.

For example, an accomplished public speaker can use a TV commercial on a local cable channel to get into the homes of small business owners. For substantially more money, a network affiliate provides broader coverage. If you do well on the telephone, radio ads on network business shows tap a sizable auto commuting market. On the other hand, trade magazine ads reach a national or international audience. Local newspaper ads hit a local audience. The *Wall Street Journal* or *Barron's* reach a more upscale, but wider readership.

Advertisements in national publications are very expensive, however, and unless a firm is already well established, local advertising probably results in the best coverage for the money.

Q. How do I lay out a magazine or newspaper ad without spending a lot of money?
A. Formats vary. Some consultants prefer full page ads with a clip-out coupon that readers can remit for more information. Most, however, stick to small quarter, eighth, or sixteenth-page ads. I've used this very small format for advertising in the *LA/C Business Bulletin*, a monthly publication covering Caribbean and Latin American business and published in cooperation with the Department of Commerce and USAID. This ad ran for three months and resulted in four new clients.

Fig. 3-1

INTERNATIONAL FINANCIAL CONSULTING

ZYX-VU, Ltd., offers international financing services to small and mid-size companies trading or investing in the Caribbean and Latin America. This U.S. based firm specializes in coordinating U.S. and foreign government sources, multilateral and bilateral agencies, development banks, and multinational and local banks to arrange trade finance and direct investment funding.

Contact: Mr. XXX, President
Box XXX, Southeastern, PA 19399
(215)xxx-xxxx; Fax: (215)xxx-xxxx.

Here is a sample of a very effective ad for a local weekly newspaper aimed at small businesses.

Fig. 3-2

RESKE & TOMAS
Management Consultants to Small Business

Stop the IRS from robbing you blind
Protect your business and personal assets from creditors
Control your markets

For 15 years RESKE & TOMAS has helped small businesses. Specialists in tax and estate planning, market/product analysis, and market control tactics, this premier SMALL BUSINESS consulting firm can make your business profitable and put you in control of your growth curve.
Call one of our principals today for an appointment:

Richard Reske   Paul Tomas   Kathleen O'Brien

RESKE & TOMAS
10000 Landow Road
Blandon, Pennsylvania 17632
(717) 123-9876

OTHER ADVERTISING METHODS

Q. Can you give me some ideas for attracting clients in a specific industry other than advertising in trade journals?

A. Consultants focusing on a specific industry—machine tools, publishing, toys and games, farm equipment, food processing, and so on—have successfully attracted clients through participation in trade shows. A large, fancy booth is not necessary—in fact, it's often not even desirable. The approach should be the same as with other advertising mediums: keep it simple, keep it tasteful.

Sharing a booth with complementary businesses—banks, insurance agencies, law firms—keeps the price down and provides the same exposure as having a private display.

One consultant who specializes in companies that manufacture, distribute, and charter pleasure boats regularly shares a booth at the annual trade shows in Annapolis and Miami. Over the years he has shared space with a variety of small service businesses but claims the best results occurred when sharing with a bank or finance company. He sits at a small table stocked with his brochure, a one-page advertising flyer, and a return postcard. He claims that the latter generates an average of fifteen to twenty inquiries per show. Of these inquiries he lands about five to ten clients. Not a bad ratio!

Q. Any other advertising ideas that won't bankrupt me?

A. I tried an approach one year that worked reasonably well. At the time I was trying to establish a secondary business to provide consulting services to small and mid-size companies interested in setting up a foreign sales corporation (FSC) in one of several qualified Caribbean island states. It seemed that the best way to reach prospects was through one of the FSC conferences sponsored by Chase Manhattan, Price Waterhouse, and other large financial service organizations.

I chose a three-day St. Thomas conference sponsored by Chase. Not only did this provide a welcome brief vacation, it gave me a chance to hand out brochures and business cards to company representatives that already had an interest in my services. The entire scheme cost $1,850, including handouts, but it did net me two new clients.

Indirect advertising is also a low-cost way to get your name in front of prospective clients.

Q. What is indirect advertising?

A. Indirect advertising means getting your name and your company name on qualification lists provided to clients by third parties. This costs virtually nothing. Although it isn't as forthright as direct advertising, such qualification lists provide entree that competitors might not think of.

Examples of a few major organizations that qualify consultants for recommendation to members or customers are: the World Bank of the United Nations, the Department of Commerce, Department of Defense procurement offices, the various departments of Eximbank, and the Inter-American Development Bank (along with its subsidiaries).

For consultants involved in international trade of any type, it also helps to send a recap of credentials to local export development organizations and the transactional non-bank financing organizations, such as MTB Bank in New York. More information is available from the International Trade Administration in Washington, D.C.

DIRECT MAIL ADVERTISING

Q. Does direct mail advertising work?

A. I have never had much success with this medium. Neither have any consultants in my consortium.

On the other hand, I have known consultants who swear by direct mail. They claim this as the only cost-effective way to reach a narrow audience. Others decry direct mail as too passive, a waste of brochures, and, with postal rates continuing to escalate, too expensive.

Direct mail advertising seems to work fairly well for narrowly defined markets in certain parts of the country. For example, targeting companies within a small radius of your office—such as a county or city—that already use and need the type of services you offer keeps the mailing list to a minimum number. Consultants in rural areas or small cities with a limited number of businesses frequently find direct mail the only feasible way to make direct contact with prospective clients.

Q. What should be included in a direct mailing?
A. Earlier we talked about using mailings as a direct solicitation for work. The key there is to pinpoint your targets. Such a highly focused pitch is directed to a very selective list of prospective clients or third-party referrals. Mailings are generally small and appeal to one specific need of the recipient.

Direct mail advertising takes on a different flavor. In this case the mailing list can be expanded to a wider geographic area, to larger (or smaller) prospects, and can include descriptions of a firm's complete range of expertise—not merely one specialty.

The copy should not include a request for work. The purpose of the mailing is to alert prospects of the special services offered. It should very briefly describe the credentials of partners in the firm—but only in one or two sentences. The main thrust is to grab the recipient's attention enough to ask for more information.

A favorite response technique utilizes a return post card, pre-stamped and addressed, enclosed with the mailing.

The mailing should consist of a one-page, eye-catching description of services and one or two short sentences explaining credentials. Include a business card.

A brochure could also be included, although this is often a waste of money because of the sparse response. I have found it more effective to send a brochure only to those responding for more information.

Don't expect a massive response from direct mailings. One inquiry for every fifty mailed out is very good. Of course, every inquiry should be followed up; first with another brief personal letter and brochure, then with a phone call asking for a meeting.

A PROMOTION PACKAGE

Q. Other than advertising, what steps bring in new clients?

A. The other half of an effective public exposure program is promotion. For most consultants, a well-planned, continuous promotion program brings in far more clients than advertising. In many cases, consultants decide to forego advertising completely in favor of an emphasis on promotion. In the early going, this may be the best course. But I emphasize "well-planned" and "continuous."

As described earlier, an effective promotion package consists of a dynamic publicity program and a vigorous public relations campaign. The two go hand-in-hand. It's virtually impossible to marshal one without the other.

To be cost-effective, any promotion package must be well-conceived and measured. A scattershot approach doesn't work. Nor does an occasional appearance at a local Chamber of Commerce dinner. For years, consultants have debated the structure of promotion campaigns and the coordination of promotion and advertising with production work. However, no one debates the *wisdom* of promotion.

Q. How do I measure the effectiveness of the campaign?

A. Measuring the effect of promotional efforts on a business is at best difficult: at worst it is impossible. Yet without some way to measure benefits against expenditures—either in money or time—it's impossible to judge what brings in business and what is merely socializing.

One measuring technique that I have used is to query new clients about where and how they learned of my firm. Many are more than willing to tell me, although comments such as "I heard about you from a friend" are as common as they are frustrating. When I ask how the friend heard about my firm I get a blank stare or "I have no idea." Still, the positive responses we do get help select the promotion schemes to emphasize.

Not infrequently, the source of new clients is obvious; perhaps an introduction at a Rotary meeting, a seminar, or at the local PTA. It pays to keep track of where new clients come from. You can end up saving a lot of time and money.

Q. What do you mean by "continuous" promotion? How do you find the time?

A. Success in any service business, and especially consulting, calls for constant selling efforts. One never knows where new business will originate; an overlooked opportunity means lost income.

It won't do to overtly push our consulting expertise with everyone we meet, all the time. Being an obnoxious pest may sell cars, but it certainly doesn't sell consulting services. On the other hand, if people don't know what we do for a living and therefore cannot recognize our expertise, we will never get any business. Therefore, I promote my business in a tactful and professional manner whenever I am in public and recommend others do the same. That's what I mean by continuous promotion.

Q. I have heard that the most effective promotion efforts result from becoming a joiner. Do you agree?

A. Personally I dislike belonging to social, civic, or business organizations simply for the sake of belonging. I find their meetings boring, time-consuming, and of little use to my business. Membership in many (although certainly not all) of these organizations consists of other consultants, lawyers, public accountants, doctors, dentists, insurance agents, real estate agents, and therapists, all trying to solicit business, and caring little for the purpose of the organization.

Many other consultants find organizations a lucrative source of clients. One member of my consortium especially likes Rotary, Kiwanis, and similar civic groups. She believes in their social missions and takes active roles whenever possible.

One day we chatted about the business benefits of joining. She claimed that she gets so many new clients through this avenue that she has completely stopped advertising and seldom spends time on other promotional efforts. She specializes in setting up and monitoring administrative activities—insurance, accounting, tax planning, investments—for health care professionals. Maybe that explains her success as a joiner.

Q. What organizations do you recommend I join?

A. I like business organizations: the Chamber of Commerce, local development councils, export and international trade groups, and local chapters of similar business-oriented associations.

I also find community organizations in education, crime prevention, and mental health to be quite accessible, with membership comprised of a cross-section of business, political, professional, and educational people. Not only do I believe in the mission of such groups, I find active members very interested in my consulting specialties—especially the international side.

In addition, I have obtained several clients from participation in international activist groups such as Greenpeace, Amnesty International, and the Rainforest Action Network.

I stay away from professional organizations for accountants, lawyers, health care workers, actuaries, and engineers. I find organizations specifically geared to consultants a waste of time and money.

PUBLICITY

Q. How can I promote my business in a broader sense?

A. That's where the publicity part of a promotion package comes in. The purpose of a formal publicity program is to promote your name and credentials to a wide audience. The emphasis is on showing the public what a terrific consultant you are and how well-versed you are in your specialties. A formal publicity program accomplishes the image-building we discussed earlier, but on a much larger scale.

Q. What about TV and radio publicity? How does this differ from advertising through the same media?

A. Both TV and radio are terrific mediums to reach wide audiences, providing a person gets on the right stations in the right time slots.

To be effective, a publicity program must take advantage of our strong points and play down our weaknesses. This must be done in such a manner that it doesn't sound like we are blowing our own horn too loudly. In other words, at least in the consulting business, publicity should utilize subtle selling to a broad audience, as opposed to a hard-hitting advertising campaign that targets very specific market groups.

Compare, for example, the two different approaches to TV exposure. Advertising on TV consists of purchasing a time slot and displaying a short, provocative message, directed exclusively to a specific audience that one hopes is watching.

An effective TV publicity stint might get you on a talk show, answering questions from the host, aimed at the entire viewing audience. The question-and-answer session might cover a very narrow topic, but usually it is broad enough to interest all viewers. The show might last for half an hour, or a full hour, allowing plenty of time to develop a pitch and project an authoritative image without appearing too terse.

The same comparison can be made for radio broadcasts. An advertising slot requires squeezing in as much information about the business as possible in the allotted time. Radio talk shows generally provide an opportunity to cover a wider range of topics.

Q. How do I determine the right stations and the right time slots?
A. A lot depends on your location. In New York or Los Angeles, the choice of stations multiplies. In Rogers, Arkansas, or Altoona, Pennsylvania, choices are more limited.

The geographic dispersion of the audience is also crucial. A local-access TV channel or local radio station attracts viewers and listeners from the immediate neighborhood. This is a terrific way to reach small businesses. Broadcasting about a mergers and acquisitions specialty will require a station in a major city.

Choosing the right programs to find the biggest audience is far more difficult. All-business TV channels and radio stations would appear to attract the largest business audience, but my experience has been that this is not always the case. A shot at the "Oprah" or "Donahue" shows attracts far more publicity than an interview on a business TV channel, even if much of it is not directly aimed at businesses. (Of course, landing a national talk show may take some doing! Don't be surprised if you end up with a "second-tier" show—that has great potential, too.)

Timing is as important as the station or program. Audiences interested in business subjects generally don't have the time to tune in during the day. Programs during early evening hours or prime time slots work best. Weekend shows are practically worthless.

Q. Other than TV and radio, what types of publicity programs are effective?

A. The list is endless. Management consulting fits perfectly into a variety of publicity options. Business audiences are interested in a broad range of topics, permitting a wide choice of effective mediums.

The choice really depends more on a person's selling skills than on anything else. Some people are very comfortable speaking to a large audience. Others can speak to small groups but not crowds. Still others prefer a one-on-one atmosphere.

Several publicity options exist for those with strong writing talent. Of course the choices are really endless for a person who can handle public speaking, small groups, *and* written communications.

Let's look at some examples of highly effective publicity exposure in each of these areas.

Q. What about public speaking before large groups?

A. Let me relate an example of how one consultant parlayed his public speaking talents into an entirely new market niche.

Bob ran his own consulting business for seven years, specializing in organizational development. He saw competition increasing from three larger firms and decided to scout around for a new market niche. Bob held several jobs in hotels prior to starting his consulting business and, projecting a sizable national growth in the hotel development field over the next ten years, he decided to beef up on current hotel organization problems. Research led him to the conclusion that an increasing number of new hotels were facing the problem of union representation, especially on the East Coast.

His first step was to get the names and membership rosters of the major hotel trade associations. He then wrote a concise, pointedly controversial article of about eight hundred words and sent it to the American Hotel Association requesting publication in a monthly hotel newsletter mailed to AHA members.

The article brought a call from the AHA program director asking Bob to speak at the association's next regional meeting in Boston, which he did. The topic was, "How to Keep Unions Out and Stay Within the Law." Two years later, Bob had presented eight speeches about union-blocking to AHA groups, honing his presentation each time. Over this period, nine new hotel development companies hired Bob to help them solve labor problems. Bob is still specializing in this very unique market, and doing quite well.

Q. Are speaker's bureaus helpful in landing public speaking dates?

A. Speaker's bureaus are in business to make money from speaking engagements. Some take a cut of the speaking fee. Others charge the sponsoring organization. Either way the amount is sizable, often one-third of the total fee paid a speaker.

Speaker's bureaus *do not* place speakers who are willing to perform without charge for purely promotional purposes.

Very few speaker's bureaus operate nationally. A handful out of New York; a couple from Washington, D.C.; one or two from the Chicago area; and a few scattered between the larger cities in the South and West are worth researching. A trip to the reference section of your library will point you in the right direction.

Beware: Speaker's bureaus are also very particular about who they choose to accept as speaking clients. Only well-known figures in business, politics, entertainment, athletics, or other high-profile areas benefit from speaker's bureaus. Bureaus are not interested in doing business with unknowns.

Q. How about participating in panels and giving speeches at seminars?

A. Both are excellent publicity channels.

Panel participation offers an excellent opportunity to voice opinions on several topics and to be observed by large audiences. Although a wide range of organizations sponsor trade shows, conventions, and conferences that utilize panel discussions as supplementary programs, local trade and business groups tend to bring in clients quickest. Functions sponsored by state and city trade development agencies usually attract business owners and managers from the immediate area who are looking for advice or resources to achieve a specific task.

The 1991 nationwide tour of Department of Commerce officials to stir up interest in exporting was a prime example. Led by Commerce Secretary Robert Mosbacher, the group promoted exporting by small and mid-size companies from Alaska to Maryland.

These promotional events were sponsored by the joint efforts of Eximbank and local trade development councils. Many featured two- and three-day conferences, replete with panel discussions by experts in exporting and related topics. Several management consultants participated.

Q. Does participation in seminars bring results as good as those from panel presentations?

A. I believe seminars can be just as effective as panel discussions, provided the seminar focuses on one of your specialties and the sponsoring group attracts sufficiently high-stature attendees. The main idea behind publicity is to demonstrate a person's special abilities to large audiences of prospective clients.

If the seminar topic doesn't fit, the publicity will be wasted. If the group isn't sufficiently large, exposure will be too limited. If attendees are lower echelon employees without the authority to recommend consultants, few if any new clients will be attracted.

Take American Management Association (AMA) seminars, for example. Most attendees are young managers climbing the corporate ladder, and have little or no authority. Others, also lower-level managers, attend expecting to learn a new technical skill. A few AMA seminars are specifically designed for senior executives, but not very many. These attract mostly department managers from large corporations, generally not the type of audience that generates clients.

On the other hand, "how to" seminars sponsored by technical trade groups, such as those dealing with new tax laws, setting up foreign sales corporations, export management techniques, business acquisition financing, or strategic resource allocation often attract executives and managers with the responsibility for resolving these matters in their companies. Such attendees frequently do have the authority to bring in qualified consultants.

Q. How about putting on my own seminar?
A. This depends on your competition. Consultants located in or near large cities specializing in small business consulting compete not only with other consultants, but with public accounting firms, the Small Business Administration, local banks, venture capital groups, and a variety of other organizations who also put on seminars for the same audiences.

Competition in smaller communities usually isn't as great, especially for more exotic topics. For example, I recently received a request from the owner of a $10 million manufacturing company in Omaha, Nebraska, to put on a local seminar about entering international trade. He had read my book *Going Global: New Opportunities for Growing Companies to Compete in World Markets* and believed that he could easily round up enough local business people trying to get started in international trade to make the seminar worthwhile.

The primary danger in sponsoring a seminar is the potential lack of enough attendees to provide broad exposure. It's bad enough spending the money to advertise and rent facilities, and then put on the seminar without sufficient attendees: it's even worse trying to do a good job for an audience of five or six people. As for publicity value, it's essentially zero.

Q. What publicity value is there in writing articles for magazines, trade journals, and trade newspapers, or in writing books?

A. If the publication sports a wide circulation, this is an excellent medium in which to broadcast your talents. Choose one whose readership is centered on managers and executives of companies in your industry (if you choose to concentrate in an industry), or in your technical specialty if you choose a technical publication.

As we discussed earlier, a published opinion, whether it be in a book, a magazine, a trade journal, or a trade newspaper, immediately stamps you as an authority in your field. This kind of publicity cannot be purchased. It is invaluable in getting your name and credentials in front of a wide audience already interested in what you have to say. It is also one of the least expensive publicity techniques. It never ceases to amaze me how many letters, phone calls, and eventual clients my books and articles have generated—from all over the world!

The three keys to using articles in magazines or trade publications as a publicity tool are that these periodicals should be:

1. Specifically targeted to subscribers whose business needs fit a consulting specialty.
2. Directed to specific geographic markets—local, regional, national, or international—that represent the client coverage you are after.
3. Focused on one or two business facets, such as magazines about secured financing, international marketing, quality control techniques, strategic planning, and so on.

Unfortunately, few publications accept freelance articles. In fact, very few of the larger-circulation magazines (*Business Week, Fortune, Forbes*) or newspapers (*Barron's,* the *Wall Street Journal*) will even read an unsolicited submission, much less publish it. Therefore, as far as articles are concerned, smaller-circulation industry or trade publications are the better outlet.

Writing books is an excellent publicity method. My books have brought several clients and engagements that I could never have reached otherwise. Compared to magazine articles, books publicize a consultant's talents to a wider audience. However, the mechanics are significantly more difficult. Here are some guidelines:

1. The topic must display a special expertise and be timely and marketable. This means that covering the same topics, with the same twist, that other authors have used, is *verboten*.
2. You have to find a publisher to handle your work. Self-publishing is very costly and, without a marketing organization, wide circulation is nearly impossible.
3. Writing a book on business topics requires a sizable amount of research, which takes time and effort away from a consulting business.
4. The actual writing process takes even more time—usually 6 to 12 months, and often longer. During this time competitors may publish similar books, the dynamics of the topic may cause major variations from your research, or your publisher may go out of business or change its publishing objectives (thus making your book obsolete for its marketing effort).

It is extremely difficult to write a business book during leisure time. Doing so definitely steals a significant amount of time from a primary consulting business. And, except in rare cases, authors *don't* get much publicity help from publishers.

Q. Does it make sense to hire a publicist to make arrangements and handle the details?
A. It's possible, but you'll have to do some research. Publicity and public relations companies thrive in New York, Chicago, and Los Angeles. They are much less common in cities like Philadelphia, Houston, Kansas City, and Miami. Smaller cities are lucky to have any publicity or public relations firms. If you live in a rural community, forget it.

Even when such firms are accessible, there are two other hurdles to overcome. First, most of these firms are not interested in working with a single consultant or a small consulting firm. They go after the Fortune 500, notable entertainers, athletes, politicians, and other well-known clients. Second, those who will take on a small job charge exorbitant fees, beginning at $10,000 to $20,000 and ranging upward.

If you do elect to go this route and have access to publicity and public relations companies, the best choice is usually a one- or two-person publicity firm. Small publicists take a limited number of clients at any one time and therefore are more apt to concentrate on your needs. They are also a bit less expensive.

Hooking up with a qualified publicist eliminates much of the strain and uncertainty in developing a well-conceived, continuous promotion campaign. But it is very expensive, and there's a reason for that. These specialists know what media best serves your special needs. They write copy, arrange meetings and interviews, and schedule appearances. (The one area they cannot help with is the writing of articles or books. That's not in their job description.)

Publicity, public relations, and advertising are all important facets of selling consulting services. They play an important role in providing a continuous high profile. This not only helps to land new clients, it gives assurance to existing clients that we are staying on top of our field and are worthy of further assignments.

These are not the only effective ways to get new clients, however. Unique promotion techniques for certain types of consulting specialties work just as well, and in many cases even better. Let's look at some of these unusual methods.

Chapter 4

PROMOTIONAL FREEBIES
How to Make Money by Not Charging

Q. Why should I give away advice? It's the only product I have to sell.

A. For three reasons:

1. free work is the least expensive form of promotion
2. everyone loves to get something for nothing (it builds egos)
3. a small but increasing number of businesses are doing it. That final point means that to remain competitive we really don't have any choice.

The key to turning freebies into paying jobs is to convert what appears to be merely goodwill into a dynamic promotional tool.

This isn't as difficult as it sounds. When agreeing to perform the free work, we make it very clear to the recipient or the sponsor that our business is selling business advice, and therefore we expect something in return for our efforts, even though it may not be a cash payment.

The next step is to be sure that donated advice is less than complete. This encourages the recipient to enter into a consulting contract (resulting in billable hours) to obtain the full benefit of the suggestions.

These may sound like harsh or even unethical approaches, but they are not. So-called professionals do it all the time, so why shouldn't we as practical business people?

How often do litigation lawyers offer free advice about the specifics of winning a court case? They may quote chapter and verse from the law books. They may even donate their time and advice to preliminary preparation. But defending a client in court without a fee? I've never seen it happen, except of course through a Legal Aid Society program. In that case, lawyers make sure these "donated efforts" are well-publicized.

And how about health care professionals? Many give free advice of a general nature, but does a heart surgeon offer free operations? Or a dentist free fillings? Or a psychiatrist free consultation? Some donate skills and a small amount of time to inner-city poverty pockets and depressed Third World cultures. These efforts, however, are usually partially funded by either government or social welfare agencies and therefore not completely free. If not, the providers likewise make sure their contribution is made known to their paying patients and to their community.

CHARITABLE WORK

Q. It sounds as if you are talking about two types of free-bies—those donated to charity and those given directly to clients or potential clients. Is there a difference as far as promotion is concerned?

A. Yes. Donating consulting time and skills to charitable organizations can have a wider impact than performing free consulting work for clients or potential clients.

With at least one organization per week begging for money I finally called a stop to *all* cash donations, regardless of the cause. Instead, I responded with offers to help charitable organizations by donating my time and skills.

Most don't want any part of donated skills—just cash—but I firmly believe that those who accepted my offer have benefited more than they would have by taking my money. And I benefit from publicity in the local media or trade organization, or receive some other type of promotional value in exchange. A few times I have picked up new clients through charitable work.

An example of turning charitable work into a full-fledged promotion occurred when a local congregation was stalemated in a campaign to raise funds for an addition to the church building. I volunteered to organize a raffle with food donated by local farmers as the prizes. I also saw that when the farmers brought their goods and the raffle was held, the news crew from a local TV channel knew all about it: not only about the raffle, but that a local business consultant (me) donated time and organizing skills.

The cameras zeroed in while I conducted the raffle, an interview followed, and the film ran on two newscasts that evening. The local newspaper picked up the idea and interviewed me about the organizing techniques I used to conduct such a successful fundraiser.

This helped both the church and my consulting business far more than a $100 donation!

Q. Cal you actually win clients through charitable work?
A. Actually, I have landed several new accounts through charitable work. The first occurred some years ago when I helped refinance and restructure a charitable foundation.

The foundation was practically bankrupt. We were in the middle of a recession. Costs were skyrocketing, and at the same time cash donations were dropping dangerously low.

The foundation was about to fire all its staff, close down its single office, and liquidate its few assets. I refused to donate cash but did volunteer my turnaround expertise. Within a week I set up a cost control system, helped structure a five-year strategic plan, and convinced a bank to make the foundation a three-year balloon term loan. The foundation eventually pulled out and is still in operation.

Two outside directors of the foundation each owned manufacturing companies. When they witnessed what I accomplished, both signed up as new clients.

FREEBIE PSYCHOLOGY FOR NEW CLIENTS

Q. What about using freebies as a technique to get new clients other than through charitable work?

A. Many consultants, including myself, use the same psychology as with charitable work. The "something-for-nothing" dream pervades our culture. Lotteries, magazine sweepstakes, vacation development giveaways, and a variety of other gambling-like promotions are popular because people continue to look for that pot of gold at the end of the rainbow.

I find that freebie psychology works especially well in the business world, and I'm surprised more service-oriented businesses haven't caught on. On the other hand, it's probably just as well that they haven't, or the tactic would soon be overworked.

Here are my five rules for benefiting from free work.

The first rule is, never advertise or broadcast free work. This immediately negates the advantage of surprise, which is an important part of its psychology.

The second rule is a bit more difficult: get in to see a prospective client before springing the freebie. It won't work by phone or letter.

The third rule stipulates that you must really want this client, either because of the potential for a long-term or high-priced engagement, or because this client is an entrée to other clients.

The fourth rule is to play on the assumption that executives do not or cannot identify the root causes of company problems.

The fifth rule assumes that these root causes can be identified quickly and parlayed into a paying job. Time is money to consultants. We can't afford to be too generous.

Q. How do I use the technique to get clients?

A. Let's assume that, through a bank referral, we manage a first interview with a live prospect, a small, profitable company with sales of $10 million. The owner is concerned about losing market share to two large foreign competitors. His banker suggests that he get independent consulting help to develop a strategic marketing plan; however, he isn't sure he wants to spend the money. Friends tell him that consultants can't do anything that he can't do himself.

Somehow you schedule a meeting.

After pleasantries subside, you make your sales pitch. The owner asks how much a strategic marketing plan will cost and quickly follows with the "poor boy" routine, stressing that the only reason for this meeting is to pacify his banker.

Of course, you understand his reluctance to spend money foolishly, especially on consultants. Undoubtedly he knows more about his business that you ever will. You certainly wouldn't be so presumptuous as to suggest that after this ten-minute conversation you could contribute anything. However . . .

Now hit him with the freebie pitch.

However, perhaps when you get to know his business better, you might have one or two helpful ideas. To accomplish this you are willing to make a half-day business survey with a written report of your findings—all free of charge!

Now this reticent business owner is hooked. Maybe this free survey will pacify his banker and he won't have to go any further.

But being a hard-nosed entrepreneur, he wonders what you expect to get out of it? Why donate your time and expertise? Are you that hard up for clients?

The answer is simple. The banker that referred you has several other accounts in the area that you hope to land as clients if you do a good job here.

Of course, if the business owner wishes, you will be happy to assist him in implementing any suggestions resulting from the survey. When the report is completed you will provide an estimate of the cost and time to implement these suggestions.

Nine out of ten times business owners or high-level executives cannot resist this pitch. It's logical, it helps them immediately, and best of all, it's free!

From your side, it opens the door wide to a potential client; it gives you a chance to define the root of the problem and assess the scope of the engagement; and it costs nothing, except time. If you don't get the client, at least doing the referral contact a favor should lead to other jobs. And finally, a half day or even a full day of marketing time isn't that much.

Q. Is there any other way to get clients with freebies?

A. The methods for setting the situation up are limited only by a person's imagination. Freebies can be worked into practically any sales pitch.

To be pragmatic, it's impossible to scope out an engagement or come up with cost estimates without at least a cursory grasp of the client's business. Except for large companies or wealthy business owners, few prospects willingly pay for a scope survey.

Of course, a survey can be included as part of an engagement, and many times this makes the most sense. Smaller clients, however, or clients in financial difficulty want to keep the price as low as possible. Free surveys accomplish this and at the same time build goodwill that in many cases is beyond measurement.

Bearing in mind the five rules for free work, here are a few examples of tactics for getting in the door to set up such a promotion:

1. Make it clear in your promotional materials that the initial interview is free (just like the ads from many law firms). Once in the door, make a sales pitch for a free survey.
2. Selectively and discreetly let referral contacts know that free surveys are available under special circumstances.
3. Use an informal setting for the initial client interview (e.g. breakfast, lunch, or a ballgame or other outing) but make sure the referral contact is also present to hear the pitch.
4. Interject anecdotes in public speaking engagements about how consultants use no-charge surveys. Be sure to stress that they always expect referrals or engagements in return.

USING FREEBIES TO CULTIVATE EXISTING CLIENTS

Q. I understand the benefit of using freebies as a selling tool to land new clients. Is there any way to use the same technique with existing clients? If so, what benefits can I expect?

A. One of the major dilemmas for management consultants in any specialty is how to parlay short-term engagements into long-term billable hours. Far too often, clients disappear once the current job is completed. Then we start all over again marketing to new prospects.

For multi-partner firms this is bad enough. For single practitioners it creates severely fluctuating income. As long as we have long-term clients, at least some income is available to fall back on. Without continuing assignments, however, marketing takes up a lot of time, and that creates income voids.

We constantly fight the battle of allocating hours between marketing and production work. When we have too much work we complain about the lack of marketing time. But that's a good problem. With too little work, we tend to take whatever clients we can get, and frequently at reduced fees. Obviously, that is a bad problem.

Although other sales techniques also prolong existing client work, free work is probably one of the most effective means.

I can hear experienced consultants moan and groan that I must be crazy to suggest such a ploy. Why give away advice to an established client?

It took me many years to understand the ebb and flow of client relationships. When a job begins, the client is full of hope that we will come up with a miracle cure. As the job progresses, boredom and impatience set in. How long must I keep paying you? When will you finish? What's taking so long? Don't you have any solutions yet?

If consultants aren't careful at this stage, clients perceive that they are merely milking the job, making it last as long as possible. This can result in getting thrown off the job, regardless of the scope contract. Fees get severed and reputations damaged.

As the engagement winds down we meet with company officials to disclose our findings. Reports get written and distributed. The final billing goes out. *Finis*.

The client may or may not act on these recommendations. It's quite possible that suggestions will be shelved as too costly or impractical, or because the business has changed and those particular recommendations don't apply anymore. Any number of circumstances prevent clients from implementing a consultant's advice.

Happy to be free of our probing, relieved that weekly billings will no longer drain their cash, clients forget about consultants and go on to other operating matters. A follow-up call or letter now and then keeps our firm on file, but we don't get called for another engagement. Eventually, competitors get in, and a client is lost forever.

That's a tough scenario but it frequently happens. Too often, we have a knack for selling new clients but can't hold on to the ones we already have.

Free consultations work wonders for preserving client relationships. The identical psychology prevails as with prospective clients. The temptation to get something for nothing is more than most people can resist.

Here's one example of how it works.

Assume that a distribution client engages you to refinance the company. An estimated time schedule and rate are negotiated. As the engagement proceeds you find that in addition to new financing the company needs more sales volume to absorb its fixed overhead. This could be accomplished by expanding its market area. Your analysis indicates that expansion can best be achieved by acquiring another distributor in a nearby city. It also becomes obvious that the company needs to replace three nonperforming managers and to develop a strategic market/product plan covering the next seven years.

The company president is immediately turned off by these suggestions, fearing an acquisition will cost too much and will diminish his control. Furthermore, he states, once the new financing is in place, he can't afford any more consulting services.

Realizing the long-term potential of this company, you decide to use the freebie approach to overcome the president's resistance. First you offer to set aside a weekend for the two of you to hash over the company's future—at no charge.

After this session, the president decides to pursue an acquisition, but is still hesitant about paying consulting fees. You negotiate a three-month contract with a contingency fee payable out of the financing proceeds on closing.

When the three months expires and a closing has not transpired, the client is hooked. *Now* is the time to negotiate a retainer contract.

What has been gained? A mergers and acquisitions job with a retainer and a potentially high closing fee. The opportunity to lead the client into a full strategic planning assignment. And the high probability that other work, such as recruiting three new managers, will evolve.

Most important, a client that you were about to lose has been retained.

Your cost? A weekend that probably would have been unproductive anyway.

Q. That all sounds fine except for the contingency M&A fee for a three-month contract. Isn't that unethical when you know the odds are against closing in three months?

A. Not at all. Although most business acquisitions take longer than three months, I have closed several within that time frame.

The client can't lose, unless of course the acquisition search continues long enough to eat up the entire closing fee in retainers. This is possible, but if it looks like that might happen, the search can always be stopped, or a new fee arrangement negotiated.

Not only is such an arrangement perfectly ethical, it in fact preserves the client's cash flow for three months: a major saving for most companies.

ALLOCATING TIME TO FREEBIES

Q. Is there some rule of thumb to use as a guide for allocating my time to free promotion work?

A. Not really. It depends on how busy you are to begin with, whether you are just starting or have an existing business, and how effective your other marketing efforts are.

Let's go back to a point we covered earlier about allocating time.

I certainly don't mean to be dogmatic about time allotments. Every consulting business is different. Multi-partner firms have more flexibility than single practitioners. The use of consortiums, networks, and informal partnerships increases available hours. Specialties that require extensive travel, such as international consulting, dictate a different approach to allocating time than those adaptable to production work in a consultant's office—such as small business accounts.

Generally speaking, however, most consultants try to follow the age-old rule of thumb—approximately 50 to 60 percent of available hours for production, 30 to 40 percent for marketing, and 10 percent for administration. For short periods, say one year, these percentages vary widely. Over the long pull, however, they can't vary too much or there won't be enough income to live on. The alternative is a radically fluctuating client base causing long open spaces without billings.

The amount of free work donated to charitable organizations is really up to the individual. Just try to get something in return—such as a little publicity.

The amount of time spent on promotional freebies for new clients is also a matter of individual taste, although clearly no one can afford to be too liberal. Since it's necessary to get through a prospect's door to use the tool, free work is really a secondary selling gimmick. I use this aspect of freebies frequently because I am comfortable with it. Others are not and employ it sparingly.

I try to remember that freebies represent marketing hours. I still have to turn out at least 60 percent of my hours in production to stay in business.

Free work for existing clients is different. I consider this pure client relations, the same as taking clients to ballgames or dinner. Looking at it this way means that the time I spend on free client work must come out of my annual client relations budget. Also, client freebies are hard to plan. We should simply be ready to take advantage of the opportunity when it presents itself.

Q. How do you feel about free public speaking or written articles as promotion pitches?

A. We have already discussed public speaking and writing as part of a publicity program. As you recall, the objective was to get your name and credentials in front of as many potential clients as possible, in the shortest time period, at the least cost. Both public speaking and writing accomplish this.

Normally, event sponsors who need a public speaker expect to pay a fee. Although not much, it does help defray travel costs and compensates for time away from the business. The same holds true for writing articles. Most magazines expect to pay something for the article, even if only a few hundred dollars. Books, of course, are never freebies, but generally compensation is so minimal that it is practically non-existent.

Only under certain circumstances does free speechmaking or writing amount to anything. If the sponsoring organization or periodical is a not-for-profit organization, of course, the probability of getting paid is about zero.

Still, most of these groups put out some form of newsletter to members. A good write-up of your speech, including the topic and the name and specialty of the consulting business, can provide excellent publicity at no cost. Readers might include business owners or executives who could use these services and this is one way of reaching them.

Donating articles to carefully selected not-for-profit newsletters also brings results, provided the organization's membership includes business leaders who might turn into clients. One such organization is the American Association for Retired Persons (AARP). Each AARP monthly newsletter includes several articles by outsiders on a variety of topics. Furthermore, since the minimum age to join AARP is 50, many members are still active in the business world.

Periodic bulletins from the American Automobile Association, the American Chamber of Commerce, a variety of agencies from the U.S. Department of Commerce, humanitarian groups such as the Rainforest Action Network, and many not-for-profit groups also accept freelance articles. I have never had much success in this area, but some consulting friends have. It's worth a try, and it doesn't cost anything.

FREEBIES FOR INTERMEDIARIES

Q. Is there some way to use freebie promotions to increase referrals from bankers?

A. Bankers (one of the best sources of referrals) are human. Just like everyone else, getting something for nothing stimulates them. The approach to any third-party referral source takes a different tack than approaching client prospects. As we saw earlier, the key to getting intermediary referrals is to identify why certain clients or customers are causing them headaches, then convincing them that you can provide the antidote.

The intermediary doesn't do the hiring, so whether a client or customer engages us or not, efforts to this end don't cost the intermediary a penny. Consequently, you don't get much promotion mileage offering them free services. A different approach must be used.

Nonperforming bank loans are a major headache for banks. In an effort to bring some level of expertise to bear on problem loans, banks have set up so-called workout departments.

In a sense these departments are in direct competition with independent consultants. They offer the same service, but have far less experience. Gradually, many bankers realize that their in-house workout experts aren't experts at all and turn to management consultants for help.

In addition to a significant lack of experience, banks have a hard time forcing the issue on nonperforming loans short of outright foreclosure, which most are not equipped to administer because they are restrained by conflict-of-interest laws from directly interfering with the decision-making process of a customer's business. This doesn't stop their meddling: it only encourages them to employ more subtle means to get their way.

These conditions give management consultants an excellent opportunity to pick up new clients, assuming bankers can be convinced that a consultant can resolve the loans with little or no loss to the bank. One way to gain this entrée is through freebies.

One of our consortium members takes to the following steps when using freebie promotions for selling to banks:

1. He first convinces banks in his area to put his firm on their "qualified consultants list." When the bank decides a customer could use an independent consultant, it gives the customer this list of three or four consulting firms to choose from.

2. To win a bank's recommendation, my consulting associate offers the bank a one-day free survey of the customer's business condition, complete with a written report to the bank.

3. If the report indicates that by taking specified steps the company should be able to repay the loan, the bank pressures the company to hire the consultant. Although the bank cannot directly force a company to do so, it can use persuasion—such as threatening foreclosure or reducing the company's borrowing base.

This associate has kept one of his staff busy full time for two years with clients obtained through workout bank referrals.

Q. Can a similar free-work method help get referrals from lawyers and public accountants?

A. That depends on your specialty. If your clients make sufficient use of lawyers and/or public accountants, they will listen to recommendations from these professionals. On the other hand, an annual audit or occasional legal advice won't place these professionals in a high enough standing to make promoting to them worthwhile.

Assuming that these professionals do carry weight with prospective clients, and that they do not engage in management consulting work themselves, freebies work almost as well here as with bank intermediaries, although with a twist.

Lawyers are notoriously poor business people, although very few smaller law firms admit it. Larger, multi-partner firms normally maintain a full complement of business management people—controller, business manager, accounts payable and accounts receivable staffs, and so on—to handle the firm's business affairs. Presumably these individuals have the responsibility for keeping the law firm on a sound financial path and in compliance with all federal, state, and local tax laws and other regulations.

The same holds true of large public accounting firms. Even though accounting and management consulting partners pride themselves on their business acumen, they maintain administrative staffs to perform the business functions of the firm.

In the early 1990s, it became obvious that several legal and accounting firms depended too heavily on the business perspicacity of these administrators. Although inadequate audit standards certainly weighed heavily on the downfall of Laventhol & Horwath, along with several smaller firms, and inappropriate legal advice challenged the staying power of some of the country's largest law firms, insufficient attention to the details of running their businesses also played a role.

Smaller legal and accounting firms cannot afford the luxury of separate administrative staffs. Partners in these firms must manage their own affairs.

The need for competent independent consulting help exists in both large and small professional firms. Once in the door, management consultants can provide the business guidance to avoid a host of financial and administrative problems. The trick is getting in the door.

It is rare, though, for professional firms to actively seek consulting help, for the reasons previously mentioned. Getting in demands a serious selling effort. Freebies are one way to open the door, albeit a back door at times.

Q. So how would the freebie approach apply in practice?

A. Here's an example. During the 1980s, I made extensive use of referrals from lawyers to source acquisition and divestiture candidates. One firm that I called on had seven partners, several legal assistants, and an administrative staff consisting of a controller and two accounting clerks.

While visiting one of the partners, I noticed that the office seemed to be in chaos: the controller was running around trying to get checks signed, secretaries were waiting to use copying machines, suppliers were calling partners demanding their money, and so on. I mentioned the apparent confusion to the partner. He responded that it was always like this, and considered the disarray to be one of the administrative headaches of running a law firm.

Sensing the opportunity for a new client, I asked if he would let me spend a day in the office interviewing people and observing the routine. I promised not to disrupt anyone and to give him a confidential report of my findings—free, of course. As an excuse for the free work I mentioned that it was in repayment for referrals he had provided in the past.

One month later I signed the law firm up as a client for an organizational restructuring engagement. The partners were pleased with the results and referred me to two of their clients for the same type of work.

Q. What about public accountants who are supposed to be experts in business matters?

A. The same something-for-nothing psychology works with public accountants. Again, the process is best illustrated with a brief example.

As an ex-CPA, I have always worked closely with public accountants, referring clients who needed accounting or tax help and receiving referrals back for clients needing help in management areas.

One March I was out of work and visited one of my CPA friends, trying to solicit client leads. She was loaded with tax return work and didn't have much time to talk. I noticed the pile of returns on her floor and, having done my share of tax work, I volunteered to help for a few days with the initial preparation of some of the more mundane returns. She was grateful for the assistance but couldn't afford to pay me.

I actually prepared tax returns without charge for an entire week, with the understanding that in exchange, she would actively encourage several of her clients to engage me. Voila—four new small business clients!

Although this situation as well as the previous one with the law firm are isolated cases, the underlying principle does work, and should not be dismissed out of hand. Even one new client in exchange for a half-day or a day's free work is a pretty good trade-off.

Before leaving the subject of freebie promotion, I feel obliged to once again caution against relying too heavily on this technique. When starting a consulting business or changing markets, new clients are hard to come by. Hours and days of free time arise. Disappointment, frustration, even boredom, are not uncommon during this period. The temptation is great to volunteer free services just to make something happen, to get the ball rolling.

As discussed throughout this chapter, free promotions serve a very real purpose in an *overall* advertising and promotion program. They are also costly in terms of time taken away from other marketing efforts. A modest amount of free work brings good results. Too much can drive you out of business.

Chapter 5

DOING IT THE RIGHT WAY
How to Make Ethical Consulting Pay

Q. What do you mean by "ethical consulting"?

A. We spoke earlier about the lack of uniform standards for soliciting and performing consulting engagements. When compared with the body of standards legislated by the American Bar Association, the American Medical Association, or the American Institute of Certified Public Accountants, the field of precepts that guide management consulting is indeed barren.

One normally thinks of ethics as a system or code of morals for a particular person, religion, profession, or other group of individuals. Ethical conduct generally means conforming to the standards of conduct of that group.

Not all standards of performance are ethical standards, however. Good examples are those set by federal and state government agencies or industry groups: Underwriters Lab, the EPA, OSHA, the EEOC, and so on. These have nothing to do with a code of moral behavior and obviously do not influence ethical conduct.

Management consultants cannot look to a national standard-setting body. Nor do we fear decertification for even the most flagrant immoral conduct. We can cheat, lie, deceive, and use just about any devious means we choose as long as we don't get caught violating a law. Our only constraints are conscience, the possibility of losing clients who won't put up with dishonesty, and/or developing a bad reputation that makes it more difficult to get new clients.

If you plan to be in business only a short time and don't have any personal problem with engaging in unethical behavior, go to it. You may not have many friends. Referrals or decent references will be hard to obtain. Clients will certainly not stay around very long. But if you don't care about those things, be my guest! Most of us, however, plan to be in business for longer than a few months. Most of us need referrals and references to get new business. And most of us feel guilty about lying or cheating.

Now, what do I mean by ethical consulting?

Ethical consulting refers to conducting a consulting business according to a code of moral standards. This code doesn't differ markedly from the way we live, or should live, in our everyday existence. Simply put, ethical consulting demands that we conduct our business affairs honestly: that we provide a fair day's work for a fair day's pay, that we don't claim to be an expert when we are not, that we retain all information learned about a client's business or personnel as confidential, that we relate all facts uncovered in our work to the client, that when expressing an opinion we label it as opinion, not fact, and that we do not claim someone else's idea or recommendation as our own.

Several years ago I gave a speech to a group of MBA near-graduates planning to become consultants. The title of the speech was "Morals and Money," and it dealt with the temptations consultants face. As part of the presentation I gave the group my "Do's and Don'ts of Ethical Consulting".

Do:

1. Tell a prospective client the truth about yourself and your abilities.
2. Take only those engagements you are qualified to perform competently.
3. Report your findings and recommendations to the client fully and totally.
4. Maintain complete confidentiality regarding everything relating to a client or a client's personnel, regardless of what may already be public information.
5. Ask for help when you run into obstacles.
6. Conduct yourself at all times in a professional manner with the highest moral standards.

Don't:

1. Pretend to be what you are not.
2. Pretend to know what you don't know.
3. Express someone else's recommendations or opinions as your own.
4. Bill more hours than you actually incur.
5. Be judgmental.
6. Intentionally lie, deceive, or omit.

Q. What's the difference between ethical consulting and "activist" consulting, that is, advocating ecological preservation, energy conservation, social welfare programs, brotherhood and community, human rights, and so on?

A. Ethical consulting relates to the moral code under which we conduct ourselves and our business, not the type of clients we take. If you believe in saving the earth, by all means structure a consulting business around that market. It's a big one. But don't confuse humanitarian or conservation objectives with ethical superiority.

Many people regard saving the whales as an ethical imperative, but just as many or more do not. Don't mix up assisting the local Habitat for Humanity chapter with ethical consulting. There are just as many unethical consultants advising "activist" organizations as advising private enterprise business.

ETHICS TRENDS IN MANAGEMENT CONSULTING

Q. Is there a significant movement toward ethical standards within the management consulting ranks?

A. Unfortunately, the answer is no. In fact, any recognizable movement seems to be in the opposite direction.

The earlier illustration of how unethical business brokers began taking over the small company M&A field toward the end of the 1980s was a prime example. Many other instances are less obvious, but unethical nevertheless.

Q. Can you give me some examples of unethical consulting behavior?

A. How about padding an expense report presented to the client? Or billing a full hour while working only forty-five minutes, or a quarter-hour for a three-minute telephone call? (Lawyers are famous for this!) What about persuading a client's employees that work beyond the original scope contract is necessary so that they will persuade the CEO to extend the engagement? Or being critical of top management to a client's employees?

How about calling on one banker to arrange new financing for two separate clients, then billing each client full time? Or making derogatory remarks about a client to a banker, public accountant, or other third party?

How about lying to a client's supplier about the client's ability to make payment? Or persuading suppliers to extend credit or loans knowing that the owner will pocket the cash?

It goes the other way too. It is just as unethical to make recommendations to a client that a consultant believes cannot be implemented with the client's resources. Or advising a client to arrange new financing when the likelihood of success is nil, given the current condition of the client's balance sheet. Or recommending a totally unrealistic sell price for a client's divestiture.

Sad to say, conversations with clients and consultants, articles in newspapers and trade journals, and observing consultants' actions at trade shows, conventions, and seminars, lead me to the inevitable conclusion that management consulting is rapidly becoming less, rather than more, ethical.

Q. Then why bother with ethical consulting when no one else does?

A. Because growing our businesses requires a competitive edge. Something that sets us apart from the run-of-the-mill consultant. Something that convinces a client to hire our firm rather than our competitor. Something that will ensure our longevity when others fall by the wayside.

With so few consultants practicing ethical consulting, I believe that by so doing, my reputation will precede me and give me that edge. Most reputable companies, of course, *want* a consultant to be ethical.

If most consultants were ethical, this wouldn't result in a competitive advantage. The fact is, however, that they don't seem to be, and therefore an ethical reputation becomes an effective selling tool.

Last but not least, I sleep better at night knowing I have tried to conduct my business ethically.

UNETHICAL REFERRAL SOLICITATION AND SUBCONTRACTING

Q. How do I develop a reputation as an ethical consultant?
A. Let's examine some broad principles in each of the major facets of the consulting field: marketing, production, and administration.

Q. Okay, how about marketing?
A. We previously examined a variety of marketing tactics that work with a varying degree of effectiveness, different market niches and for different personalities. They included soliciting referrals, subcontracting, advertising, public relations, publicity, and promotional freebies.

We all know what ethical marketing consists of. Let's take a look at some unethical examples, beginning with referral solicitation.

When we are desperate for work, with cash reserves running low, and when nothing seems to bring in clients, we turn to referrals as a "court of last resort." We also tend to inflate our abilities. We request referrals for work we haven't done for a long time, if ever. We propose cut-rate fee structures with the hope of buying a job.

When times really get tough we try bribes, promising to bring intermediaries work if they will only refer us to a client. Even kickbacks and fee-splitting are not unheard of.

These are all unethical practices. By stooping to such means to get referrals, we have, in effect, prostituted ourselves. And worse, unless the intermediary is oblivious to what's going on, or unless he or she is equally unethical, these practices virtually kill any real opportunity for legitimate referrals—now or in the future.

No one wants to deal with someone who blatantly lies or cuts fees out of desperation. In other words, no one likes a loser, and unethical referral solicitation smells like rot.

Q. How about subcontracting? It seems this offers the least temptation to be unethical.

A. You are probably right. It's doubtful that another consultant would agree to a subcontracting arrangement with you without knowing your capabilities. If evidence from your prior engagements isn't available, references will obviously be verified. Even if the consultant conducts an unethical business, he certainly won't hire you knowing in advance that you can't be trusted.

However, once again, we normally avoid subcontract work unless we don't have enough to keep busy. If conditions get too tight, the tendency is to stretch the truth (lie) about our background and competency just to get work, any work. Lying about qualifications may not be obvious enough to warrant verification, but it is still unfair to our employer, the consultant we subcontract from.

Even worse, once on the job and presented with problems we cannot handle, instead of deferring to the consultant who hired us we too often try to bluff our way through. Or denigrate our employer. Or actively push the client for a direct engagement next time around. Or take any number of other unethical steps to ensure continuation of the assignment or to grab the client for our own.

Let me explain what happened when I subcontracted a systems installation job to another consultant. The assignment was an outgrowth of a strategic planning engagement. I didn't feel competent either to design the system or to recommend an appropriate computer hardware configuration. On the recommendation of an associate I brought in a consultant I'll call Sally.

While I was on assignment for another client, Sally designed the system and then assisted the client to select hardware and install the system. She did a solid, competent job.

When I followed up with my client a month later to make sure everything was running smoothly, I was not-so-politely informed that I did not have to bother coming back, that Sally had convinced the CEO that she could handle strategic planning, organizational development, and any other assignment that might come up.

Sally had been a systems designer and programmer her entire working life. She had no management experience. I never learned what tactics she employed to steal my client.

UNETHICAL ADVERTISING

Q. What about ethical standards for advertising?

A. The advertising business has certainly become one of the prime breeding grounds for unethical practices. Short time periods or limited space in which to persuade companies to buy our services encourages the use of hyperboles and inferred guarantees, both of which stretch the truth. Advertising executives, on the other hand, argue that product truth remains inviolate, that the use of flattering descriptions to glamorize the customer's product or service are not intended to deceive.

Regardless of the intent or means employed, the fact remains that most advertising is structured to lead viewers or readers to assume that buying the product or service will satisfy needs and wants beyond that of competitors. In some cases this may be true. In many others, one product or service performs the same function as another.

Practicing ethical consulting certainly does not mean that a person cannot or should not advertise. Properly worded and displayed, ethical advertisements can be as effective as those making exaggerated claims. In the long run, most service-oriented companies find ethical advertising pays off.

Q. Can you give me a comparison between ethical and unethical advertisements for consulting services?

A. Let's compare two small ads recently appearing in a national business magazine. Both consulting firms specialized in sourcing export financing for American companies. (All names have been fictionalized.)

Ad #1 looked like this:

FINANCIAL CONSULTANT

Fifteen years of helping export clients arrange buyer and supplier credit, bank guarantees, government assistance, and commercial and political risk insurance gives us the background and experience to help you tailor a financing program to fit your exporting and importing needs. For free, initial consultation call

BRYAN AND SMITH
International Financial Consultants
and ask for Mike Smith, at
(212)XXX-XXXXX.

I would consider this a completely ethical advertisement. It truthfully explains the firm's qualifications, identifies what it is selling, and offers individualized service. It's hard to imagine how this could deceive any reader.

Ad #2 presented a different picture:

GET THE MONEY YOU NEED FAST

MELBOURNE INTERNATIONAL CONSULTANTS arranges export financing packages our competition only dreams about. Our private funding sources in Europe, Japan, and Washington stand ready to finance your international business regardless of current credit problems. When your bank says no, we say YES. For further information and application forms use your company letterhead to write to:

MELBOURNE INTERNATIONAL CONSULTANTS
P.O. Box 111
Hong Kong

This advertisement says nothing about the firm's qualifications. It claims financing from "private sources" without clarifying their legitimacy, and it infers that financing is available even for poor credit risk companies. The inference of assured financing is unmistakable. Although the ad makes no outright guarantees, the inference is unmistakable. In addition, the ad smells suspiciously like a money-laundering scheme.

To me this is an unethical advertisement. More to the point, it's a sleazy way for consultants to conduct business.

ESTABLISHING AN ETHICAL REPUTATION THROUGH ACTIVISM

Q. How can I structure a publicity and public relations promotion campaign that clearly identifies me as an ethical consultant?

A. This is not an easy task. It's one thing to avoid a negative, unethical impression in an advertising medium; it's another to actively promote the practice of ethical principles.

As a society, we have become so jaded that when someone holds out an ethical banner we become skeptics. We wonder what the hidden agenda may be. We ask ourselves, what's in it for this "honest John"?

I have been in the consulting business for over 15 years and in the business world for more than 30 years. Over that period society's values have changed. They seem to have shifted away from a traditionally American attitude of tight moral standards for the individual and freedom from constraints from ruling organizations (government or corporate). Values have, in my mind, moved toward permissiveness for the individual and tight regulations and laws from ruling organizations as the primary means of solving society's problems.

This shift seems to encourage individuals to try to get by with anything they can. Customers rely on laws and regulations to keep sellers from going too far. Litigators have certainly benefited from this state of affairs, but it's unclear how much gain there has been for individual entrepreneurs and businesses.

This societal shift in values leads to the distrust of individual motives, especially the motives of business people trying to follow ethical principles. Such practices run contrary to the "get what you can while the getting is good" philosophy.

Several publicity and public relations avenues can be used to create an ethical image. In one of our earlier discussions we saw how taking a stand can bring your consulting credentials to the public eye. The same approach establishes you as an ethical consultant.

Once again, the clearest way to illustrate the point is by the use of an actual case.

Mary ran a consulting business focusing on organizational development for architectural and engineering firms. Many of her clients specialized in selling environmental clean-up procedures to help companies comply with EPA regulations. As her business grew, Mary decided to expand her industry coverage to the distribution side of the auto parts aftermarket, which was commensurate with her background.

Mary ran a few ads in an industry trade journal, joined the appropriate trade organizations, and even tried a local direct mail solicitation. She wasn't getting very far and was about to drop her expansion plans.

A community group was trying to convince the county commissioners to mandate a trash recycling program, and, considering her environmental background, Mary was asking to participate. She became extremely active, speaking at rallies, writing opinion letters for the local newspaper, and soliciting petition signatures from local businesses, including three auto parts distributors.

To this day, Mary attributes her new-found success with auto parts distributors to the visible stand she took to promote trash recycling. In this very cut-throat, hard-nosed, male-dominated industry, Mary's reputation as an ethical, community-minded consultant has brought her more business than she can handle. She now has three offices in three states handling more than thirty auto parts distributor accounts and has expanded into market niches far removed from organization development.

Whether you call it publicity or public relations, taking a stand for a cause frequently establishes an ethical reputation.

Q. How can I market ethically when my competitors don't?

A. Begin with the assumption that most consultants are ethical. That means that we need to follow suit just to stay even. Conversely, beginning with the assumption that most competitors are not ethical (which is probably closer to the truth), we have a chance to gain an edge by offering something they do not, namely honesty, confidentiality, and more than a little caring for the welfare of a client.

I'll grant you that in some markets this may not win friends or clients. Playing softball when everyone else is playing hardball has its perils. An associate of mine was an especially ethical consultant, believing strongly in the old-fashioned work ethic of a fair day's work for a fair day's pay. He won a bid to design and install a computer network system for a state liquor control board.

The second week, he was still on schedule when a minor official informed him that he was working too fast, to slow down, or strange things might happen. He kept his pace.

The following week he was asked to leave the job because another consultant was starting on Monday. He learned later that the new consultant was the brother-in-law of the minor official issuing the warning.

I believe this case is an exception to the rule, however. Most clients appreciate a consultant's honesty, confidentiality, and all the other facets of ethical business. Furthermore, on at least three occasions I have been told by clients with whom I have major, long-term engagements that I won the jobs not only because of my reputation as a skilled consultant, but because of my reputation as an ethical person.

ETHICS IN PRODUCTION

Q. I realize you have already referred to several instances of ethical practices while performing a job. Can you give me any more insight into how to retain clients and engender additional work by performing production work ethically?

A. We haven't talked about production very much, and that's the second half of a consultant's success equation. The first step is to contract with clients: the second is to perform the work, frequently referred to as "production."

Some consultants, in some markets, strive to develop a small base of long-term clients, preferring to perform a variety of jobs for the same client rather than devote time to marketing new ones. This is certainly understandable. As we have already seen, marketing consulting services is a tough road, even for a super salesman.

The success in developing long-term relationships with clients is nearly always predicated on establishing a good working rapport, both with top executives and lower echelon employees. Developing a good rapport usually means developing mutual trust as well.

Once a consultant proves expertise in solving a specific problem, the emphasis shifts to personal relationships. Proving technical capabilities doesn't take too long once the job starts. A few days or weeks and the boss has a fairly strong opinion of your expertise.

Developing strong personal relationships takes longer. We all know that first impressions may or may not prove valid. We also know that in the glow of a new engagement, we try extra hard to impress; not only the boss, but employees as well. During short engagements, this euphoria might very well carry to the end without a conscious effort to develop relationships.

Reaching mutual trust, however, takes a while. On some assignments, especially those requiring constant interplay with lower echelon employees, I find it fairly easy to develop a relationship of mutual trust. It takes much longer on engagements that keep me in the office of top management, or performing work off-site.

The entire foundation for building trust rests on ethical principles. Few of us would continue to trust a client who promised payment on presentation of our invoice and then reneged.

On the flip side, we can't expect client personnel to trust us if we promise to deliver a report on a given date and then don't. Or if we criticize employees behind their backs. Or if we discuss the company's affairs with outsiders. Or if we belie confidences to employees that have been extended by top management. Or if we waste time. Or if we don't return client phone calls. I could go on forever, but you get the general idea.

Q. What do you consider the most serious potential ethical violations during production?

A. I think most consultants would agree that confidentiality is the most important facet of a consultant's business ethics. Many would also agree that I consider the second major ethics problem is pretending that we can perform a job without adequate knowledge or background.

Probably the easiest way to blow a client's trust is to not honor the confidential nature of information we obtain or discussions we have while on the job. Such breaking of trust is inexcusable for an ethical consultant.

As consultants we gain access to the most confidential information available in a company: far more, surprisingly, than a company's external auditors or lawyers. Although communications with consultants are not protected under the privileges the law grants to communications with lawyers and doctors, to be ethical we must nevertheless do everything in our power to honor a client's confidences.

One last comment about ethics during production. We all encounter problems during engagements that we know we do not have the ability to handle: a technical problem we don't understand, an organizational conflict we cannot resolve, personality clashes that prevent us from doing our work, and a myriad of other circumstances. Honesty demands that we bring such circumstances to the attention of the executive or manager who hired us. As ethical consultants we are also bound, if it is within our power, to offer remedies, even if it means bringing in another consultant to do the work for us. Next to breaking confidentiality, leading a client to believe that we can perform work we are not capable of doing is the most serious ethical violation during the production cycle.

Q. Is it common for consultants to fudge their billable hours?

A. I don't think that fudging billable hours is a widespread practice. If anything, consultants tend to be horrible timekeepers and *forget* to bill legitimate hours.

Cheating on hours does happen, however. It seems to be most common with work that consultants take back to their office. Not infrequently, telephone calls, emergencies from other clients, or administrative glitches interfere with doing a thorough job. With time constraints pressing from all sides the tendency is to broad-brush the work, even if it's a final report, just to get it done. That's unethical enough. To bill for hours devoted to other clients or for resolving administrative hang-ups is unconscionable.

I have also talked to consultants who have reneged on their hourly fee structure. After executing a scope agreement and beginning the work, a consultant might find that he or she has grossly underesti-mated the quoted hours or not-to-exceed price. Rather than renego-tiate a new contract, the contracted hours are billed, but at higher than contracted rates. If the client complains, the argument runs that the actual work performed ended up different from that envisioned in the original scope agreement and this new, upgraded work com-mands a higher hourly fee. Consultants may get away with this once, but I can't imagine a client engaging them for a second time.

ETHICAL CLIENT RELATIONS

Q. What are client relations?
A. In its simplest form, it is the term applied to those actions we employ to develop and maintain the goodwill of clients. Client rela-tions activities range from ballgames to dinner at a fancy restaurant; from sailing to a fishing weekend in Canada; from dinner parties at home to bridge games with spouses; from a golf or tennis outing to a professional boxing match.

Most of these activities involve harmless, relatively low-cost entertaining. I can't think of any instances where one of the above activities involves ethical questions.

Q. I've heard that overseas business is conducted with one hand under the table and the other in someone else's pocket. Is that true?

A. International consultants, those who must travel overseas on behalf of clients, or consultants whose clients are foreign companies, face a special client-relations problem: kickbacks, payoffs, bribes, and a variety of even less savory activities. The U.S. Foreign Corrupt Practices Act forbids an American company from engaging in any type of bribe or payoff to obtain business favors or to influence business decisions.

Except for some of the very large multinational corporations that maintain separate foreign subsidiaries to deal with such matters, most American companies try to keep their records clean. Unfortunately, they have been known to lean on their management consultants to do the dirty work for them.

Clearly, this question must be resolved by the individual consultant on a personal level. I don't know of any clear-cut, worldwide consensus.

However, the legality of performing such activities for American clients is another matter. Not being a lawyer, I can't provide legal advice. But I would certainly check with a qualified American attorney before engaging in any seemingly questionable activity.

Q. How can I improve the ethical management in my own office, especially regarding employees?
A. Ethics begin at home. It's practically impossible to follow two sets of standards, one in your own office and another one when dealing with clients.

Nearly all consulting markets require a significant amount of time away from the office, either working at a client's location, marketing, or traveling. Partners in multi-partner firms try to schedule their time so that at least one is present in the office at all times. At some times, however, it just doesn't work out. Single practitioners constantly confront this problem.

Someone must mind the store when we are away, and this usually means either full or part-time employees. The rule of thumb stating that approximately 10 percent of available hours should be devoted to administrative work holds true whether we perform the chores or let someone else do them.

Entrusting employees to run a store, a warehouse, or a shop in the owner's absence, necessitates hiring qualified, reliable people. In a consulting office it goes one step further. Clients seem to be constantly phoning to ask one thing or another; referral contacts want to talk to you personally; new clients ring up wondering when you can see them; client reports must be prepared, marketing presentations put together, and a myriad of other activities relating directly to the success or failure of the business must be attended to competently in your absence. This is in addition to pure bookkeeping functions such as paying bills, collecting accounts, filing compliance reports, and maintaining records.

With this level of responsibility, a person cannot afford to treat employees other than ethically. Employees hold the business together. They have the ability to hold clients or lose clients. They also play a major role in keeping the business solvent. It's just too big a risk to treat them any less ethically than clients.

Chapter 6

DEFINING THE JOB
How to Write Winning Proposals

Q. Lawyers, doctors, public accountants, and other professionals don't usually bother with written proposals. You tell them what you want and they do it. Why complicate matters when it's faster and easier to communicate orally?

A. Perhaps the professionals you mention would be better off if they did make use of written proposals. Some of the more successful corporate lawyers are beginning to do so.

In the consulting business, written proposals and accompanying scope contracts are accepted as standard operating procedure. Management consultants use written proposals first and foremost as a selling tool.

In earlier discussions we saw how clients seldom define the real problem, merely the results. They run out of cash, but don't have the vaguest idea how to rectify it. Frequently, company officers can't even correlate the results they observe with a problem; they just know that something is wrong.

As a selling tool, written proposals clarify and define a consultant's interpretation of the client's problem and propose definite courses of action to resolve the issue.

A duly executed written proposal that includes a scope contract is a commitment by the consultant to perform specific tasks and by the client to pay a specific fee for these services.

It's worth noting that consultants have used proposals more than once as an effective defense against client claims of nonperformance. Aside from legal aspects, an executed document that clearly defines the scope of work prevents misunderstandings at a later date about the extent of a consultant's responsibilities. It also prevents disagreement over invoices for services rendered.

Q. When should a proposal be submitted?
A. This depends entirely on the relationship between consultant and client. When soliciting new clients you might choose to use the proposal itself as a means to close the order. In this case, it should be submitted early in the discussion cycle—perhaps at the second meeting. It then serves as a discussion document. As the meeting progresses and the client's needs become clearer, specific points can be added to or deleted from the original document to arrive at a mutually acceptable definition of scope.

A different approach is appropriate when submitting a proposal to existing clients. Presumably a good working relationship has already been established, and if both parties agree in principle that the consultant should take on an additional assignment, the proposal can be submitted before finishing the current engagement.

Many find the informal approach works best, either while entertaining the client or immediately prior to beginning the job. The scope is probably already mutually agreed upon so the proposal becomes merely a clarification of previous discussions.

Q. I'm confused between a proposal and a scope contract. Can you explain the difference and when to use one or the other?
A. A proposal offers the client your specific services to solve a specific problem or problems. A scope contract defines the criteria surrounding the type of services to be performed. Another way of looking at it is that the proposal describes the "what" of the engagement: the scope covers how and when the work will be performed.

Very often the same document can be used for both a proposal and a scope contract. In this way the scope description is included in the body of the proposal.

This works fine for most jobs, provided the services to be rendered are easily definable. Most project-type engagements fall into this category: an acquisition or divestiture, the installation of a computer system, the identification of solutions to environmental hazards, and so on. These projects have a beginning and an end, with easily measurable results. A simple one- or two-paragraph scope statement suffices and is easy to include as part of the proposal.

Continuing engagements aren't as straightforward. This type of work is far more complex, longer-term, and somewhat nebulous, with results often not visible for two or three years. Attempting to define the scope of such an engagement in one or two paragraphs nearly always leads to misunderstandings and disagreements.

Normally, a separate scope contract should be negotiated for complex assignments, spelling out both the consultant's and the client's responsibilities in sufficient detail to avoid later claims of nonperformance or litigation.

WRITING THE PROPOSAL

Q. I realize that every proposal must match the needs of the client, but can you recommend general guidelines for proposal content?

A. Every proposal *is* different. The client's needs, the consultant's style, and the primary purpose of the proposal all influence format as well as content. A few general guidelines do apply, however. Let's deal with proposal content first, then cover scope contracts.

In addition to identifying the names of the consulting firm (or consultant) and the client, simple proposals should include a minimum of three points:

1. What services will be performed.
2. The fee to be charged for these services.
3. When payment is due.

Here is a sample of a simple proposal that excludes any definition of scope.

Fig. 6-1

PROPOSAL FOR CONSULTING SERVICES

On July 15, 1988, discussions were held between Joe Expert, a principal of DO-RIGHT CONSULTANTS ("consultant"), and Peter Freezout, president of NONLEAK BATTERIES, INC. ("NONLEAK") for the purpose of exploring NONLEAK's interest in expanding into international markets.

In response to these discussions, consultant hereby proposes to help the Financial Manager and other managers of NONLEAK structure and develop an export program for the Grade EE battery line.

Consultant's fee for this service will not exceed $20,000. This fee will be based on the number of actual hours incurred by consultant on behalf of NONLEAK at the consultant's billing rate of $150 per hour.

Consultant proposes to submit an invoice to NONLEAK every Monday for the actual hours incurred the previous week. This invoice is payable upon presentation.

In addition, upon approval of authorized personnel of NONLEAK, consultant will incur various out-of-pocket expenses while performing these services. NONLEAK will reimburse consultant upon presentation of a biweekly expense report detailing these expenditures with appropriate receipts.

The execution of this proposal does not bind either party; however, both parties agree to negotiate a contract within the next 30 days that defines the scope of the engagement, the time frame within which it will be completed, and the detailed work to be performed by consultant. If such a scope contract is not executed within this time frame, this proposal becomes null and void.

FOR DO-RIGHT CONSULTANTS	FOR NONLEAK BATTERIES, INC.
_____ Joe Expert, Principal	_____ Peter Freezout, President
_____ Date	_____ Date

This proposal states a "not-to-exceed" price for the project. Although most consultants hesitate to go this route, it does serve as an attractive selling tool for new clients. I have never landed a new client that didn't ask how much the job would cost. The smaller the client, the more important it is to respond to cost concerns in the proposal.

Clients nearly always underestimate what a consulting job will cost. It doesn't make much sense to proceed with a review of client operations and then, when you try to negotiate a scope contract, learn that the client has $10,000 in mind while you are looking at $50,000.

Remember, a proposal is a non-binding document, submitted with the clear understanding that the scope contract to follow sets the estimated project time and price.

If you are hesitant to use "not-to-exceed" words, as a minimum give a broad range—"from $10,000 to $30,000."

By executing a proposal agreement in advance of a scope contract, you have hooked the client while allowing time to further define the exact nature of the engagement. It also prevents the client from equivocating while preliminary reviews and research are being accomplished as a basis for negotiating the scope contract.

WRITING THE SCOPE CONTRACT

Q. What items should be included in a scope contract?

A. The specific terms of a complex scope contract result from a review of the company's business including production capability, product lines, and market position, as well as an assessment of managerial personnel. Such a review may be free, as we discussed earlier, or the actual hours may be included in the first invoice after executing the scope contract.

Some consultants try to scope out an engagement without such a review. This is usually a bad practice. It can lead to grossly underestimating the amount of time required to do the job, resulting in a loss to the consultant. Even without a guaranteed fee ceiling, clients invariably have a figure in mind beyond which they become very uncomfortable.

Less frequently, executing a scope contract without a preliminary review leads to an overstatement of projected cost. More often than not this loses an otherwise viable client. A pre-scope review nearly always results in better client relations, longer-term relationships, and in the end, substantially higher billings.

Whereas a proposal can be drafted relatively quickly, a scope contract deserves as much care and detail as one can muster.

Some consultants continue to execute very general scope contracts, without a detailed explanation of the engagement. This is a drastic mistake. It invariably leads to client distrust, misunderstandings, and a reluctance to see the project through.

More than one consultant has started an engagement without a detailed scope contract only to find halfway through the job that the client has become disenchanted with the time and money expended and is now severing the contract.

As a minimum, whether embodied in the proposal or executed separately, a scope contract should include the following:

1. Succinct statements of the specific tasks to be undertaken by the consultant.
2. A clear description of the consultant's responsibilities.
3. A clear description of client responsibilities.
4. A disclaimer of any guarantee of results.
5. An estimated time frame to accomplish each step of the engagement.
6. Clear statement of the right of either party to cancel the engagement.
7. Billing and payment terms.
8. A method for adjudication of disputes.

Within this framework, negotiations may lead to additional clauses or clarifications as well as references to follow-on jobs.

Q. Can you give me an example of a scope contract supporting the export program proposal?

A. Here it is. One caveat, however: don't copy this sample contract word for word. It is not meant to serve as the model for all contracts. Bear in mind that each situation calls for different wording.

Fig.6-2

SCOPE OF CONSULTING SERVICES
TO BE PERFORMED BY DO-RIGHT CONSULTANTS
FOR NONLEAK BATTERIES, INC.

As an adjunct to the proposal for consulting services to NONLEAK BATTERIES, INC. ("NONLEAK") submitted by DO-RIGHT CONSULTANTS ("consultant") on August 1, 1988, and subsequent to consultant's business review of NONLEAK, consultant will perform the following services relative to helping NONLEAK personnel establish an export program.

Marketing Representation

Consultant will present to NONLEAK the names, qualifications, and references of at least three export management companies (EMCs) qualified to market NONLEAK products to overseas buyers. Consultant will help company personnel negotiate a marketing contract with the EMC that NONLEAK personnel select as the most appropriate.

Shipping

Consultant will assist NONLEAK personnel evaluate the scope of the EMC's role, not only for marketing but also for arranging shipping, documentation, packing instructions, and freight haulers.

Insurance

Consultant will present NONLEAK with an evaluation of commercial and political risk insurance options and arrange for such coverage as is selected by company personnel.

Financing

During the preliminary review, NONLEAK financial personnel indicated a desire to use external financing to fund working capital requirements for the export program. Accordingly, consultant will utilize its best efforts to help NONLEAK qualify for and obtain working capital financing through Eximbank or other appropriate sources.

Collections

Consultant will instruct NONLEAK personnel in the drafting and use of international letters of credit and will help NONLEAK representatives select a bank with an appropriate international department to handle letters of credit and other international banking activities.

Other Matters

One phase of the preliminary review was to evaluate the competence of NONLEAK personnel to handle export business. Because of NONLEAK's general lack of experience in export management, consultant will, as an additional service, undertake to train selected personnel in the essentials of managing an export program.

Length of Engagement

The nature of this engagement precludes the guarantee of a completion date. However, it now appears that the engagement should be completed between 90 days and 180 days from the execution of this contract, assuming all company and external parties are available when needed and will proceed with diligence.

Fees and Terms of Payment

Even though the proposal preceding this agreement stated a not-to-exceed fee of $20,000, the results of the preliminary review and the extended services desired by NONLEAK invalidate this estimate. It now appears that the total fee for this engagement will range between $22,000 and $50,000, depending on the hours incurred, although consultant does not guarantee that the total cost will not exceed $50,000.

Consultant will invoice NONLEAK every other Monday for the actual hours and out-of-pocket expenses incurred during the previous two weeks. Such invoice is payable upon presentation.

Termination

This contract may be terminated by either party upon seven days verbal or written notice.

Liability of Consultant

Although consultant will use its best efforts to achieve the results desired by NONLEAK management, it cannot and does not guarantee or warrant that these results will be forthcoming. In addition, by executing this contract, NONLEAK agrees to hold consultant harmless from any liability or claim arising from this engagement brought by NONLEAK, its employees, or parties external to NONLEAK.

Adjudication

This contract is executed under the laws of the state of Alaska. If arbitration is necessary to resolve disputes, each party to this contract will select one arbitrator and the two selected will choose a third. A ruling by a two-thirds majority of arbitrators will be binding on both parties.

FOR DO-RIGHT
CONSULTANTS

FOR NONLEAK
BATTERIES, INC.

Joe Expert, Principal

Peter Freezout, President

Date

Date

Q. You said earlier that for relatively simple project-type engagements I could incorporate a scope statement within the context of the proposal letter. How about an example of that?

A. It's important to recognize that when incorporating a scope statement, the proposal becomes a contract, not merely a letter. I guess that statement requires a short explanation.

When we agree to take on work from a new client, we inevitably spend several hours, perhaps days, at the beginning, just learning about the client's business and personnel. This is non-productive time, similar to the business review previously mentioned.

If you don't want to donate this time, a separate scope contract provides the flexibility to include these hours in the first invoice. Also, completing a review permits a much better understanding of how long the job will take.

Executing a proposal and scope contract combined doesn't leave any room for preliminary review. It's easy to underestimate the length of the engagement. It's equally easy to misinterpret the client's real problem and hence real need.

By giving the client a not-to-exceed price or even a minimum/maximum ("min-max") range of hours or fees, the odds are high that you are shooting in the dark. Contracting for a two-week job that ends up taking two months could be a catastrophe.

Granted, with an "at will" termination clause either party can get out, but stopping work will also probably result in the loss of a client.

With that in mind, here is a combined proposal and scope contract for a clean, one-project engagement.

Fig. 6-3

PROPOSAL FOR CONSULTING SERVICES

On December 3, 1989, discussions were held between Roger Rover, a principal of TOP NOTCH CONSULTANTS ("consultant"), and Henry However, president of STRETCH HOSIERY, INC. ("STRETCH") for the purpose of exploring STRETCH's interest in a computer-based accounting system.

In response to these discussions, consultant hereby proposes to use its best efforts to assist the Controller of STRETCH design and implement a new accounting system using a PENTIUM II computer and the Peachtree accounting software package.

Consultant will invoice STRETCH weekly for the hours actually incurred at a billing rate of $150 per hour, plus out-of-pocket expenses approved by STRETCH. This invoice is payable on presentation.

Consultant estimates it will take two to three weeks at three days per week to complete this engagement, although, because of the unknown capabilities of STRETCH accounting personnel, consultant cannot guarantee this completion date. Furthermore, consultant cannot guarantee STRETCH's complete satisfaction with the system.

This contract may be terminated by either party upon three days verbal or written notice.

This contract is executed under the laws of the state of Texas. If arbitration is necessary to resolve a dispute, each party to this contract will select one arbitrator and the two selected will choose a third. A ruling by a two-thirds majority of arbitrators will be binding on both parties.

FOR TOP NOTCH	FOR STRETCH
CONSULTANTS	HOSIERY, INC.

Roger Rover, Principal	Henry However, President

Date	Date

NEGOTIATING THE SCOPE

Q. Are there any pointers you can suggest for negotiating a proposal or scope contract?

A. Too many consultants, both beginners and experienced, shy away from negotiating the scope and fee structure of a new engagement. With a minimum understanding of the client's business, they run an enormous gamble by proposing and agreeing to do a job at fixed or not-to-exceed fees, or even fee ranges, without going through a negotiating process.

Refusing to commit to a fixed or maximum fee doesn't do the trick. Too often, when clients insist on knowing how much the job will cost, we insist on billing by the hour at our standard rate. This may work for lawyers, but it seldom works for consultants—especially with new clients.

When a client says, in essence, "give me a price or you don't get the job" we back off, quote a price range, and then try to compensate once on the job. This invariably leads to overruns and loss of billings. Negotiating a mutually satisfactory fee structure brings much better results.

Instead of arbitrarily establishing a minimum/maximum range of hours or fees, or worse yet, acquiescing to a client's demands, put on your negotiating hat, bring out the gloves, and have at it. When a prospective client sees you are serious about negotiating, one of two conditions will occur: (1) a mutually satisfactory arrangement will be negotiated, or (2) the client will acquiesce to your original hourly fee proposal without a fight.

As far as negotiating techniques are concerned, all consultants have their own. Successful negotiators know what tactics work for them and stick with them. If you can't negotiate, no tricks I come up with will help very much.

Nevertheless, here is an outline of four basic tactics that work for me—what I refer to as the "Four P's". "The Four P's" first appeared in my book *Buying In: A Guide to Acquiring a Business or Professional Practice* (McGraw-Hill).

The "Four P's" of negotiating strategy are:

1. *People.* Know your opponents. Get to know as much about the people on the other side of the table as possible. Look for weaknesses. Identify strengths. Try to figure out what turns them on and off.
2. *Plan.* Establish a negotiating strategy before you ever get to the table. Decide how far to go to get the job. Identify points you can live without: which must be won?
3. *Perception.* Trust your intuition. Nine out of ten times the situation as initially perceived ends up being true. Don't backtrack when an opponent shows signs of weakening.
4. *Patience.* Don't be in a hurry. Let points ride. Don't lose your cool. Let the opponent tip his hand, and then go for the jugular.

DISAGREEMENTS ABOUT SCOPE

Q. What do I do if the CEO wants to change the scope of the engagement after I have already started?

A. You have two choices: renegotiate a new scope to include the changes or terminate the engagement. That's one reason it's so important to have an instant termination clause in the scope contract.

When you are engaged to sell a company on a contingency fee, without retainers, and the owner decides not to sell, all hours incurred to date are lost (a very good reason to insist on a retainer!). On the other hand, if the client wants to shift the scope to, say, refinancing or restructuring the company, merely renegotiate a new contract. Just be sure to include the lost hours.

Q. What if the CEO interprets the scope contract differently than I do?

A. That's a real problem.

The solution differs between a project engagement and a continuing management engagement. Let's look at projects first.

As we discussed earlier, a project engagement has a beginning and an end. It has definitive parameters. The results can be easily measured.

Without getting into a detailed discussion of various project engagement fee structures, let's assume that a contract calls for a fixed fee for a stated number of hours or days, to design an inventory control system. Terms of payment are 10 percent up front; monthly billings of 80 percent of the actual hours incurred; and 10 percent upon completion of the project. One of the reasons for structuring fees in this manner is to minimize a loss if the client breaches the contract.

Halfway through the job the CEO claims that you agreed to train employees to operate the system. Although this was not part of the scope contract, the CEO is adamant. Now what do you do without losing the rest of the job, including the 10 percent holdback, and probably the client?

Your course of action depends on the future potential of the client. With long-term potential for additional work, perhaps it makes sense to acquiesce and write off the training hours as a free promotion.

On the other hand, if the inventory control project is the last job you expect to do for this client, you might say, "OK. We each interpret the scope differently. How about a compromise? I'll spend the extra time training your employees for one-half my normal billing rate for the extra hours I incur. The total extra charge should be about $10,000. I'll do it for $5,000, if you will pay my invoice upon presentation without any holdback. In addition, I would like a reference letter from you now acknowledging your satisfaction with my work."

If the CEO remains adamant that the training be included as part of the original bid, I would seriously consider walking off the job and writing off the balance of the contract. Obviously, a reference letter will not be forthcoming.

Q. What should I do when and if I have disagreements with client management?

A. One of the lessons consultants learn early in the game is that we can't please all our clients all the time. Disagreements frequently arise during an engagement, either about scope interpretation, about the way we conduct the assignment, or about the benefits the client receives. Disagreements over scope interpretations seem to be the most prevalent.

I don't have an easy answer. Success in selling services, and especially business services, depends to a large extent on reputation. Reputation is most easily substantiated by references from previous clients.

When a disagreement results in our walking off the job, it's impossible to get a good reference from the client. If the disagreement is serious and we continue working, we become frustrated, the quality of our work suffers, and any reference probably won't be very good.

This is one reason that negotiating talent ranks right up there with selling ability as a prerequisite for consulting success. Except in rare situations, I have found that a cool head, coupled with tactful but firm negotiations, can resolve most disagreements before they fester. Neither consultant nor client may be entirely satisfied with the negotiated settlement, but making the effort should at least keep the parties on speaking terms.

Severing a relationship in anger doesn't help either side.

CRITICAL CONTRACT CLAUSES

Q. Can you give any tips about which clauses are more important than others—and if so, how they should be written to avoid later conflict?

A. The entire scope contract is a vital part of any engagement. If the scope of work can't be translated into a mutually agreeable written document, don't take the job.

Still, you should remember that most executives do not have legal training. They shy away from anything requiring commitment to a complex legal document.

The primary objective in committing an engagement scope to writing is to prevent misunderstandings during the job. It is not to strangle either party with a complicated contract. Therefore, I have always felt that the most important clause in a scope contact, or any written agreement for that matter, is an escape clause granting either party the right to terminate at any time. (If marriage contracts were written this way there would probably be more happy marriages and far fewer divorces!)

An escape clause doesn't have to be complicated. A single sentence serves the purpose. The termination clause in the scope contract between Do-Right Consultants and Nonleak Batteries, Inc. is as good as any:

"This contract may be terminated by either party upon seven days verbal or written notice."

Q. Other than an escape clause, are any other clauses particularly crucial?

A. I won't bother going into too much detail about descriptions of fee arrangements. You know how important they are.

One other clause seems to confuse consultants. That's the one covering a consultant's responsibility for results. Psychologically, we accept that a lawyer doesn't always win his case in court; a doctor's prescription doesn't always cure; a CPA automatically disclaims responsibility for the accuracy of audited financial statements. Still, we engage these professionals without as much as a second thought about guaranteed results, knowing full well that mandated perfection is impossible.

Not so with management consulting. When clients hire consultants to do a specific job they expect perfect results: a workable strategic plan, new financing, smoothly functioning systems, gains in market share. Clients hire consultants to solve problems they cannot handle themselves and expect that the value received, namely the satisfactory solution to the problem, is commensurate with what they pay the consultant.

None of us are magicians. Serious client problems cannot be solved with short-term simplistic approaches. Implementing a consultant's solutions requires long-term efforts by client personnel and (usually) outsiders: customers, banks, suppliers, legal counsel, and so on. Obviously, consultants have no control over either client personnel or outsiders. Therefore, it is pure fantasy to expect consultants to recommend solutions that will always solve a client's problems.

Nevertheless, clients expect perfection and consultants can only guard against dissatisfaction by incorporating disclaimers in the scope contract.

Q. Can you give me some examples of disclaimers that clients will accept?

A. One of the favorites is a "best efforts" clause. This states that consultants will use their "best efforts" to reach the solution the client desires. "Best efforts" does not mean a guarantee, only that all means within the consultant's control will be exerted to solve the problem.

Some consultants flatly refuse responsibility for results with the statement:

We do not guarantee or warrant that our recommendations or efforts will bring expected results.

I find this disclaimer unsatisfactory because it sounds as if we are telling the client up front that our recommendations might not work. If that's the case, why should the client hire us in the first place? Many consultants use this phrase, however, and seem to get by with it.

A third way to handle disclaimers—and one that works especially well in complex, multi-project or-step scope contracts—is to use language within the description of each project or step that effectively disclaims responsibility for results. This language might consist of phrases such as "assist company personnel," "present alternative options," and "evaluate opportunities." None of these phrases calls for a specific solution, and therefore no guarantee is made.

Q. Why should a client pay a consultant to install an accounting system if the consultant implies that it might not work?

A. Again, consider the CPA, who routinely denies responsibility for uncovering anything during an audit. Yet business people pay huge amounts to get a certified statement that really means absolutely nothing. One result is that fewer and fewer companies voluntarily purchase certified audits. They buy an audit only because some government agency or bank requires it, not for their own benefit.

That's an important lesson for management consultants. While it is extremely important to disclaim responsibility for the results of our work when other parties have a major role in the implementation of our suggestions or in the long-term maintenance of a project, it's equally important to accept responsibility for our own actions. This is why the words "assist," "recommend," "evaluate," and "present" are used so frequently. We certainly can, and should, accept responsibility for assisting, recommending, evaluating, and presenting, if that's what the scope contract calls for.

USING LAWYERS

Q. With such a strong emphasis on saying exactly what I mean in a proposal and scope contract and to be sure these important clauses get included, isn't it mandatory that I get an attorney to help?

A. No. Using an attorney to draft either a proposal or a scope contract too often ends in disaster. The client gets suspicious, misunderstandings occur, negotiations are impossible, and worse, you don't get the engagement. Lawyers don't *always* create these circumstances, but they frequently contribute heavily.

If an agreement is so complicated that either consultant or client needs legal assistance to draft or interpret it, the agreement will never hold up. Contracts or agreements between consultant and client should be relatively informal. It's the only way to establish mutual trust, and as we saw previously, mutual trust is the foundation of ethical consulting and sound client relations.

Beware of clients who insist on involving their legal counsel in discussions or agreements. In isolated cases there may be merit in seeking legal advice, but normally a company's legal counsel and consultant work together on the same problem. To bring counsel into the negotiations between client and consultant may just be company policy, but may signal something is amiss. This might be that the client is litigious, looking for a reason to bring suit against you. Nobody needs that type of client. On the other hand, it might just reflect the client's past experience.

Q. Are you saying that consultants and attorneys are adversaries, that we should never bring legal counsel into our dealings with clients?

A. Not at all. Consultants and lawyers should not be adversaries. We're in the same business: helping clients solve problems. And, as we've seen, lawyers are an excellent source of referrals in some markets.

Lawyers can be an invaluable source of information and assistance in situations that require legal interpretation or advice about peculiar laws or regulations that seem to conflict with the implementation of your recommendations. In that case, by all means seek legal advice.

Several years ago, while performing a restructuring engagement, I recommended that my client consider using the threat of filing for protection from creditors under chapter 11 of the federal bankruptcy code as a method of restructuring liabilities.

This company had been in financial difficulty for several years. The CEO and I worked out a plan to increase sales, decrease costs, and recapitalize the balance sheet—a plan that would bring the company out of its financial mess. With suppliers threatening to stop shipment and banks pushing for foreclosure, we didn't have time to implement the survival plan.

At the time, I did not have a strong background in prepackaged bankruptcies and wasn't exactly sure how to reschedule debt prior to filing and then develop a reorganization plan that would bring the client out of chapter 11 in thirty to sixty days. The client's attorney had no experience in this area either. I called in an attorney friend who specialized in bankruptcies to help work out the details.

In this situation, legal advice was *essential* to protecting my client's interest. Without a competent attorney we could not have resolved the issue.

The point I am trying to make is that you should use competent legal counsel to help solve client problems, but you shouldn't let lawyers interfere with writing an agreement or establishing a working relationship with a client.

Chapter 7

CHARGE THE RIGHT PRICE
How to Get Clients to Accept Your Fees

Q. Do different types of engagements necessitate different fee structures or is there a standard method?

A. There is no standard way to structure fees or terms of payment. We use a variety of methods, depending on the type of engagement, how well we know the client, a client's financial condition, the competition, and several other factors unique to specific situations. Also, fee structures and terms of payment are separate considerations, and should be viewed independently.

Fees can be quoted by the hour; by the day, week, or month; for a project; or on a contingency basis. On some jobs, consultants guarantee that the total charge will not exceed a maximum amount. In other cases they quote total charges within a minimum/maximum ("min-max") range.

Terms of payment are even more varied. Scope contracts might specify payment on receipt of invoice; thirty-day terms; weekly or monthly retainers; payment in full at the end of a job (such as for buying or selling a company); equity in exchange for services; or barter arrangements, to mention only a few of the more prominent terms.

Q. With all those variations, how do I choose the most appropriate fee arrangement? What is the starting point when establishing a fee structure?

A. The starting point is always an estimate of how much time the job will take. Although many variations exist, as a general rule, engagements can be divided between project work and continuing or long-term jobs.

For projects, we normally estimate how many person-hours the project will consume.

For continuing engagements, we estimate how many days per week or per month will be allocated to the job.

Once the estimated time is established, we merely apply a billing rate to arrive at an estimated price.

Q. How do I estimate how much time a job will take?

A. That's where experience comes in. As we have seen, this is a major point to be negotiated in the scope contract.

Unfortunately, there is no easy or standard method for estimating time. Beginning consultants experience a great deal of difficulty forecasting billable hours, although once a few jobs are completed it becomes easier.

The forecast of a specific number of days per week or month takes into consideration the availability of both consultant and client personnel. It is usually arrived at through negotiations.

The best way to demonstrate the estimating process for a project engagement is by example. Let's assume we're preparing a quote for the design and installation of a computer-based inventory control system for a company manufacturing kitchen cabinets. First, divide the job into its smallest logical time segments. Then estimate the hours for each segment. The estimated time schedule might be as follows:

		Estimated Hours
1.	Analysis of raw material and hardware purchasing sequence	10
2.	Analysis of work-in-process inventory stages and flow	12
3.	Analysis of stocking levels of finished products	6
4.	Selection and purchase of appropriate computer hardware and software	24
5.	Preparation of back-up manual inventory records for parallel run	48
6.	Training client personnel	24
7.	Implementation of system for raw materials and hardware	40
8.	Implementation of system for work-in-process	40
9.	Implementation of system for finished products	21
10.	Coordination of all systems—test and adjust	24
11.	Full documentation delivered to client	18
	TOTAL HOURS	267

The multiplication of 267 hours times a billing rate of $125 per hour produces an estimated quote of $33,375.

It might be possible to stay with actual hours on a job like this. More likely, however, the client will want either a not-to-exceed price (which would be $34,000) or a min-max range (which might be $30,000 to $35,000). If a similar job has been performed for other companies, a fairly accurate estimate of hours should be possible, making either approach feasible.

If the preliminary review indicates that the client does not utilize a manual inventory control system or that employees are unsophisticated in computer applications, it might be wiser to quote a min-max range.

If client personnel seem likely to resist a new system or if the business could change radically before the system is completed, then either a not-to-exceed or a min-max range would be foolish. In such cases, you must insist on billing actual hours.

If the client balks, try a "best efforts" clause against a min-max range, with the option of reviewing progress and renegotiating the range half-way through the job.

Q. How about estimating hours for a long-term continuing assignment?
A. Continuing engagements normally do not have logical endings. In nearly all cases, these assignments result in substantially more work, in more diversified areas, than originally anticipated, making an estimate of hours impractical.

As an alternative, many consultants favor guaranteeing so many days per week or per month for the engagement. To give the client at least some idea of the total scope, they also quote a maximum time limit for finishing the job or for renegotiating both scope and price—for example, two days per week for three months, or eight days per month for five months.

The best tack is to negotiate the committed days and the maximum time limit. Then quote a daily rate, such as $1,200 per day. Quoting a not-to-exceed price or a min-max dollar range for these jobs is dangerous. The client may want more than two days for some weeks, or more than eight days for some months. And by fixing a maximum dollar limit, it's possible for you to end up with a substantial loss.

As a practical matter, project hours cannot be quoted with any real accuracy for continuing assignments. Neither consultant nor client knows specifically what tasks will be involved in the engagement.

These suggestions and those previously stated for project-type work are guidelines. Actual fee structures depend on too many variables for you to follow standard procedures. In addition, you should remember that consultants tend to get into some very special situations that require uniquely structured fee schedules to satisfy the needs of both consultant and client.

FEES FOR SPECIAL ENGAGEMENTS

Q. Can you give me an example of what you would consider a special situation?

A. Take mergers and acquisitions (M&A) work. Every acquisition or divestiture job is different. I have performed several of each and no two have been alike.

Four basic fee structures are used for M&A jobs, plus an unlimited number of variations to the basic structures:

1. Lehman scale contingency closing fee based on total purchase/sale price. (The Lehman scale is defined below.)
2. Monthly retainer cumulatively applied against a contingency closing fee.
3. Up-front or monthly retainer plus a closing fee.
4. Actual hours incurred plus a closing fee.

The first method is obviously the cleanest. The Lehman scale contingency fee structure is acknowledged as a standard for M&A work, although increasingly consultants are demanding upward modifications (i.e., twice the Lehman scale). Lehman scale fees are calculated as:

5 percent for the first $1 million of purchase/sale price
4 percent for the second $1 million
3 percent for the third $1 million
2 percent for the fourth $1 million
1 percent for the fifth $1 million
1/2 percent for anything over $5 million

Since the fee is contingent upon a successful closing, if the closing falls through, no fee is paid and the consultant loses the hours worked. The low probability of reaching a closing is one reason this fee structure is so high. Very few true M&A consultants adhere to this structure any more. Too many things can go wrong, resulting in huge losses.

The second method is much more common. Typical monthly retainers are structured on the number of days per month committed to the client at a daily rate. This method ensures compensation even though a closing (the point at which a company is sold) never occurs. Generally, clients insist on a maximum number of months (usually six to nine) to get the company sold or to acquire one. If a closing doesn't occur by then, either the project gets dropped, or a new fee arrangement is negotiated.

For small acquisitions or divestitures commanding low prices, many consultants use the third method. The up-front retainer runs between $15,000 and $30,000 and is not refundable. This rather sizable amount attracts only those clients genuinely interested in an acquisition or sale and financially viable—two crucial ingredients in M&A work. One variation of this theme allows the client to offset the up-front fee against a closing fee, although normally it is in addition to the closing fee. The monthly retainer in such cases should be calculated in the same way as in the second method.

For very complex or difficult acquisitions or divestitures I insist on billing actual hours incurred rather than gambling on a retainer. I do the same when the job must be completed quickly. For example, a client trying to capture a new market before competition gets in frequently has no patience for a long acquisition search or negotiation and wants the job done now—not six months from now.

Actual hours should also be used when a fixed number of days per month becomes impractical to estimate. For instance, when an overseas client wants to acquire a company in the United States or an American company wants to sell a foreign division or subsidiary, it's nearly impossible to estimate with any degree of accuracy how many days it will take.

Q. Are there any other jobs requiring special fee structures?
A. Yes—too many to cover here. But I should comment on one that consultants are being increasingly called upon to perform: raising capital.

With a credit crunch hitting both American and foreign companies, financing has become a very popular market niche for consultants with connections in international finance circles. Many small and mid-size companies think only of their not-so-friendly bank when it comes to raising external working capital, funds for expansion, or financing for international trade or investment. Banks, on the other hand, are increasingly withdrawing from the small loan market. Creative financing is needed, and consultants are frequently called upon to source it.

Some financial consultants charge the traditional finder's fee, ranging from 1/2 to 5 percent of the funds raised. The trend, however, is to include capital raising activities with related consulting work—such as restructuring or long-term planning so you can offer a complete package. For this type of job, retainers or committed worker days can easily be wed to a modified finder's fee structure.

I met a consultant at a seminar on Eurosecurity financing who related an interesting combination of financing and management consulting. His client needed to raise $20 million: $13 million for starting an assembly plant in Madagascar, $4 million for new equipment in his U.S. plant, and $3 million for working capital to bring a new product to market. The client also wanted help sourcing a joint venture partner and recruiting suitable management staff for the Madagascar plant.

The consultant structured his fees as follows:

1. Finder's fee equal to 1.5 percent of the financing package.
2. Monthly retainer of $10,000 for six months.
3. Equity in the new Madagascar subsidiary equal to 5 percent of total capital.
4. The use of the company's American Express card for six months not to exceed $10,000 per month.

About a year later I ran into this consultant again and asked how he made out. Without going into details, he said that he had earned enough on this job to start up a branch office in Johannesburg and that he was now specializing entirely in international financing markets.

DIFFERENT RATES FOR DIFFERENT WORK

Q. I'm curious about setting hourly or daily rates. How do I know what rates to charge?
A. Setting billing rates involves three distinct issues: how much your services are worth on the open market; how much the competition charges; and how much a client is willing to pay.

A related element also enters into the equation: the type of work involved. Quite often, while trying to build a business, consultants overlook this last point. That's a major mistake.

Some jobs are more difficult than others and should be priced higher. Some jobs require a higher level of expertise or more training than others and command a higher fee, as do those entailing a greater risk.

No rule or custom dictates that we must charge the same hourly rate for all types of work. On the contrary, it's more logical to establish a range of hourly rates applicable to the various types of work we expect to solicit.

Q. Are clients willing to pay higher hourly rates for high-risk jobs or for those requiring more effort or more training than others?

A. Yes. Most business people are not blind to these factors. They realize that a consultant, or anyone else, should be compensated according to the complexity of work done and the risk taken.

Q. How can I evaluate how much my services are worth on the open market?

A. The easiest and most equitable way is to compare what you do with salaries paid employees performing similar work. For example, assume a client wants help installing a new computer-based accounting system and training personnel to operate it.

A full-time employee with the ability to do this work would cost the company approximately $40,000 to $50,000. On an annual basis, a $50,000 salary works out to an hourly rate of $26. Fringe benefits raise the rate to $36. Locating and training a new employee adds another $15, bringing the total to $50 to $55 per hour.

Factor in executive search fees, severance pay when the job is completed, and other miscellaneous costs, and $75 to $85 per hour is easy to justify. Add in the convenience of beginning the job immediately and an hourly rate between $90 and $100 is not unreasonable.

Engagements involving work assignable to an executive earning an annual salary of $100,000 to $150,000 obviously justify a much higher rate.

Q. How do I find out what my competition is charging?

A. This is far more difficult. If competitors can be identified as other management consulting firms a few phone calls might provide the answer. Be cautious, however. In an effort to encourage newcomers to price themselves out of the market, we tend to overstate our answers. Although rates vary substantially in different parts of the country and even more by client size and type of work, non-consulting competition provides a more reliable guideline than other consultants.

Lawyers, public accountants, engineering firms, financial planners, and a variety of other personal-service businesses all compete with consultants at one time or another. It's usually much easier to get a fix on hourly rates from these competitors than from management consultants.

A quick call to a major office of one of the major accounting firms can establish rates for partners, managers, supervisors, and juniors. The same holds for large legal and engineering firms. It's also easy to get rates from export management firms for an export job.

Q. Can you give me some idea of currently acceptable fee levels?
A. It's always dangerous to generalize about fees. However, here are some broad guidelines.

In the late 90s, hourly rates for management consultants on the East Coast (excluding New York City) were approximately as follows:

For small business accounts	$75 to $100
For project work, mid-size clients	$125 to $150
For management assistance on continuing assignments	$125 to $175
For export/import jobs	$150 to $250
For overseas work	$250 and up
For M&A work	$150 to $200 plus closing fee
For finance sourcing	0.5 to 5 percent of financing package

Q. How do I find out how much a client is willing to pay?
A. Weigh your judgment call against rates charged by competition. If the two are in the same ballpark, that range should represent what clients are willing to pay. Whether they will or not depends on their financial situation, how much they really want your service, and how adept you are at selling and negotiating. In the end, assuming the client does want the service, the price must be a negotiated amount that both parties can live with.

SETTING THE TERMS OF PAYMENT

Q. What about setting payment terms?
A. A variety of payment terms can be used, depending on the client's financial standing, the type of work, client/consultant relationships, and a consultant's needs. If you are broke, you'll

want to be paid very quickly indeed. A financially secure consultant can afford to be more flexible. The more flexible you can be, however, the greater the probability of your getting the job and the higher the fees.

Although the variety of payment terms is limited only by the creativity of both client and consultant, here are a few of the more common methods.

1. Payment on receipt of monthly invoice
2. Payment on receipt of weekly or biweekly invoice
3. Advance payment of weekly or monthly retainer, offset against weekly or monthly invoices for actual time
4. Up-front payment equal to a percentage of total fixed fee, usually in tandem with a percentage holdback to completion of job; the balance payable as invoiced weekly or monthly
5. Up-front payment and/or monthly retainer offset against percentage fee at closing of transaction (as with an acquisition or divestiture)
6. Total fee payable upon completion of job (as with contingency fee for M&A work or finance sourcing)

Q. When should I insist on an up-front payment or a weekly or monthly retainer?

A. It's always a good idea to negotiate advance payments when taking on a new client. Once a working relationship exists and a track record of prompt payments has been established, advance payments can be stopped. Until then, however, lawyers, doctors, and other personal service professionals nearly always demand advance payment. So should consultants.

The size of the client doesn't seem to make much difference. Many giant corporations are the slowest payers, especially during a business downturn. It's bad enough when giant automotive, aerospace, and retail companies push their product suppliers into accepting 60- to 90-day payment terms. Pulling the same stunt with small, service businesses can easily lead these smaller firms and their owners to the bankruptcy court. With bankruptcies continuing to rise at a rapid rate (mostly entrepreneurs and small businesses) the phenomenon is clearly no abstract theory.

Smaller clients may not be as bloodthirsty, but they are generally short of cash. It's very easy to pay product suppliers first and let lawyers, public accountants, and, of course, consultants wallow in the dust.

WHEN A CLIENT IS CASH-POOR

Q. Most of the new clients I solicit are small and mid-size businesses. Several have told me that they would like to hire me but can't afford it. How can I get around that problem?
A. One way is by taking an equity share in the client's business as part payment. This doesn't cost a client anything. If the company's cash shortage emanates from growing pains rather than financial difficulties an equity share could be a good investment.

I do not recommend, however, taking an entire fee in equity shares, regardless of a company's growth potential. The reason is purely psychological. When clients get the benefit of consulting advice without paying anything except equity shares, they tend to undervalue your expertise. Let me offer an example.

Some years ago I picked up a new client, a small publisher of two trade magazines for farm equipment dealers and dairy farmers. At the time, agriculture was a booming business in the Upper Midwest and the publisher was doubling its subscribers every nine months. When negotiating the scope contract, the owner convinced me to take a 25 percent share of the company as my entire fee.

The engagement entailed setting up a strategic planning procedure, recruiting two top executives, and assisting the owner with market research for a new publication he planned to add. The job lasted seven months. When the engagement ended, I went on to other clients, convinced that I had made a substantial contribution to the growth of the company. How wrong I was!

Within three months the owner junked the strategic plan and fired one of the new executives. Furthermore, he told his banker and several suppliers that my work was only marginally effective: although I was a capable consultant, nobody willing to work as cheaply as I did could possibly have the experience to provide sound advice. That was the first and last time I agreed to take an entire fee in equity shares.

Q. I would think that taking an equity share in a high-growth company could eventually be extremely lucrative—far more so than taking cash fees. What's your opinion?

A. There's no question about it: taking shares in a company that eventually goes public could result in hitting the jackpot! If the company doesn't go public, however, stock certificates could be worthless paper, regardless of how fast the company grows.

To prevent this from happening, make sure that the client agrees to buy back the shares on a predetermined future date if the company doesn't go public. Such an agreement should also specify the buy-back price. And of course, the price should not be less than the cash fees that normally would have been charged in the first place.

One convenient way to handle this is to make the minimum price equal to the amount of cash fees normally charged, regardless of the company's fortunes. Try to negotiate a buy-back price equal to some multiple of book value or prior years' earnings, with the cash fee amount as a floor.

Such a buy-back agreement can be included in the scope contract, although it gets a bit cumbersome. Writing a side agreement with a reference in the scope contract works better.

BARTER

Q. Suppose the company is not in a high-growth pattern. Is there another way to take the job and still make out all right?

A. Yes. I have found that old-fashioned barter arrangements work wonders under certain circumstances. In fact, I used barter techniques to successfully build a business (a computer training school) that was completely divorced from the rest of my consulting business.

Bartering is a different ballgame than taking equity shares. Equity requires waiting an indeterminate amount of time to recoup an investment. It may never be recovered if the company doesn't prosper. With a barter deal you receive something of value immediately.

The psychology is different, as well. Equity shares don't cost the client anything right now, and maybe never. Therefore, in a sense the client gets consulting services free. With barter, on the other hand, the client gives up something of value immediately in exchange for consulting advice. The greater the value placed on the bartered goods or services, the more consulting advice is worth.

Q. Can you give me some examples of types of goods and services I could expect to receive for consulting services?

A. Here are a few of the barter deals I have made. Some of these products and services were for the total consulting job; some represented only partial payment with the balance in cash:

- Secretarial services—typing, copying, mailing
- Restaurant dinners
- Legal services—contract reviews, real estate advice
- Tax return preparation
- Office table, chairs, desk, and lamps
- Carpet cleaning
- Charter air service
- Hotel rooms
- Flower arrangements
- Wall hangings—paintings, posters, etc.
- An automobile
- Snow removal and lawn care
- Computer instruction on new software
- Auto repairs and tires
- Copying machine and fax machine
- Tree service and landscaping
- Advertising service and brochure printing

This represents only a fraction of what I have bartered for over the years. Most of the goods and services came directly from clients. The automobile, the auto repairs, and tires came from third parties in three-way barter arrangements.

Each of these goods and services had value to me in the sense that I would have purchased them if they hadn't been bartered. But this is not always the case. Many barter deals involve goods that you can't use yourself and must be sold to recoup your investment.

Q. How does reselling bartered goods work?
A. It's not as complicated as it seems. As long as a person has a pretty good idea who will buy the goods and knows the approximate market price before setting the barter value, it's hard to lose. For example, when taking used office furniture that you don't need, it's easy to arrange a resale to a used office equipment and furniture dealer. Just be certain to get a quote first.

On the other hand, I have known consultants who have a terrible time recouping the value of their services. A friend performed an acquisition with a Lehman scale closing fee that amounted to $150,000. He negotiated payment of $75,000 in cash and $75,000 worth of products from the acquired company, which distributed electrical fixtures for industrial and commercial applications.

My friend ended up renting a small warehouse to store the goods. It took him three years to find buyers for *half* of the goods. He held an auction for the balance and claimed he lost his shirt on the deal.

In the international consulting market, getting paid with bartered goods is quite common, especially if the job involves setting up or acquiring a foreign manufacturing facility. Not infrequently the consultant becomes a player in a buy-back or co-production countertrade arrangement between the two principals. Goods acquired in this manner are normally best disposed of through a third party broker who knows how and where to sell them.

Q. How does acquiring bartered goods through a third party work?
A. Let's say that a client sells me laundry supplies, maintenance hardware, restaurant supplies, and other consumables to hotels. I don't have any use for these products but want to arrange a barter contract.

The first step is to determine what volume of these products matches the consulting fees I would normally charge. Once that's established, the client and I work out a swap with the hotel. The client gives that volume of supplies to the hotel. The hotel grants me free rooms and meals equal in value to the supplies. I perform the consulting services for the client. Voila—a three-way swap in which everyone makes out.

The same principle applies to four- or more-party swaps but obviously, the more parties involved the more difficult it becomes to value the bartered goods and services and to coordinate timely delivery.

Q. Can you summarize the pros and cons of barter arrangements for a layman?

The plus side first:

1. When new or existing clients don't have the cash to pay consulting fees, a barter deal might be the only way to get the job.
2. If you can use the goods or services yourself and would have purchased them anyway, there is no gain or loss in bartering versus cash payments.
3. Even if you can't use the goods or services yourself, if you know of a third-party market for them it's possible to make more on a resale than from cash fees.
4. Under certain conditions tax savings can be realized using barter. I do not hold myself out as a tax expert, however. Consult a competent and qualified tax advisor to get all the particulars for your situation.

On the minus side:

1. The value of the bartered goods or services must equal or exceed normal cash fees for the engagement.

2. Disposing of bartered goods on the open market can be difficult.
3. The client may be in a better position than you to know the value of the goods or services and could take advantage of your ignorance.
4. Three or more parties to a barter increase the complexity geometrically. So does utilizing a barter broker for disposal of foreign-acquired goods.

KEEPING TRACK OF HOURS

Q. How do I avoid overruns?

A. So far we have discussed setting fees and terms of payment for establishing a price in the scope contract or bid. But that's only half the picture. The other half is a system that flags potential overruns from estimated hours. The system should provide ample warning to take corrective action or to renegotiate the balance of the contract before you go too deep in the hole.

A variety of methods can be used to keep track of where we are relative to the original scope contract. The choice of one over the other is a personal matter. Most of us develop our own system to fit our bookkeeping abilities. Two of my consulting associates don't use any formal system, preferring to keep track intuitively. This seems like a dangerous path, however, and I certainly don't recommend it.

An hour/day tracking system is also necessary if the scope contract calls for weekly or monthly billings of actual hours or days worked. A record must be kept in case the client challenges an invoice.

Over the years I have developed several tracking systems for different types of engagements. All work fairly well as long as I remember to keep posting my hours currently. If I don't, none of them work. I use different methods for short-term projects, continuing engagements, and special assignments.

Q. Can we take a look at a short-term project system first?

A. Let's construct a very simple example using these facts:

Project description: to evaluate the market size for a new product line and the competitive positions of major players.

Estimated completion date: 12 weeks

Estimated person-days of work:

    Market analysis   12

    Competitive survey   10

    Report   2

Below is a simple, one-page budget to account for twenty-two peson-days. Note the milestones marking the "red flag" date of each of the two steps—market analysis and competition survey. If the actual person-days are behind budget at either of these dates, corrective action must be taken or renegotiations started.

Fig. 7-1

HOURS BUDGET

Client: XYZ Corp.
Project: market analysis and competition survey

Week	Market Analysis		Competition Survey		Total	
	Budget	Actual	Budget	Actual	Budget	Actual
1	2				2	
2	2				2	
3	2				2	
4	3				3	
5	2				2	
Milestone check						
6	1		1		2	
7			1		1	
8			2		2	
9			2		2	
10			2		2	
Milestone check						
11			2		2	
12						
Total	12		10		22	

Q. How do you construct a time budget for a continuing engagement?
A. That depends on how the scope contract reads. If it calls for billing actual hours incurred without any top limit or time constraint, then a piece of paper is sufficient to keep track of hours incurred. Several inexpensive software programs with predesigned time sheet forms can also be used.

I find it a chore to use a computer merely to post daily hours, however. Manual posting to a spreadsheet or 3 x 5 cards works just as well.

The number of simultaneous jobs influences which system is the handiest. I normally have about three or four jobs going concurrently, plus half a dozen marketing projects in various stages. Some hours are billable; some are not. A handy deck of 3 x 5 cards—one per client—provides easy access and a quick reminder of unbilled hours. I use the same cards to track collections against receivables for those clients who do not pay promptly.

A 14-column spreadsheet serves the same purpose, although I find it too awkward.

For continuing management assignments that call for a finite completion date or a guaranteed number of hours or days per week or month, a modified schedule similar to that used for projects fills the bill.

For example, assume a turnaround engagement that calls for a commitment of three days per week to perform a variety of activities. The fee structure calls for billing actual hours incurred every two weeks. The scope contract calls for interim status reports every two weeks. The engagement is supposed to run for a maximum of six months. You have agreed to terminate earlier if the company cannot be restructured or saved through other means, at which time a bankruptcy filing or liquidation will be recommended.

Here is a time sheet structured to fit this assignment, up to the decision point for bankruptcy or liquidation.

Fig.7-2
TIME SHEET

ABC CORPORATION

Actual Hours

	Monday	Tuesday	Wednesday	Thursday	Friday
Week					
1	9	8		8	
2		10	7	8	
Report #1					2
Total hours	9	18	7	16	2
3	8	8	8		
4		8	9	8	
Report #2					2
Total hours	8	16	17	8	2
5					
6					
Report #3					
7		The balance of the form would be similarly completed.			
8					
Report #4					
9					
10					
Report #5					
11					
12					
Report #6					

Milestone decision point—GO OR NO-GO
(NOTE: The same format would be repeated for the second three months)

Q. What variation in these forms would you recommend for special assignments?
A. That depends on the terms of payment, the fee structure, and the type of engagement. For jobs calling for billings by the hour or day either one of the forms works well.

For M&A jobs calling for an advance monthly retainer offset against a Lehman scale closing fee, there isn't much need for a time sheet, unless a fixed number of hours or days per week or per month are guaranteed. On the other hand, it is helpful for planning. The idea is to keep track of how many hours go to productive work and how many to marketing and administration, even though that information might not be needed for billing purposes.

Time management can be especially crucial when starting out or when shifting to new market niches. Without a disciplined system to account for time, it's far too easy to get bogged down on non-productive projects.

I also find it very helpful to budget hours by job and by task and then periodically match up actual hours incurred. Many consultants find this a useless task, but it does help in planning our time. I find this approach especially necessary when performing an international assignment that takes me away from the office for weeks at a time. By budgeting my time, I know if and when I need to make provisions for assistance to handle administrative tasks and marketing at home.

Regardless of the format, most experienced consultants would agree that keeping track of billable and non-billable hours nearly always helps when establishing fee structures for future jobs.

Chapter 8

BIGGER IS BETTER
How to Make Your Business
Look Bigger Than It Is

Q. I've found that once I land an engagement, the client wants me to get into areas beyond the scope contract. What do I do if I'm not capable of handling this work?

A. Consultants have struggled with this problem, it seems, since the beginning of time. All too often, we get into situations requiring skills or knowledge beyond our expertise, usually during continuing engagements.

Recently, while I was working on a refinancing assignment, a CEO asked me to participate in a review of the company's new laser sensor product marketing program. I soon realized that without a background in engineering (not to mention laser technology) I was lost. When I told the CEO that I wasn't qualified, I also suggested he allow me to bring in an associate, an ex-employee of the GE Space Center with twelve years of experience in electronic instrumentation. That saved the day and I continued on the refinancing assignment.

One of the consultants in our consortium handled a similar situation differently. An expert in organizational development, his client needed help setting up an export program. Instead of calling me, he tried to do the job himself, failed miserably, and lost not only the organization restructuring job, but the client as well.

It doesn't pay to attempt a job if you don't have the expertise. Nine times out of ten we botch the assignment and end up with a very unhappy client, or no client. If you can't find someone qualified to handle the task, admit your shortcomings and go on to the next job.

Q. That's easy to say but not so easy to do. How do I find these people? And how should I organize my business to utilize their talents without losing clients?

A. Let's start at the beginning. Multi-partner firms use different approaches than single practitioners. In fact, diversification is the major advantage of multi-partner firms. Although the talents of two or three partners are not likely to cover the waterfront of skills, there isn't much reason to form a partnership unless the principals bring complementary but diversified talents to the table.

Another advantage multi-partner firms enjoy relates to size. A business large enough to support three or four partners usually requires one or two junior partners or staff personnel. These employees with specialized or technical skills open the talent door even further. With a variety of talents in house, these firms have little need to call on outsiders.

Single consultants face a different problem. For a variety of reasons, many prefer to work on their own, unencumbered by formal partnerships. I certainly do.

Although freedom of action is clearly an advantage of being alone, one person's breadth of skills and experience can't match that of larger firms. Client companies obviously recognize this shortfall. As long as we continue operating as individuals we will have a difficult time competing with larger firms for the better and more lucrative jobs.

The answer is to continue running our businesses as individual consultants but present the image of a multi-partner firm.

Q. Is that lying?

A. Absolutely not. Lying about our capabilities, of course, will only get us in deep water if we do get the job. But presenting the image of a larger firm is not lying, if in fact the same diversity of capabilities can be assembled as in a multi-partner business. This can be accomplished by forming consortiums, networks, or informal partnerships.

CONSORTIUMS

Q. What is a consortium?

A. A consortium is loosely defined as a temporary alliance of two or more businesses in a common venture. In the management consulting field, consortiums normally include only consulting businesses, not complementary professional firms.

A consortium is not a legal entity. No contractual documents are executed, although non-binding written agreements help to define the consortium structure and the responsibilities of each participant. Here is a sample of a typical consortium agreement. It is not intended for use as a model to cover all the specifics of your business situation; use it as a general guide.

Fig. 8-1

CONSORTIUM AGREEMENT

The following management consulting firms do hereby form a consortium for the purpose of utilizing each other's skills and talents for obtaining and performing consulting engagements:

Thompson & Co., Inc.
Ross Lowe Associates
PNF & Associates, Inc.
Retlan A. Plain & Company

Each of the parties to this agreement will hold each other party harmless from any liability arising from that firm's actions of any type.

The parties also agree that if and when occasions arise, either in marketing or production, that require expertise not resident in the firm soliciting the engagement, that firm will first seek assistance from a member of this consortium, provided that a member has the required skills or talents. If such skills or talents are not resident in the consortium, then assistance from non-member firms may be solicited.

If one member assists another member, the fee structure and terms of payment will coincide or be compatible with the practices of the engaging firm.

All client billings and collections will be handled by the consortium member actually performing the work. No member is responsible for the billing or collections of any other member.

This agreement is non-binding. A member firm may withdraw at any time. The consortium may be totally disbanded at the discretion of two or more members.

Additional management consulting firms may be asked to join the consortium from time to time, provided that all then-current members agree.

_____   Thompson & Co., Inc.

_____   Ross Lowe Associates

_____   PNF & Associates, Inc.

_____   Retlan A. Plain & Company

DATE   _____

Q. Where do I find the appropriate consulting firms to form a consortium?

A. After being in the business for a while, it's pretty hard not to meet other management consultants. New York City is probably different, but in most parts of the country we keep running into the same faces at seminars, promotions, lawyers' and accountants' offices, banks, alumni gatherings, and civic and social functions.

Having met five or six consulting firms, it's easy to decide which ones fit your modus operandi and ethical standards. If asked, most consultants are more than willing to join a consortium.

There's no reason for not belonging to more than one consortium, provided the types of engagements and clients don't clash. For example, a consortium of international consultants is unlikely to infringe on a consortium of small business consultants. Firms specializing in turnaround work seldom compete with those focusing on Fortune 500 clients. And so on.

Consultants just starting out or in the early years of building a business have a little more difficulty locating appropriate consortium participants. Old-timers tend to be skeptical of joining forces with the new kid on the block. Staying power comes from experience, and few of us are willing to risk our reputation on a newcomer's ability to make the grade.

One way around this hurdle is to team up with other consultants who are also trying to build a business. This type of consortium doesn't provide as much experience, but when you're starting out any help is usually welcome.

If appropriate firms can't be located, try setting up a network, which isn't as difficult to break into.

CONSORTIUM BENEFITS AND RISKS

Q. What are the specific benefits of participating in consortiums?
A. Consortiums are helpful in two areas: marketing and production.

I mentioned the desirability of presenting new clients with the image of a diverse repertoire of talents. Large consulting firms do this by displaying the capabilities of partners and staff associates. Single consultants accomplish the same objective with consortiums. Even if members are never called upon for assistance, just having their names and qualifications in sales literature creates a "big firm" image.

Q. Should I have brochures printed with this information?
A. Why not? As we saw earlier, brochures won't be the deciding factor in getting clients, but they will cut down on the time it takes to explain qualifications.

One way to keep the printing cost down is to have separate "slip-in" pages for each member of the consortium. That way, if someone drops out, or new consultants join, the entire brochure doesn't have to be reprinted. When marketing to international prospects, I don't see any need to include members who specialize in troubled companies. For government contract work, promoting specialists in computer systems design won't help.

Alternatively, some consultants feel that consortium participation does not belong in a brochure, that describing the breadth of qualifications is better handled with separate sales literature. A one-

or two-page description of the consortium and its membership can be distributed to prospects as needed.

I have yet to meet a client who didn't feel more secure hiring a consulting firm with a wide breadth of talents and skills. Consortiums provide this depth. Promoted with the proper flair, consortium membership is one of the best marketing tools around for single practitioners.

Q. What about production benefits?
A. Production benefits are obvious. None of us is expert in all business areas. Many of us have a wide range of talents and skills, but it's impossible to be strong in every technical facet of business management.

Most smaller and mid-size companies prefer a small consulting firm or a single practitioner to a large organization like Andersen Consulting: some of the big companies do, too. We provide personalized service, more flexibility in our scheduling, and generally charge less than the giants. In many cases, Andersen, A.T. Kearny, and the other large consulting organizations get jobs because clients feel they have the diversity of talent to take care of any exigency that may arise.

Even though flexibility, personalized service, and competitive rates are important factors, smaller firms can only survive over the long haul by offering a skill range similar to the industry leaders. Consortiums fill the gap.

An excellent example of how this works occurred several years ago. I was engaged in a very complex strategic planning job that involved restructuring an organization and installing production and inventory control systems.

As the job progressed, it became obvious that the client also needed help in two distinctly different areas: developing an application engineering system to move customer change orders through to production, and conducting site surveys for a satellite manufacturing plant and distribution warehouse. Not only did I have my hands full already, my experience in these areas was nil.

The client was leaning toward engaging the local office of Peat Marwick, which at that time had a strong consulting reputation in application engineering and site evaluation. I had a strange feeling that once this giant got in the door, I would never see my client again.

At the time, two members of my consortium, from Texas and Colorado, sported engineering and real estate credentials equal to or superior to Peat Marwick's. I brought them in for a meeting with client personnel. Once the client saw their credentials and understood the flexibility and personal service they offered, Peat Marwick didn't stand a chance. The CEO was so pleased with the results that the company remained a good client until it merged with a larger corporation some years later.

This is only one example. I could offer two dozen more. On the production side, even more than with marketing, single consultants cannot compete for major jobs without a diversified consortium to draw from.

Q. Doesn't a consortium also involve risks?

A. It certainly does, especially when it consists of several firms scattered throughout the country. Two of the biggest risks are mismanaging long-term coordination of market specialties, and cheating.

Every successful consulting firm keeps one eye on changes in the marketplace. As new trends develop, new regulations occur, and new companies are formed, smart consultants develop strategies to exploit them. This might mean recasting client bases, originating innovative ways to handle new marketing directions, retraining in state-of-the-art skills, or (for larger firms) hiring or retraining staff specialists.

Even with modern-day communications, it's hard to know what changes occur in each member firm. Seldom if ever do all participants get together for a summit meeting. Computer telecommunications, letters, fax, and telephones work well enough to keep the group informed if everyone uses them conscientiously—but it's easy to forget to communicate when you're running to keep up with a growing business. Changing patterns in consulting firms make current sales literature difficult to maintain and frequently create confusion in determining who has what skills.

The second risk, cheating, happens less frequently but is nevertheless a concern. The cheating I'm referring to occurs when we bring a consortium member into our marketing or production cycle and the client ends up dropping our firm and going with our associate.

Consultants are notorious for protecting their clients: that's why they seldom talk to each other. They are afraid that another consultant will steal a client. Fortunately, this fear is usually groundless, at least between smaller firms. It definitely is not groundless when the big firms get a toehold.

Since consortium participants normally consist of smaller firms or single practitioners, cheating should not be a problem. It does occur, however, and we must stay alert to the possibility.

Another tip on cheating: don't count on suing an offending member based on a consortium agreement. It hardly ever works and only damages your reputation. Remember, the agreement is non-binding and can be terminated by anyone at any time.

Some hyperconservative consultants who are wary of losing clients insist on executing a noncompete agreement among consortium members. Signing such a clause is your option, of course, but I have never seen consortiums last very long that rely on noncompete covenants.

BILLINGS AND CLIENT RELATIONS WITH CONSORTIUMS

Q. Can you tell me a little bit about the mechanics of consortium billing practices?

A. When two or more consortium firms do a job together, the client always knows the identity of the separate entities. If camouflaging identities is important, you can use the network route.

Normally, although not always, consortium members bill the client separately. Obviously this means that each firm also does its own collection follow-up also. Since the originating firm executed the scope contract, and assuming the scope has not changed materially, fee structures and terms of payment must follow the original contract, commensurate with the originating firm's procedures.

If this becomes a sticking point between consulting firms, side agreements can be used to compensate consortium members for fee concessions or payment delays. Clearly, this cuts into the profit of the originating firm and is not common practice. However, if the client provides a major source of billings over an extended period, compensating a consortium member might be a good trade-off to losing the client.

Q. Do occasions arise when fee splitting is the way to go?
A. Because each firm bills separately, fee splitting is not common in consortiums. Exceptions do arise, however. One such exception occasionally occurs in M&A work. Assume a single practitioner gets a complete acquisition job—sourcing, due diligence, financing, negotiating, and perhaps assisting in transition management. If it's a large acquisition in a remote location, a consortium member near that location might be called upon to perform one or more of the steps: sourcing targets, due diligence, locate appropriate financing, or assist in the transition.

In this case, member firms provide a service to the originating consultant, not the acquiring client. Fee splitting is quite common. The client pays the originating consultant who in turn splits the fee—either retainer or closing fee—with the consortium member.

Q. How about maintaining the "big firm" image?
A. Regardless of how fees and billings are structured, an in-charge image must be sustained. It doesn't make any difference how many consortium members participate or what functions they perform. It is your client, you negotiated the fee structure, terms, and scope, and you should expect to continue getting new assignments long after your associates are gone.

The originating consultant must assume total responsibility for everyone's work as well as retain an active liaison role between the client and other consultants. The last thing any client wants is to make several consulting firms responsible for the same job. They just won't do it.

GETTING OUT OF A CONSORTIUM

Q. How do I get out of a consortium gracefully if the occasion arises to do so?

A. As I previously discussed, consortium agreements should be written to permit any participant to leave at any time. So getting out is never a problem.

Q. How do you dissolve a consortium?

A. Legally there's no problem. All participants merely agree that it is dissolved, and it's finished.

However, from a client relations perspective it gets more difficult. The fundamental reason for forming a consortium in the first place is to present the image of a large, diversified firm without losing the flexibility, personal service, and potentially lower rates of a small firm.

Sales literature refers to multiple capabilities. Prospecting, referral solicitations, and promotion and advertising spreads all speak to a diversified capability. Existing clients expect a firm to have the capability of handling practically any assignment that might come up.

When the consortium dissolves, a small firm (perhaps a single practitioner) once again has limited credentials. If the situation is not handled properly, this causes all kinds of problems, including driving consultants out of business.

Q. Are you saying consortiums can never be dissolved without severe hardship on all participants?

A. Not at all. If that were the case, no one would use consortiums. All I'm saying is that the dissolution must be handled properly with your future and the client's well-being in mind.

To start with, all participants must agree that clients for whom work was performed through the consortium belong to the originating consultant. They must also agree not to solicit or otherwise steal current or prospective clients. This can only be an "honor system" agreement, not enforceable by law. On the other hand, if you have all worked amicably together for several years, there's no reason to suspect foul play upon dissolution.

Second, the dissolution should be based on a sound economic reason, not merely the fact that members can't get along any more. This is crucial. Clients and referral contacts expect a rational reason for the dissolution.

Third, all recent or current clients, as well as likely prospects, should be notified personally, either by phone or in person. This shows concern for the client's welfare and provides an opportunity to offer explanations and answer questions. Use the same approach with referral contacts.

Fourth, be ready to offer a substitute for the consortium's capabilities. It won't do any good to merely announce your withdrawal. That destroys a diversified capabilities image. Set up a network that includes a broad range of capabilities; something even broader than a consortium. An informal partnership will serve the purpose, but is far less convincing than a network.

USING A CONSULTING NETWORK

Q. What's the difference between a consortium and a network?

A. I defined a consortium as a temporary alliance of two or more businesses in a common venture. Consortiums are normally formed between consultants or consulting firms. A network is entirely different.

A network is an informal working arrangement between businesses selling different but complementary services. It normally consists of small service businesses that cannot afford to maintain a complete complement of skills or talents, or are not licensed to sell certain types of services.

In the consulting field, we run into all types of client needs. Most fall within a range of typical consulting qualifications, but on occasion we come across some that require the expertise of non-consultants. For example, say a client needs to raise capital to acquire a new plant in Toronto. A qualified U.S. management consultant can source the financing but probably doesn't have the knowledge or the license to locate and close a real estate deal in Toronto.

Working with a Toronto commercial real estate agency, the consultant could provide a very real service for the client, probably saving several months of searching out an appropriate agency. The consultant might also be able to work some billable hours into advising the client about suitable properties.

Q. What other types of service businesses are good candidates for a network?

A. That depends on location—whether you are in a city or a rural community—and market niches. Generally, although certainly not always, companies in large metropolitan areas already have established ties with legal and accounting professionals, real estate and insurance brokers, and so on. In small communities this may not be true, and network contacts could be very helpful.

In both the M&A and financing niches, a range of network contacts nearly always proves helpful, mainly because this type of work crosses many disciplines. The same holds true for most engagements in international consulting.

Here is an example of how I used subcontractors to handle a complex international acquisition engagement.

A certain firm sold industrial fasteners in the United States and decided to acquire a complementary business in England to serve the European Community market. My assignment was to source targets, negotiate a deal, perform appropriate due diligence, and coordinate the financing and the preparation and negotiation of the buy/sell agreement.

I used subcontractors with the following expertise at various stages of the engagement:

1. A London chartered accounting firm.
2. A British solicitor experienced in acquisition work.
3. An American money broker with confidential sources in Switzerland and the Netherlands.
4. An expert in both United Kingdom and American tax laws.

This network had been built up over a period of several years, so I knew each person's capabilities—and they knew my standards. Furthermore, each had brought me business before, so our working relationship was a two-way street.

Since I remained responsible for the entire engagement, the only one of the four that my client met personally was the British solicitor—at the closing.

BILLING CLIENTS FOR WORK DONE BY SUBCONTRACTORS

Q. How do you handle the billings? Does each firm bill separately, as with a consortium?
A. No. Networking doesn't work that way. Networking is a form of subcontracting. The originating firm gets paid under the terms of the scope contract. In turn, it pays the subcontractors. Therefore, all billings go out on the originating firm's invoice.

Q. Wouldn't I be losing money that way?
A. No. Then there wouldn't be any sense in subcontracting. The easiest way to handle the cost of subcontractors is to bill them to the client as out-of-pocket expenses, the same as travel or telephone expenses.

Q. Won't clients get upset if I do that?
A. They shouldn't—not if they grant permission to hire these specialists in the first place. Most clients are more than happy to delegate the responsibility for arranging and supervising such activities. It relieves them of extra administrative bother and ensures that only one person, the consultant, is held accountable.

Q. Can you give me some more examples of the types of non-consulting service businesses I might network with?
A. Here are a few that I and my associates have used with varying degrees of success:

- Contract lawyers
- Bankruptcy lawyers
- Real estate lawyers
- CPAs—auditors
- CPAs—tax experts
- Computer software specialists (especially for computer networks)
- Internet specialists
- Financial planners
- Insurance counselors
- Estate planners
- Small venture capital firms
- Securities underwriters
- Commercial real estate brokers
- Export management specialists

SUBCONTRACTING WITH OTHER CONSULTANTS

Q. How about networking with other consultants? Does that work as well as consortiums?

A. It depends on the type of engagement and a variety of other considerations.

Networking among consultants is one of the most common ways to increase the diversity of a firm's services. It is a completely informal arrangement and does not require any written agreement.

Networking can involve any number of consultants or other service firms. In fact, the more the merrier. Hooking up with consultants in other parts of the country provides excellent national exposure.

Networking is also a good source of work during slow periods. It seems that I always have more requests to work on a subcontract basis than I have time for.

Finally, subcontracting is an excellent training ground to pick up new information or to brush up on unused skills.

Q. What about the downside? There must be risks in networking, just as with consortiums.

A. Yes, that's true. Three major problems keep cropping up.

Not being intimately familiar with the honesty and work standards of network participants probably creates the biggest risk. A limited number of consortium participants get to know each other well in a relatively short time period. With a broad network, either of consultants or other service businesses, the risk of running into a bad apple is always present.

A second problem relates to workload. When I contact network participants I generally need help quickly. But they have their own businesses to run, and most are not about to drop everything to give me a hand. This happens more frequently in multidisciplinary networks than those consisting of consultants.

Finally, and more often than one would expect, there is the problem of competence. People may claim expertise in taxes, but that doesn't make them experts. Although lawyers must be licensed to practice, I have run into more incompetence in the legal profession than in any other service business. Computer specialists who claim they can handle any type of business frequently are lost in at least a few. Retailers don't know manufacturing. Hotel experts are unfamiliar with distributorships. Large company experience doesn't apply to small companies.

This is still further proof that consultants (or others) who haven't seen fit to specialize often can't do any job well.

MARKETING WITH A NETWORK

Q. You have mentioned only the production benefits of networks. Can't they also be effective for marketing?
A. Networks do not sell as well as consortiums. Clients may be eager to know which skills are available if needed, but a network seldom lands a job.

I would never advertise specific network firms especially nonconsulting businesses, in sales literature. Cluttering up a brochure with names and credentials of non-consulting companies detracts from the primary message of selling our own consulting expertise.

Q. If I can't use my brochure, how can I advertise the network's diversity?

A. By treating the subject separately. Use a separate sheet or announcement to promote full-service capability. Mention the services within the network—tax planning, estate counseling, computer specialities, and so on—but not the names of the network firms. Network participants subcontract work. The name of the company shouldn't make any difference to a client as long as the originating firm (yours) retains responsibility for the quality and timeliness of the work.

One consultant in my consortium came up with a unique marketing tool utilizing a network. When an interesting news event, book, tax change, or other pertinent item comes to his attention that might be of interest to prospective clients, he writes a one-paragraph description of the event. He then faxes it, on his letterhead, to the other seven network members. These members, in turn, re-fax it to seven of their contacts, who presumably fax it to seven more. My friend claims this pyramid approach works as an inexpensive, broad coverage, advertising method and has actually attracted new clients.

INFORMAL PARTNERSHIPS

Q. In addition to consortiums and networks, you mentioned informal partnerships as a third way to diversify. How does that work?

A. Informal partnerships can be especially helpful to consultants just starting out or in the process of rebuilding a business. Such structures also are used by single practitioners who are temporarily overloaded with work but do not want to hire either part-time or full-time employees.

An informal partnership differs from a formal partnership in several ways. Under an informal structure:

- The business operates under the name of the primary partner.
- The arrangement has a defined termination date.
- Partnership liabilities remain the sole responsibility of the principal partner.

- All income and expenses of the organization fall to the principal partner (with one exception).
- Each partner continues to manage his or her own business.

An informal partnership is not recognized as a legal entity. No federal or state identification numbers are required. No partnership tax return is filed.

Q. That sounds like a very loose structure. Is any type of partnership agreement necessary?
A. Yes. A duly executed agreement is mandatory. The reason will be obvious when we talk about handling the billing function and paying for administrative and marketing expenses.

Here is an example of a typical agreement between two parties to an informal partnership. It is a broad model only, and is not meant to cover all business situations.

Fig. 8-2
INFORMAL PARTNERSHIP AGREEMENT

This agreement between Zyco Associates, Inc. ("Zyco") and TWL and Company ("TWL") establishes an informal partnership for the purposes of soliciting and performing management consulting services.

The parties to this agreement acknowledge that:

- The business shall be conducted under the name of Zyco Associates, Inc.
- TWL will maintain its own identity independent of Zyco but will not solicit clients nor perform consulting services other than under the name of Zyco Associates, Inc.
- Zyco will retain all decision-making authority but will consult with TWL on marketing and production matters in which TWL is involved.
- TWL will invoice Zyco for all billable production hours at 75 percent of TWL's standard billing rate.
- Zyco will pay TWL's invoices within 10 days of the receipt of payment from clients for work performed by TWL.

Furthermore, both parties agree that 25 percent of all client payments against Zyco invoices will be retained in a separate bank account to be opened at the First National Bank under the name of Zyco Associates, Inc. The principal of Zyco will have sole signatory authority and will pay all administrative and marketing expenses of the informal partnership out of these funds, including but not limited to office rent, telephone, secretarial services, office supplies, electricity, gas, and water.

Such funds will also be used to reimburse both parties for out-of-pocket expenses submitted on appropriate expense report invoices to Zyco Associates, Inc.

If and when such expense funds are exhausted, both parties mutually agree to contribute equal amounts of cash to cover future expense payments.

Furthermore, both parties agree that within 30 days after the end of Zyco Associates, Inc.'s fiscal year, all remaining funds in the special bank account will be distributed in equal amounts to Zyco and TWL.

Furthermore, both parties agree that this agreement may be terminated by either Zyco or TWL within 60 days of serving written notice on the other party. Upon termination, the principals of Zyco and TWL will jointly prepare and distribute an announcement to all clients and potential clients notifying them of the severance.

Furthermore, Zyco agrees to hold TWL and its principals harmless from any liability arising from the non-payment of Zyco expenses or other cause other than for claims from clients served by TWL.

Furthermore, this agreement will end on January 1, 1995, provided that neither party has invoked a termination prior to that date. All of the above-described dissolution actions will be executed effective on that date.

FOR ZYCO ASSOCIATES, INC.   FOR TWL AND COMPANY

_____   _____

_____   _____
          Date   Date

Q. If one party breaks the agreement, can the other party sue? In other words, is this a legally binding contract?

A. Yes and no. The intent of both parties should be that the agreement is *not* legally binding. We consultants tend to be an independent breed. We don't like to be tied down or coerced into doing things we don't agree with—characteristics that seem to be predominant throughout entrepreneurial ranks.

Although some consultants feel a need to execute binding contracts for virtually anything, I don't like the idea: I suspect that most others in the field would agree with me.

As a matter of fact, great care should be taken to write the agreement so that it is specifically not binding. If either party questions the wording, just insert a separate clause specifically stating that the agreement does not bind either party. The termination clause should take care of this concern, however.

Can one party sue the other? Of course. But the whole question of whether consultants should sue consultants comes back to ethics. If two consultants cannot trust each other to take the actions they agree upon, no partnership, network, or consortium relationship will work. If one or more in a group is unethical, the only solution is to get out. And get out fast.

FEES AND BILLINGS IN AN INFORMAL PARTNERSHIP

Q. How about fee structures and billings? Does each party bill its fees separately?

A. No. In this respect informal partnerships are similar to networks. Each participating firm accounts for its own billable hours, but the client gets one bill at the fee structure originally negotiated in the scope contract. Internally, informal partnership fees and billings are handled the same as subcontracting. Partner B invoices the principal, partner A, for work done. Partner A incorporates B's hours with his own and submits one invoice on A's letterhead or invoice form to the client. The client pays A, and A pays B.

The client deals with one entity, the firm bearing A's name. How A and B split the income is not the client's concern.

For tax purposes, A and B each file a return for their own company, reporting their individual income and expenses.

Q. How does this differ from a normal subcontracting arrangement?

A. In two ways: in the marketing of consulting services and in the way partners share administrative expenses.

Let's take marketing first. To clients, or prospective clients, the organization appears to be a partnership, consisting of one or more principals depending on how many consultants are included. Sales literature includes the names, credentials and skills of all consultants. All advertising and promotion casts the organization as a normal partnership. This achieves the same "big company with diversified skills" image as a consortium.

In the administrative area, an informal partnership typically maintains one formal office, that of the principal partner, A. Partners B, C, D, and all other consultants as are included in the arrangement, use the office and share the expenses.

Although the method of paying administrative expense varies, the example we discussed earlier is typical:

- Partners charge the partnership a lower fee than their normal billing rate, say 75 percent.
- Client billings reflect the full fees of all partners.
- The partnership pays partners at their 75 percent rate, keeping the excess in a partnership bank account from which all administrative and marketing expenses are paid.
- Excess cash in the account at the end of the year is distributed to all partners based on a predetermined ratio.

SHARING ADMINISTRATIVE FUNCTIONS

Q. You mentioned that one of the benefits of informal partnerships is sharing administrative expenses. Does this hold true for consortiums and networks also?

A. It could, depending on the location, type of business, and needs of other consultants in the group. If an office must be located outside your home, or if administrative personnel are required, sharing expenses can be a big help, especially for single practitioners.

Sharing office space kills two birds with one stone. It provides administrative cover when each consultant is in the field marketing or performing an engagement. It also reduces expenses.

Q. Can you list the types of expenses that can easily be shared in such a situation?

A. Assuming we're talking about an external office and employees, consultants normally incur the following types of administrative expenses, all of which can be shared with other businesses utilizing the same office:

- Rent, electricity, gas, water
- Office equipment—fax, copier, typewriters, computers
- Liability and casualty insurance
- Secretarial and clerical salaries and payroll taxes
- Office supplies
- Telephone, answering service
- Security services
- Subscriptions

Some service businesses extend sharing to group auto insurance, group health insurance, and certain advertising and printing expenses.

Q. Does it make sense to share administrative expenses with other than consulting firms?
A. Why not? At one stage in my consulting career I shared an office with a two-partner CPA firm, a lawyer, two insurance brokers, and an industrial psychologist. We all got along fine and seldom if ever had a dispute about which office expenses needed to be cut or added. Furthermore, we all acted as referral contacts for each other—almost like a network. In many respects we *were* a network, even the psychologist, whom I brought into two jobs requiring personnel evaluation expertise.

I realize that many consultants shy away from sharing offices, fearing that this presents the wrong image to clients. They may have a point. Clients like to believe that a consulting firm is big, diversified, and can afford its own facility.

On the other hand, clients also recognize that by keeping administrative expenses to the bone, consulting firms can afford to reduce rates. It's hard to beat lower prices as a competitive edge. I have never met a CEO willing to pay higher fees to enable a consulting firm to support a lavish office.

Chapter 9

REPORTS AND PRESENTATIONS THAT WORK
How to Write and Deliver Them

Q. I've never been much of a writer. In fact, I hate to write: reports or anything else. What do you suggest?

A. Get out of consulting.

Q. What if I had told you I can write fairly well, but I'm terrified of giving a presentation to a group?

A. Same thing. Get out of consulting.

Q. In all seriousness, are reports and presentations really that important? Why can't I just tell clients verbally what I've found?

A. I am quite serious. If you can't write and make presentations, find another career.

Sure, verbal communications are important, even crucial to getting and keeping clients. But saying something isn't enough. Clients expect to receive something tangible for their money, in addition to favorable business results from your advice. That "something tangible" is a piece of paper, a report, or a document the CEO can read, digest, and pass on to bankers, employees, managers, or professional advisors.

Even if your recommendations never get implemented, the mere fact that a document defines the problem and includes recommendations for solving it makes a CEO happy—at least most of the time. Psychologically, a written report proves that the company's money was well spent.

Multinational accounting firms have understood the psychological impact of reports for decades. If you have ever been in a company audited by one of these firms, you have probably seen the report they present to management at the end of an audit outlining the strengths and weaknesses of the company's internal controls.

The report has nothing to do with the audit, but it looks good. It gives company management something to show off: "See, our company is doing all right, this internal controls report says so!" The company can be near bankruptcy but, if the internal control report glows, everything is all right. Many managers can't read an audit report, but give them an internal control report and they're suddenly experts.

The same psychology applies to management consulting reports. You simply can't get by without them.

Q. How about presentations? Why are they so important?

A. On many occasions, a written report doesn't, by itself, convey the importance of our findings. Since a picture is worth a thousand words, in addition to a written report, it may be appropriate to make a formal presentation either to the CEO or to a group of managers or staff personnel.

Presentations frequently help to get a point across at some critical juncture. For example, an associate of mine was engaged to help a mid-size company develop a strategic planning process. She spent several weeks strategizing with the CEO and the company's top three senior vice presidents. Now it was time to delegate downward; time for the eight department managers to develop their segments of the plan.

She met with each manager but didn't make much progress. Finally, she decided to show them rather than tell them. Using a set of slides she had made for another client that depicted the steps and format of a detailed plan, she put on a half-day presentation for the department managers. That did the trick: the logjam burst.

Presentations also work well as a selling tool for prospective clients. I was competing with three other firms for a cost system design and installation job. Each of the three met with the vice president for finance before I came in.

Going last is never my favorite position. So I went to work with a six-color flip chart explaining what I had in mind. I followed it up with a color video of cartoon animals demonstrating the system flow and product cost build-up. After we executed a scope contract, the CEO told me the elephants and mice sold him.

Are presentations important? They are as crucial as reports for a successful consulting business, and often even more effective.

PRELIMINARY REPORTS

Q. Can you give me some idea of the most commonly used reports?

A. I find it helpful to divide reports into three categories: preliminary, interim, and final.

The preliminary report presents findings gleaned from the introductory review of the business or activity performed at the beginning of an engagement. As we have seen, this overview may be gratis, a promotion freebie, or the first step in the engagement.

Whether the client pays for it or not, the primary purpose of an overview, other than as a selling tool, is to give the consultant a snapshot of the business, the principal players, and a brief evaluation of the accuracy of the client's perception of the problem or problems. Articulating our findings in a written report forces us to organize our thoughts and clarify any fuzzy points. This report then provides the basis for the scope contract—either a reaffirmation, a chance to renegotiate it if already executed, or the information necessary to draft one.

As a secondary purpose, the preliminary report informs company management of our perception of the business and problem(s) and permits valuable feedback before starting the detailed work.

Q. What should a preliminary report look like?

A. That depends on the client, the engagement, and your findings. The larger the client and the more complex the engagement, the more points arise—and consequently, the longer and more complete the report.

Conversely, an overview for a very small company preliminary to a short, simple engagement—such as the liquidation of assets—can consist of no more than two paragraphs.

Generally, however, one or two full pages serves the purpose. The content varies with the situation, but here is one format I frequently use.

Fig.9-1

REPORT OF INTRODUCTORY REVIEW

INTRODUCTION

The introduction should be no longer than one paragraph, and should summarize the steps taken during the review and the major findings. It might read as follows:

Pursuant to beginning work on the project defined in our scope contract dated June 15, 1985, namely to help X-PAY personnel develop the techniques to construct an annual business plan and then to assist in the preparation of the plan for 1986, we conducted an overview of the X-PAY business operation. We paid particular attention to the flow of information within the company. A series of potential obstacles evolved from interviews with key X-PAY personnel.

RESULTS OF THE REVIEW

In this section, succinctly define the three or four major obstacles that must be overcome to successfully complete the engagement.

The potential obstacles as we see them are:

- Both the controller and the sales managers will be on vacation during the first two weeks of the engagement. This will make it difficult to accumulate sufficient sales and accounting information and will create the need to conduct a second training session for them when they return.
- The computer-generated "orders received" reports, currently used by the sales department to determine order backlog and to forecast sales, appear to be missing a significant number of orders.
- The 1997 audit report has not been finalized. The audit report is the starting point for 1998 projections that lead to the 1999 business plan.

REQUESTED ACTION STEPS

In this example, client management must make some decisions before the engagement can begin. This section outlines what steps are needed.

To reduce the amount of our time and hence your cost, we propose that the general manager of X-PAY take the following steps prior to our beginning this engagement:

- Request the controller and the sale manager to postpone their vacations for two months, or as a minimum, stagger them so that they are not concurrent.
- Establish a task force of sales personnel to update and verify the accuracy of the orders received report.
- Encourage your auditor to finish the 1997 annual report.

We believe that it is in the best interest of X-PAY to take these actions before we begin our work. By so doing, our fees will be in line with the scope contract estimate. If we must work around these three major obstacles, our time will be extended by at least 35 percent.

Please let us know your decision. We will then schedule our workload to begin the engagement within one week of hearing from you.

INTERIM REPORTS

Q. How about interim reports? Can't I get by without wasting time on something as non-productive as writing reports?

A. Interim (or status) reports are used to report the progress on engagements, or lack thereof, as of a specific point in time; to recommend changes in scope; and to inform management of actions required by company personnel to enable the project to proceed.

For various reasons, we sometimes find it difficult to set aside time for writing status reports. We get so wrapped up in the details of the work that we forget that top managers, intent on keeping the company running smoothly, cannot see the broad picture of what is being accomplished, or conversely, what hurdles we encounter. We try to jump these hurdles on our own and many times, if not most of the time, our methods conflict with operating procedures or personnel idiosyncrasies. Tempers flare. Next thing we know, the CEO jumps all over us because we are behind schedule or have disrupted critical company activities.

Interim reports are not only necessary to keep peace in the family; they also give us a chance to blow our own horn, to tell top management how much we have accomplished to date.

A third reason for issuing status reports is to clarify our interpretation of events that have occurred or discussions that have been held. For example, an assignment involving the preparation of business or strategic plans always involves a series of meetings with top executives and/or middle managers. A variety of topics are covered. Decisions evolve. Verbal communications in group meetings are normally very poor. More often than not, someone in the room interprets what was said differently than you do. Summarizing the content of the meeting in writing flushes out disagreements before they become dangerous.

Q. What format should I use for status reports?
A. Use a format that makes you comfortable. As long as the writing is clear and succinct, and the content includes everything germane to the circumstances, who cares about format?

If it helps to see an example, here's a format I often use to cover all three of the major objectives:

1. To report the progress on an engagement, or lack thereof, as of a specific point in time.
2. To recommend changes in scope.
3. To inform client management of actions required by company personnel to enable the project to proceed.

Obviously, I have fictionalized the client name. Since the details of this report are irrelevant to our discussion the report shows only summarized comments.

Fig.9-2

STATUS REPORT
for
GREASEY MANUFACTURING CORP.
For Period Ending June 1, 1998

PROJECT: To assist GREASEY management acquire a $20 million bearing manufacturing company in Idaho.

SUMMARY OF PROGRESS

SINCE PRIOR REPORT DATED MAY 15, 1998:

- A strategy meeting was held with top management to define the specific type of company to be acquired, its location, and its approximate size.
- Five target candidates were presented for review by top management.
- We obtained product line information and performed a market analysis for each target and presented these findings to your vice president—finance, Mr. Applebee.

RECOMMENDED CHANGES IN SCOPE OR TIME FRAME:

Based on our progress to date, we do not recommend any changes at this time.

RECOMMENDED CLIENT ACTIONS:

Although we are still following the schedule originally proposed in our scope letter, certain matters have arisen that could stall our efforts during the next month. We bring these items to your attention with the recommendation that you take appropriate action to resolve the issues. By so doing, we will be able to proceed unimpeded.

Issue #1:

Two of the five target candidates we presented do not fit the original acquisition criteria as set out at our meeting of May 16, 1998. We recommend a decision to drop these candidates immediately.

Issue #2:

Within the next three weeks, it will be necessary to begin the due diligence investigation of the remaining candidates. This will require the full-time participation of your controller and two clerical assistants, and three PCs must be allocated to the project. We recommend steps be taken immediately to make these personnel available within five to seven work days. If existing hardware is not sufficient, we also recommend leasing up to three PCs that will run with your existing software.

We would like to take this opportunity to thank all company personnel. They have been helpful in our endeavors to date. Without their active cooperation, we could not fulfill the company's acquisition objectives.

NEXT REPORT:

The next status report will be issued on July 1.

Q. But why can't I report verbally without going to the effort of writing a report?

A. Some consultants do get by without writing any interim or status reports, preferring to keep client management verbally informed of progress or glitches. I suppose that for very short or uncomplicated jobs, interim reports are a waste of time. In most cases, however, they are well worth the effort—even if the client doesn't want them or read them.

Let me give a concrete example of how reports can come in handy other than as a good client relations tool.

Several years ago, a consultant I'll call Bob worked in an informal partnership with me for about six months. He was getting started and needed work. I was overloaded and needed help. Bob's assignment was to arrange for the liquidation of the assets of a small company. I didn't have time to participate, so he was on his own.

The entire job took about six weeks. Bob didn't bother to write status reports every week, which I would have done on something as tricky as a liquidation.

Two months after the liquidation auction, our client received a check from the auctioneer for the net proceeds of the sale. It was about 50 percent of what he expected. He turned around and brought suit against us for negligence, claiming we had not told him of the estimated prices calculated by the auctioneer three weeks before the auction.

In fact, Bob *had* told the client—orally. Fortunately, he also took notes at that meeting with the auctioneer. When the company's lawyer saw the notes, the case was dropped.

The moral is that if Bob had written a formal weekly report, this information would have been included. The client would know what to expect and we would have the proof that he knew. The suit could have been avoided and we would have saved legal expenses, a substantial amount of wasted time, and a lot of headaches.

Written status or interim reports, signed by the client as being received, nearly always hold up in court as evidence of knowledge—or so my legal friends tell me.

Q. How should I handle a really serious problem, one that materially affects the company but that the CEO might not be aware of?

A. I can only think of one way to report a serious problem. Go to the top of the organization: the CEO, president, senior vice president, or someone else in charge. If the problem has just surfaced or if we believe employees are hiding something from top management, we have an ethical responsibility to bring it to the attention of the top executive.

This should *not* be a written report. It may fall into the wrong hands, and that could bring harm to you, to the company, or to the top executive. Instead, I recommend requesting a private meeting with the executive and verbally relating the information uncovered. If the executive subsequently asks for a written report, fine. But then it's the client's responsibility if it falls into the wrong hands.

FINAL REPORTS

Q. How about for final reports?

A. The final report is your "coup de grace." This is where you brag about what a great job you have done, how the company will benefit, what an enormous help the company's employees were, and any other positive statements you can conjure up.

The final report provides the best opportunity to lay the groundwork for additional work or at least a strong reference letter. Here's a chance to reap the benefits of a bang-up promotion with the stroke of a pen, and it doesn't cost a penny.

Q. How do you write a final report that accomplishes such a grandiose promotion?

A. Final reports are much easier to write than either of the other two. With the preliminary report we walk on eggs, still trying to sell the client, or at least trying to solidify our position.

Interim or status reports can often be negative, disclosing problems encountered and recommending, in some instances, harsh remedies. Company management won't want to hear about some of the matters at this stage. They just want you to overcome and complete the job.

But the final report finishes the job. By now all or nearly all invoices have been paid. The CEO begins to see the results of the efforts that commanded such high fees. Assuming these results meet expectations, everyone is happy by this time. The report merely ties the last knot.

Although consultants disagree about the length and content of the final report—and some don't even bother to write one—I prefer a short, punchy approach, complimentary to client management and personnel. The concluding paragraph is the punch line where I identify one or two areas in which I can be of service to the client in the future. (Preferably the not-too-distant future.) I also like to frame this report in the form of a personal letter. Here is a sample of a typical final report using this approach.

Fig. 9-3

FINAL REPORT
GREASEY MANUFACTURING CORP.
ACQUISITION OF BOXWELL AUTOMATIC, INC.

Dear Mr. Cleanwell:

Now that Boxwell has joined to your cadre of progressively managed companies, I'm confident GREASEY will set the pace in the industry as a major supplier of a complete line of high-quality bearings and accessories.

Before signing off completely, I want to take this opportunity to thank you and the rest of your management and employees for all the assistance given me during this very difficult acquisition engagement.

The target search was a real challenge. Recessionary pressures demanded that the financing be creative and innovative. I was also very pleased to see that the negotiating strategy I recommended paid off.

It would have been difficult to bring this one off without the skill and daring of your management team. I hope you are as pleased with the results as I am.

It has been my experience that integrating the organizations, marketing efforts, and customer service activities of a company as complex as Boxwell with those of an acquirer can be a trying experience, often taking more time and causing more headaches than initially envisioned.

Our firm has helped many clients accomplish this task with a minimum of lost time and expense. We would like the opportunity to do the same for you. At your convenience, I will be happy to meet with you and describe how we can help.

Sincerely,

REPORT CONTENT AND PRESENTATION

Q. As a general rule, should reports lean toward optimism or pessimism?

A. That depends on which report you are talking about, how confident you are of your position with the client, your assessment of the likelihood of your work meeting the client's expectations, and the position of the person receiving the report.

Presumably the client has problems or an overview wouldn't be necessary. A preliminary report should define these problem areas as accurately as possible.

The preliminary report is a sales tool, used to convince the client to either hire you in the first place or give you total support for carrying out your assignment. Therefore, emphasis should be placed on (1) succinctly defining the problem areas, and, if necessary to get top management attention, overstating their severity, which exudes pessimism, and (2) your ability to solve these problems efficiently, timely, and at minimum cost, which portrays optimism.

Interim or status reports can go either way. Some consultants use these reports to startle decision-making managers so they begin implementing recommendations. The reports reflect worst-case scenarios, painting pictures of doom and gloom if these suggestions are not implemented immediately. Very often this approach is used for reports addressed to second-level managers to stir the brew and make things happen.

I favor this approach for many engagements as a method to keep client personnel interested in what I am doing and to make sure top management knows that company managers, not me, are responsible for making my recommendations work. A copy of the report to the CEO helps immeasurably.

Other consultants don't use this approach, believing it creates animosity and therefore hinders their effectiveness. They would rather soft-pedal obstacles in written critiques and rely on verbal persuasion to achieve their results. If the problems aren't too severe, if your recommendations are on shaky ground, or if you feel that a negative report will force top management to choose sides and support the employees' position, then obviously the soft approach has merit. When battle lines are drawn, with the consultant on one side aligned against operating managers and top management on the other, the odds of winning become very slight.

The final report should always be optimistic. After all, the client has paid you to do a job, you have done it, and if you are not optimistic about its impact on the company, no one else will be. This is especially true following a succession of "head-banging" interim reports. Beat up on people to get the job done. Once it's completed, praise them for their cooperation. Clients love it. This approach shows that the CEO was right all along in supporting company managers.

When using the final report as a selling tool it's imperative to be optimistic. I have never met a senior executive who wasn't egocentric. Praising management ability and astute judgment leads to more opportunities than implying that severe problems continue to exist.

Q. Isn't that lying, and therefore unethical, unless you genuinely believe it?
A. I don't consider it unethical if I assume that in the long run top managers know how to run their company better than I do. I'm merely reaffirming that philosophy.

Very early in our discussion we talked about how consultants seem to think they can run a company better than its managers. I pointed out how this is a horrendous sales approach because managers never agree.

A second issue is involved as well. As a practical matter, these managers are right. We may be able to step into a management role in a troubled company and with specialized, short-term techniques turn it around. But these techniques utilize one-shot actions. They do not work for ongoing management. Managers who live with the day-to-day decision-making of running a company can do a better job over the long term than an outsider, assuming they have the motivation and the tools.

I don't see how cultivating client managers after completing an assignment can be unethical when all you do is state the truth.

Q. Who should reports be addressed to and how should they be presented?

A. Preliminary reports should always be addressed to the person who signed the original scope contract. Presumably this same person heard the initial sales pitch. In privately owned companies the business owner should receive this report. In larger companies, a senior officer might have the authority. If preliminary discussions involved another manager with the responsibility for solving the problem, address the report to this person with a copy to the top executive.

The addressee for interim or status reports varies. A lower echelon manager may have responsibility for seeing the project through. In that case the reports should be directed to that person, but again, with a copy to the top executive. If the owner or CEO maintains direct authority, then clearly the report should go to that person.

The final report always goes to the top executive. You may be directed to send copies to other managers or to board of director members, but the original should go to your direct boss.

As far as presentation is concerned, there aren't any rules. The nature of the engagement, the caliber of company personnel, client size, our communicative abilities, and many other factors determine whether we should send written letters or reports or use more esoteric techniques to get our points across.

EFFECTIVE PRESENTATIONS

Q. Can you give me some tips on what works and what doesn't in giving a presentation?

A. This subject opens Pandora's box. As much harm can come from the wrong presentation as benefit can come from a well-directed one. The types of presentations, the tools that can be used, and the abilities of presenters create an unlimited number of combinations. What works one time may never work again. What works for me probably won't work for you. What works for project engagements is most likely inappropriate for continuing management assignments. What works for American clients may be confusing for foreign clients. And on and on.

However, making an effective presentation is such an important topic that it can't be ignored. The best I can do is to relate what works for me in a variety of situations and let you take it from there.

First, some fairly universal ground rules:

- Time is money.
- Pictures are better than words.
- Color is more effective than black and white.
- Visual aids that don't work are deadly.
- Active presentations work better than passive ones.
- Standing creates a more authoritative image than sitting.
- Open discussions are better than lectures.
- Telephones, secretaries, open doors, and other distractions should be eliminated.

Consultants violate the first rule, "time is money," more than any of the others. Regardless of who the audience may be or how many people may be addressed, their time is valuable. They have relinquished their time to listen to your pitch.

Honor this gift. Keep the presentation short, sweet, and simple. A pitch lasting more than ten minutes is too long. If the audience chooses to extend the meeting with questions or discussion, that's a different matter. But they make that decision, not you.

Q. What do you mean by pictures? Do I have to hire a photographer?
A. Maybe. In some settings, it might be a good idea.

The next three rules covering pictures, color, and visual aids can be discussed together. Pictures may be just that—pictures. They may consist of photographs, sketches, graphs, charts, tables, or any other visual presentation. The saying "a picture is worth a thousand words" applies in spades when you are trying to get a pitch across in minimum time.

If possible, use color rather than black and white. Videos, slides, overhead transparencies, flip charts, even hard copy handouts, will attract more attention when in color. I find red, blue, and green to be most effective. Be careful not to use the wrong color at the wrong time, however. In the United States, red connotes danger and brings negative reactions. Various shades of blue seem to be soothing and remind the audience of the sky or water, implying tranquillity. Green usually works well when portraying positive action steps.

Practically any type of visual aid is effective if used properly. I prefer those not requiring a dark room. Audiences doze off. Prepared flip charts work effectively; so do overhead transparencies. Slides and videos are all right if the lights can be kept on. But the room must be small enough and without window light for the audience to see clearly.

Regardless of the method, I strongly recommend staying away from giving your audience hard copy handouts to read during the presentation. You lose the audience even faster than you would in a dark room.

If visual aids depend on mechanical or electrical parts to function, test them out ahead of time to be sure everything works. Bringing your own equipment rather than relying on that supplied by the company is the safest route. This sounds elementary, unworthy of even discussing, but rest assured, it isn't.

I once competed against two other consulting firms for a lucrative international market evaluation job. I invested in a professionally prepared video presentation. It illustrated how I had compiled market demand curves and market size statistics from interviews and surveys on a previous overseas job. The tape cost me over three thousand dollars to have prepared. The prospective client provided the VCR and TV set.

Halfway through the presentation the TV screen went dead, the VCR sputtered, and my video popped out with tape flying, completely ruined. I don't know what caused it, but it killed my presentation. I didn't get the job. I have never used client equipment since.

TAKING CHARGE

Q. What do you mean by "active" presentations?
A. The idea is to keep the audience awake and attentive. At the same time, it's important to assume an authoritative role. Even if

you're a little hesitant about the subject, an aggressive image can be convincing.

Staying on your feet, moving around, pointing to a graph or a chart, walking into the audience (if possible), and using your hands, feet, and facial expressions to make important points, all tend to keep the audience focused on what you are saying. Be as dramatic as you can.

Effective public speakers seldom hide behind a lectern. John Bradshaw, the self-help author, is a perfect example of a speaker who uses movement to make his points. It's hard to imagine a Bradshaw audience member falling asleep!

Contrast this with the approach so many consultants use. Sitting across a desk or around a table. Remaining behind the overhead projector. Operating a slide projector. Talking from a flip chart without moving to it and away from it. Or reading from a paper or notes. Boring!

There aren't too many things in this world that I'm willing to guarantee, but I guarantee that you will get a better reception by being an active speaker than by assuming a passive role.

This holds true whether you are making a sales pitch to a prospective client or presenting a report during an engagement.

Q. Sometimes I don't have any choice: I have to make my presentation across the desk from a CEO or manager. What do I do?

A. The same principle applies. Use flip charts if possible. Hard copy graphs and charts are second best. Avoid descriptive written documents as much as possible.

In any event, don't stay seated, regardless of how confining the office may be. Get up. Move to the window. Lean over the CEO's shoulder to point out items on charts.

Force the audience (even an audience of one) to stay with you. Ask questions that require answers. Offer answers before questions are asked. Anticipate the listener's moves and stay one step ahead.

Not only do these steps force attention on what you are saying, but by being an active presenter you prove your enthusiasm for the job. If a CEO has a choice between two consultants with similar credentials, fees, terms, and personal attributes, the one showing the greatest enthusiasm will win the job every time.

Here's a secret to closing a presentation, especially when soliciting an order. Toward the end of your pitch, switch tactics. Assume a more humble position. Back off. This forces the listener to ask at least one question, even if it isn't relevant. This gives the executive the last word and, in effect, command of the meeting. Playing to a person's ego has closed more than one order.

Q. How do you feel about encouraging open discussion during your presentation?

A. Open discussion has both good and bad points. Obviously a client or prospective client has the right to ask questions and deserves prompt answers. At the same time, a presenter deserves the courtesy of being heard.

Remaining in command of a presentation is probably the most difficult aspect of selling consulting services, whether you are trying to land a new client or get recommendations implemented. Once control of the meeting is lost, it's over for all practical purposes.

Most people have a difficult time staying in control with continuous open discussion. The ball keeps shifting from one person to another, depending on the question, the answer, or the debate. Once the audience members begin discussing points among themselves, it's about time to pack your bags and go home. You have lost the war.

On the other hand, the most effective presentations are structured to permit and encourage as many questions and as much discussion as the audience desires. The more the merrier—as long as the presenter controls the timing of the discussion. If the audience wants a lecture they can go to a school or church. Here, they want to participate, and that's good. Just be careful to keep the meeting under control.

Q. Can I get around this problem and still permit questions?

A. Yes. It's quite simple, as long as you stay on your feet and remain active.

Begin by asking the audience to hold questions until you have finished, reminding them that the presentation will only take ten minutes. At that time you will be happy to answer any questions that arise. Point out that you realize their time is limited and questions during the presentation will only slow it down. Once you have finished, you can let them ask all they want. By then you will have made your point.

If the audience consists of more than three people, chances are good that someone will deliberately interrupt at random with inane or irrelevant questions. Managing this situation could very well determine your success or failure in landing the job or in selling recommendations.

Being obnoxious won't help, even though you may be tempted to say, "Shut up and sit down!" Conversely, if you try to answer the question seriously, you lose momentum and, hence, control of the meeting.

I use a standard retort that seems to work, "That's a very good question. Let me continue and I'll try to answer it for you. If I miss the point ask it again when I finish." And then I immediately shift topics.

If the questioner persists, I use a much firmer voice to repeat my response and ask if it's all right to continue. My point is usually made, loud and clear to everyone in the room, without being offensive. If Mr. Obnoxious still persists, I launch into a humorous anecdote on some irrelevant topic. That always works. (It goes without saying that if Mr. Obnoxious is the CEO, you should take a more conciliatory tone.)

WHERE AND WHEN TO MAKE PRESENTATIONS

Q. The final ground rule you mentioned relates to using the right setting to make the presentation. Could you elaborate on that?

A. This is in keeping with the idea of staying in control of the meeting. Nothing is more disturbing that to have telephones ring, secretaries running in and out of the room with messages, coffee pots boiling over, or sunshine hitting someone in the face while you are trying to give a presentation. When you only have ten minutes to make a pitch, these distractions can easily kill the whole effort.

We do not always have the luxury of choosing the location for our presentations. That's up to the client. But we can certainly make recommendations, as long as we do it before the meeting begins.

The shortest, most productive, and most rewarding presentations I have made to prospective clients were in hotels—either a conference room for larger groups or a suite rented for the day. The same holds true for preliminary and status reports on engagements. No telephones, no secretaries, no interruptions.

Conversely, the worst sessions were held in small offices on company premises.

If you do get stuck on company premises, and most meetings seem to be held there, try following these pointers to avoid as many distractions as possible. (By the way, requests for modifications to the routine of company officials should be made well in advance of the meeting.)

Fig. 9-4
SETTING THE STAGE FOR A PRESENTATION

Try to arrange for the following:

THE ROOM

- Large enough to accommodate all listeners without making them climb over each other
- Without windows
- As far as possible away from the office of the top official in the meeting (i.e., the president or CEO)
- Sufficient electrical outlets
- Good lighting
- A lockable door, or a door with a DO NOT DISTURB-type sign

THE ARRANGEMENT

- Large enough table to accommodate everyone comfortably (a conference table is much better than a row of chairs)
- Plenty of room for you to show charts and move about (essential)
- Thermoses of coffee and water, along with cups and glasses *on the table* (so no one has to get up)
- Sufficient ventilation—air conditioning, heat, fan—locally controlled if possible

INSTRUCTIONS TO SECRETARY
- No telephone calls
- No entrance for messages
- No visitors

Q. Are there any special days or times of day that work best for presenting either a sales pitch or an engagement report?
A. Yes, indeed, at least from my experience. You may disagree because a lot depends on when you function best. But a lot also depends on the normal work flow in the company.

Most company executives like to clean off their desks Friday afternoon so they can start the next week fresh. Or they like to leave early to do errands or to go to the gym. Friday afternoon, then, is a terrible time for a presentation.

Monday morning is almost as bad. Executives need to set the work schedule for the week. Many have staff meetings. Perhaps they still need to clean up loose ends from Friday or answer that phone message they put off last week.

Some people prefer to have extraneous meetings after 5 o'clock to avoid wasting productive time. And many executives consider listening to a consultant's pitch extraneous. Agreeing to this is usually a bad practice. Aside from everyone being tired from a full day's work, many people have evening commitments and look forward to getting home. It's very difficult to keep their attention in the evening.

The same holds for weekends. If the boss demands a weekend meeting, at least some invitees, and probably most, will grudgingly attend, but not be very receptive to your pitch.

Stay away from "noon" meetings with box lunches ordered from the corner deli. Some executives love to do this to save productive time, and very few phone calls occur during the noon hour. From our perspective, however, people are more interested in eating their corned beef on rye than listening to our pitch.

If at all possible, try to schedule the presentation about mid-morning, around 10 o'clock, on a Tuesday, Wednesday, or Thursday. People have cleaned off their desks by then, they are not yet worn out, and if the question-and-answer period runs on, the noon bell provides a good breaking point.

One last point on scheduling. Although we can never insist on a time or day—the client is always right—we can certainly use the many tricks all of us develop to get what we want, or something close to it. In other words, don't give in merely because you are on the selling side. In the long run, competent business people will hold us in higher regard if we stick to our guns on the important issues than if we cave in at their request.

Chapter 10

KEEPING CLIENTS HAPPY
How to Use Client Relations Techniques to Attract More Work

Q. How far do I have to go with regard to client relations to be competitive?

A. Successful consultants make client relations activities an overt, planned part of their business, not a haphazard effort. On the other hand, I don't see why client relations should occupy a major part of anyone's operating budget.

Let's take a look at the various types of client relations efforts that do bring in business and compare them to those that waste time and money.

Client relations is to consulting what the combination of customer relations and customer service is to other businesses. It consists of several approaches, all aimed at providing a competitive edge.

Client relations activities are logically grouped into four categories:

1. Relationships nurtured with client personnel.
2. Relationships with a client's outside advisors.
3. Activities related to ex-clients.
4. Promotional efforts to attract new clients.

Each plays an integral role in developing new business. If well-planned and conscientiously undertaken, client relations activities provide a competitive edge that sustains and promotes the growth of any consulting business.

If ignored, clients don't hang around very long. If randomly employed, money will be spent and effort and time expended without any measurable gain.

The secret to effective client relations is to plan your steps ahead of time.

ROLE PLAYING

Q. Can you give me a few tips on how to improve my ability to develop workable relationships on the job?

A. The relationships you establish with client personnel will determine to a large extent how successful you will be on the engagement. Developing relationships that help rather than hinder can be tricky. The role you choose to play in the beginning sets the tone for the entire engagement.

Q. What do you mean by role playing?

A. By playing a role I mean the impression you give client personnel—employees as well as top management. Work habits, authority, congeniality, capability, loyalty, and so on, influence the manner in which client personnel interact with you.

Four roles predominate in the consulting field. Choosing the right one depends on the type of assignment and the demeanor of client personnel. They are:

- The good ol' boy role—"Trust me, I'm your friend."
- The professor role—"I'm a professional so you can come to me for advice."
- The good-time Charlie role—"Let's have some fun."
- The general's role—"This is a serious matter, and I'm a no-nonsense person."

The first works with smaller clients that employ an older, long-tenured work force, where the business owner works closely with employees. What I affectionately call the good ol' boy approach puts the consultant on an equal footing with employees. This makes the owner comfortable. Employees, suppliers, and even customers are treated in the same hospitable manner. No airs of superiority here, at least not with anyone important present.

Joining in as just another good ol' boy (or gal) is sometimes the only way to cope. Once you are accepted as one of the gang, information flows faster, obstacles are removed, recommendations are implemented, and helpful suggestions become the rule rather than the exception. If the engagement lasts for a while, you will probably be invited to a company picnic or Christmas party; asked to come along for a beer after work; and, often, become a confidant listening to gripes and tales of woe.

These relationships are important, however, and an integral part of a client relations program. In many cases, cementing relationships with employees is just as important as maintaining good relations with the CEO. Without their active support, it's doubtful any of us would get anything done at a client's facility.

Q. How about the professor role?
A. This is a bit harder to pull off. If the company, or department in a larger company, functions smoothly with very few serious problems, the employees and the boss are probably fairly competent at what they do. They may feel that an outsider giving advice in their domain can't possibly know as much about their jobs as they do. They are probably right.

Invisible walls quickly form. Sometimes they're not so invisible. Information is cut off. Suggestions and explanations are abbreviated. Perhaps a rumor mill is intentionally started to discredit you with top management.

When that happens, you can rest assured that the job will take at least twice as long as scheduled, and the results will be incomplete.

I ran into this problem on a systems job for a manufacturing client. The company was very profitable, the employees very competent. It took about five minutes for me to determine that I was not wanted. They didn't want the system, they didn't want me, and to hell with the boss!

I struggled for two weeks, finally telling the vice president who had hired me that if I didn't get better cooperation the job would never end. He relayed my remarks to the employees with a caveat to cooperate. The walls became twice as thick. Eventually, I had to beg off the engagement, at a substantial loss.

Q. How should you approach a problem like that?

A. A few months later I took another systems job with a smaller client. Learning from my last escapade, I immediately introduced myself with an air of professorial authority, then handed out a personal profile listing my credentials and outlining similar systems I had installed for other clients. I also asked the employees immediately for their advice, noting that they certainly knew the work flow better than I ever would. If they would help, I promised to pass this information on to the business owner.

Last, I let it be known that even though I was sure they could do the installation themselves, as an expert I could do the job quickly, efficiently, and would soon be out of their hair, wasting as little of their valuable time as possible.

In other words, I established my credentials, convinced them that I could be trusted, and showed them how they would benefit from my being there.

The professor role doesn't always work as smoothly as this example might suggest, so be careful. It can backfire quickly if you falter technically, especially when one or more employees really could do the same work. Playing the professor role requires that you know exactly what to do and how to do it.

Q. What about the good-time Charlie role?

A. This only works with top managers who are good-time Charlies themselves. If they are uptight about getting the job done or about wasting time, the "have fun" approach won't work.

It's easy to tell early in the engagement how loose these executives are. They joke, have lunch together, perhaps play sports together. They seem very self-confident and don't take the daily routine too seriously.

Very likely you will be asked to join them for lunch. Eventually you'll be brought into their inner circle and share in their jokes and stories. If you happen to be a tennis player, skier, boater, golfer, or whatever, so much the better. Once you join in the merriment and become accepted as a fun loving person, these managers will make sure you get your way with employees.

With clients like this the worst approach is to take the job, or anything for that matter, too seriously. Pretend you are having a great time, whether it's true or not. Good-time Charlie managers can be a real pain, but if you play up to them, the sky's the limit.

Assuming the job gets completed approximately on time, another assignment is practically a certainly. The good-time Charlie role works better than the others for getting more work, assuming, of course, that top managers really are as loose as they appear. Sometimes appearances can deceive.

Q. Explain the general's role.

A. Engagements in profitable, growing companies are a snap compared to working in financially troubled ones. In the latter, Murphy's Law applies daily. Nothing goes right for anybody. Employees are sour. The owner or top managers are surly. Rumors about everything from the collapse of the United Nations to the boss's latest sexual conquest run rampant. No one works very hard. Complaints permeate the air.

The only way to handle this type of situation is to become a general and take command.

It's important to establish your command of the situation quickly. Your demeanor, actions, dress, and tone should all indicate the seriousness of the job to be done.

To be viewed as a no-nonsense person you must not tell jokes, seldom laugh, keep to yourself except when you need information from someone, go about your business stone-faced, and insist in no uncertain terms that when you ask for some information or assistance you want it *now*, not tomorrow.

These jobs are seldom fun. Time is of the essence. There is never enough information, or time, to do the job the right way. Key employees seem to be either quitting or taking time off.

Nevertheless, these clients are common and therefore we must deal with them. Their cash is as green as the good time Charlies'. And in more cases than not, these companies need us so badly that additional work is a foregone conclusion. But it's important to maintain the serious, no-nonsense role. The boss thinks the problems are serious. So must we.

Q. How does planning help establish these relationships?

A. You should already have evaluated the type of person in authority when you get hired. If not, then you should certainly have some idea by the time you complete the preliminary review. In nearly all small and mid-size companies, as well as divisions or departments of larger firms, the character and personality of the boss permeates the organization. If the boss can be classified into one of the four categories chances are very good that the employees follow suit.

Knowing what will be faced once the job begins, it's easy to cast yourself in the appropriate role. Successful consultants are all good actors. It goes along with being adaptable.

RELATIONSHIPS WITH OUTSIDE ADVISORS

Q. One of my clients specializes in constructing electric power plants and substations. It seems that the company's outside legal counsel and public accounting firm constantly have their fingers in the business, giving the CEO advice about management matters. How can I work effectively when these outsiders are always there?

A. I must admit, this subject is near and dear to me. I can't count how many of my clients have relied on outside lawyers and public accountants for management advice, usually bad advice.

Lawyers are notoriously poor business people. Public accountants aren't much better, especially those from small firms or lower echelon employees of the giants. Major accounting firm partners don't seem to be quite as inane. However, many company executives do rely on these people for business advice. That means we sometimes have to develop tactics to keep them from fouling up our work. And this is a difficult, frustrating task.

I don't have a fail-safe answer. These professionals were on the client's scene long before we came along for consulting work. Clients trust them because of their professional status. Criticizing these advisors is the worst approach. Clients defend them with, "I've known so-and-so for ten years. I trust her judgment." That's tough to overcome.

Q. Is there any way to get these people on my side, rather than against me?

A. If you can get outside lawyers and accountants to acknowledge your authority and support your opinions, they will stop interfering—at least for a while.

This is as much a part of client relations as romancing the CEO or playing a role with employees. A good starting point is to meet with these advisors, at lunch or in their offices, before beginning the engagement. Bring along a personal profile and a brochure. Concentrate on winning them over using one of the four role models we discussed previously. Emphasize your desire to help them do their job more effectively. Promise to keep them informed of your progress on the job as well as any problems that might pop up relating to their field (with the client's permission, of course). This can mean more business for them.

The most critical point to get across at this meeting is your total adherence to confidentiality. Lawyers and public accountants are very conscious of client confidentiality. They will never reveal any information unless they believe it will be held in confidence. And in many cases, interfacing with a client's outside advisors at least once or twice during an engagement is mandatory. We must have their confidence, not only to keep them out of our way, but to get information from them when needed.

Q. Should the CEO or other management personnel attend these meetings also?

A. The answer is an unequivocal *no*. The CEO should make the introductions before the meeting, but should not participate in it. This makes the meeting stilted, with everyone jockeying for position before the CEO. It's impossible to establish a relationship under these circumstances.

Q. How about during the course of the engagement? Is there anything I should do to solidify the relationships?
A. Yes. I always make it a point to ask the client's lawyer and public accountant to lunch at least once and maybe several times during an engagement. I prefer separate meetings, however. It keeps them from joining forces and overwhelming me with off-point suggestions and information. These meetings provide a good setting for informal verbal status reports to keep them informed of your progress with the client.

Clearly, the client must approve of the meeting and sanction the status report. And it's crucial to tell the professional that the client has approved, as evidence of your confidentiality.

Properly managed, a client's professional advisors can be more help than hindrance. At a minimum, their ideas are not flavored by day-to-day operating hurdles nor are they subject to as much internal political pressure as employees.

Q. What happens when part of the engagement requires business advice about topics handled by outside professionals, such as tax or estate planning matters?
A. This happens frequently, especially with smaller, owner-managed clients. Nearly any type of continuing engagement involves recommendations for alternative courses of action that impact taxes, estate planning, wage and hour laws, equal opportunity laws, perhaps safety and environmental regulations, contract interpretations, and so on.

In many cases an outside lawyer, public accountant, or other professional has far more knowledge about these subjects than we do, yet to complete the assignment we must incorporate the impact of these matters in our recommendations.

Some consultants, especially when starting out, make the fatal error of trying to give advice in areas that they have no business being in. Unless we are practicing lawyers, we have no business making legal recommendations. The same holds true for tax advice, unless we happen to be tax experts. Most of us are not lawyers or tax experts and should stay away from expressing opinions in these areas.

This is when a good relationship with outside advisors becomes essential to fulfilling the contract. Having developed such a relationship it's easy to pick up the phone and ask for professional advice. Once obtained, it can be included in our recommendations, citing the authority.

Q. Should I call an outsider for advice each time I come across a contractual matter or a compliance question?
A. No. Obviously, if you have a good background in current environmental regulations, bankruptcy proceedings, or employee rights under the wage and hour law, go ahead and express an opinion. You can always recommend that the client seek further advice from a professional before taking action, although in most cases that's not necessary.

Consultants who specialize in personnel recruiting or organizational development should have a knowledge of wage and hour laws and equal opportunity regulations as part of their credentials. Those specializing in environmental consulting should be up to speed on Environmental Protection Agency regulations. And so on.

But having sufficient knowledge to offer business advice upon which a company's management can base decisions is different from offering an opinion on a complex legal or tax matter. Don't worry, most competent managers know the difference and wouldn't act solely on your advice anyway.

CLIENT ENTERTAINING

Q. Give me some tips about romancing a business owner, CEO, or other top management personnel. For instance, how about wining and dining?

A. The question of how much entertaining is enough and how much is too much has always plagued consultants. Some executives have no interest in being romanced. Time or money spent on them is completely wasted. Others, the "good-time Charlies," expect their consultants to initiate and pay for a certain amount of entertaining. But most fall between these two extremes.

Executives from larger companies nearly always pick up the tab, reimbursed by the company, of course. Executives in small cities or rural communities do the same. They like to play the good ol' boy role.

Even with changes in the tax-deductibility of business entertaining, it's still used as a viable selling tool in most companies. Many executives still expect to be entertained by suppliers of any product, including business advice.

I have always felt that it is common courtesy to invite top managers to lunch or dinner occasionally. Also, I find that sticky problems are easier to resolve in the relaxed atmosphere of a quiet restaurant than in the hustle and bustle of an office.

There's no need to be too lavish, however. I have never met a legitimate business person who expected to be wined and dined at a $100-a-plate restaurant.

Q. What about events that the client sponsors or supports, such as charitable balls, or alumni functions?

A. Whether you like such events or not, if top management supports them and invites you to one, attendance is mandatory. You probably won't get any brownie points for attending but will certainly get black marks if you don't.

I don't like these events, but if invited, I force myself to go. I pretend to have a good time, regardless of how boring it may be. The reason I make the effort is simple: I've seen it pay off. Let me give you an example.

Some years ago, a client that manufactured oil field equipment invited my wife and me to a formal dinner dance at the Waldorf in New York to honor some important industry official. The evening was so boring that I can't even remember who was honored.

We were stuck at a table with ten foreign dignitaries, most of whom couldn't speak English. My host and his wife were seated at the head table—5,100 people away. I won't go into the details, but it was one of the worst evenings—and one of the most expensive—I have ever suffered through.

The payoff? Two months later my host introduced me with a raving reference to the president of a $2 billion French company looking for a business acquisition in Texas. I got the job.

Q. How about sporting events or leisure time activities?
A. Yes. Season tickets or golf or tennis club memberships can be very helpful. Sporting events seem to appeal to a lot of people and season tickets assure you of good seats. A lot of business gets conducted at these events, contrary to what the IRS chooses to believe. Tickets are expensive but clients appreciate the gesture.

I would only take top executives, however. If you can't attend, giving the tickets to client employees helps promote their goodwill.

When romancing new clients, I prefer a less hectic environment—golf, tennis, or my favorite, sailing. It's hard to know for sure, but I'm fairly certain I have picked up more than a few clients by treating them to a Sunday-afternoon sail—sometimes a full weekend.

I don't play golf, but a consulting friend does. She suggests a golf game at the very first meeting with a prospective client. My friend has reciprocal club privileges, so even clients located in distant cities get invitations. She swears by it and claims that once she gets a CEO alone on the golf course she nearly always closes the order.

Use the entertainment vehicle you are comfortable with. But if you plan to make management consulting a career over the long haul, access to sporting events is practically imperative.

Q. How do you feel about mixing with employees below the rank of top management?
A. This is generally a bad policy. Occasionally, having a beer with the crew can help break an information logjam or convince

recalcitrant employees that you are not out to get them fired. With this exception, however, socializing with lower echelon employees can be dangerous.

In too many cases, especially in troubled companies, animosity exists between top executives and the working ranks. Distrust permeates the air. Battle lines get drawn between workers, first-line supervisors, middle managers, and the CEO and other senior executives. Each side looks for an excuse to ignite its cannons.

When we are hired by senior management, other employees jockeying for favored positions among themselves feed us information they want the boss to hear. Senior executives feed similar misinformation, hoping we'll carry it back to the workers.

Socializing with lower echelon employees puts consultants in the unenviable position of being the bearer of lies in both directions. This makes a successful engagement virtually impossible.

One-upmanship is not restricted to troubled companies. As we all know, it exists throughout the business community, affecting large corporations and small ones, profitable ones and losers. We must maintain our independence from both top executives and workers in order to view solutions objectively.

Although clients get hurt from bad consulting advice, consultants get hurt much worse. When the word gets out that you can be manipulated, your reputation and the foundation of your business can easily become tarnished beyond repair.

It's just common sense to avoid situations that could be interpreted in the wrong light. Socializing with lower echelon employees is one of those situations.

MARKETING TO EX-CLIENTS

Q. Does a client relations program for ex-clients do any good?

A. It depends on who they are, where they are located, what markets you are in, and how much time and resources you can afford to devote.

I have a standard policy to stay in contact with ex-clients, regardless of where they are located, for eighteen months. If additional work hasn't been generated in that time, I forget about them. Other consultants disagree. Several associates believe that six months is long enough. On the other hand, one consultant in our consortium never stops. He continues to send brief notes and Christmas cards, and occasionally makes phone calls to ex-clients from five years back.

The time frame doesn't seem to be that relevant, again depending on a person's resources and markets. The form of communication doesn't seem to matter either. As long as ex-clients hear from us occasionally and know we are still in business, chances are good we'll get a call when a new job opens.

I have mixed feelings about spending much money on promoting ex-clients. On the one hand, a satisfactorily completed engagement should be reference enough for additional work if it becomes available. Active promotion is overkill. The ex-client knows your abilities, how you operate, and your personal characteristics. Promotional gimmicks won't improve this image and they could tarnish it if the recipient interprets your actions as too flashy or pushy.

Conversely, I have had excellent results using luncheons and an occasional ballgame to keep in touch with several ex-clients. They haven't all resulted in new work from the same companies: but without exception, these executives have given me excellent referrals to other prospective clients, many of which have resulted in work.

Q. How do you set aside time for this in the heat of battle?
A. Maintaining relationships with ex-clients falls into the marketing category and time must be allotted from marketing hours. The more a consulting business grows, the less of a chore this becomes. The guidelines that we spoke about earlier for allocated marketing time diminish by the time a broad client base is established. The only exception is if your entire business focuses on one-shot project jobs. In this case allocating 30 to 40 percent of available hours to marketing remains essential for staying in business.

I have a terrible time keeping track of things unless I abide by written schedules. I lack the mental discipline to remember to do things one or two months in the future without a written reminder. Consequently, I maintain two client computer files. One for keeping track of appointments and commitments with current clients; the other for ex-clients.

I try to schedule follow-up appointments with ex-clients at least three months in advance, and sometimes as much as six months. Since operating executives have worse memories than mine, I also schedule a confirming letter two weeks before the appointment and then I call four to five days before the date.

Because the potential of getting additional work from ex-clients is greater than getting it from new prospects, I have no difficulty shifting marketing time to this effort. A few consulting friends think that stealing marketing time from prospecting is a sure road to oblivion, but it works for me. To each his own.

Several other techniques work as well as luncheons and sporting events, but I find these the least burdensome.

Q. What other techniques are you talking about?
A. Well, for one, newsletters. Biweekly or monthly newsletters are an excellent way to keep in touch with ex-clients. They work for new prospects also. Keep in mind, however, that cold mailings become very expensive.

Another possibility is weekend seminars. If you already use the seminar route as a prospecting tool, it's a simple matter to invite ex-clients. If not, try structuring one exclusively for ex-clients and current clients.

A weekend retreat is a third possibility. It takes time to set up, but getting away from the spouse and kids for a weekend of relaxation appeals to a lot of people and is an excellent promotion medium.

Q. How can I make a newsletter pay?
A. Public accounting firms, insurance agents, and financial planners find newsletters an excellent way to communicate new developments in tax laws, and tips for personal financing planning, investment alternatives, and estate planning. Securities brokers

constantly use the technique. A few management consulting firms have joined the parade.

Monthly mailings should be adequate. If you can't prepare it yourself with desk-top-publishing software, several small advertising and public relations firms furnish prepared newsletters. All you have to do is stamp on the name of your firm and mail them out.

Topics should be focused exclusively on your specialities. You get far more mileage out of newsletters if you prepare the copy yourself rather than using a prepared letter.

An ex-partner who branched out on his own developed a monthly newsletter covering export/import topics (his specialty). He claims an enormously successful reception, especially from ex-clients for whom he had performed export engagements. He told me that in 1989 the newsletter generated so much repeat business that he cut new prospecting time to less than 10 percent.

Q. How about seminars?

A. Normally one thinks of putting on seminars as a pure marketing device to attract new clients. However, seminars can also be used as client relations promotions for current and ex-clients. It goes without saying that the topic must be germane to your specialty. It should also focus on current developments. Some project-type markets do not adapt well simply because there isn't enough new material available to make a seminar worthwhile. Nearly all management niche markets do adapt, however.

If the seminar's primary purpose is to serve as a client relations tool, it should be structured differently than if used as a selling tool to attract new prospects. Here I'll address seminars only as a client relations approach.

Even though it should conform to your specialty, the topic should not be so informative that the seminar can be substituted for your consulting expertise. For example, if you specialize in preparing business plans or developing strategic planning procedures, don't hold a seminar to teach the audience how to do it. Encourage them to hire you for that.

Concentrate on related topics, such as current developments in government assistance programs for exporting, government contracting opportunities, new software developments for spreadsheet analyses, or financial statement analysis. These topics all relate to the planning process and should get the audience interested in learning more. Ergo, you will have new engagements.

One-day seminars held during the work week fare better than those lasting two or three days. No executive has that much time to spend. Weekend seminars are even better. They give people an excuse to get away from cutting the lawn.

Q. How about retreats?

A. Very few consultants use retreats. They fear that participants will not like each other, or will be afraid that a competitor will attend, or think that retreats are only for New Age types.

I find that clients are more receptive to retreats than practically any other client relations technique I have tried, once I convince them that it won't harm their company or their personal image. The biggest drawback is that it takes a good bit of preparation.

Actually, I stumbled across this technique by accident. I have never heard or read about many other consultants using it.

I had developed a modest client base of small businesses in a variety of industries. Many of the engagements were short-term, solving rather mundane marketing and financial problems. Advertising and other promotions weren't doing much to bring in new clients and I wasn't getting any referrals from prior clients.

The owner of one company mentioned over lunch that he had attended a weekend retreat in the Pocono Mountains sponsored by a pseudo-religious group and stated how relaxing it was to get away from the routine.

The light dawned. A friend owned a modest vacation resort in the Poconos, consisting of twelve small cabins by a lake. I arranged to rent them all for a weekend in October, his slow period. I invited all prior and current clients by phone. Nearly 50 percent accepted. We had a terrific time. Best of all, I landed four new clients on direct recommendations from two of the attendees.

I'm not sure I would go to the trouble of planning a retreat strictly as a form of entertainment for clients. It's too much work. But as a combination of client relations and a selling tool, retreats work very well.

EMOTIONAL INVOLVEMENT

Q. How do you feel about consultants that get emotionally involved in an engagement?

A. That's one of my pet gripes. We all know how important it is to maintain our independence on a job. Clients hire us to do a specific task. Losing our independence makes objective evaluations or recommendations impossible.

Yet, when we take assignments that evolve into pseudo-management activities, it's difficult not to begin believing that our efforts are so important to the company that it can't survive without us. We get upset when employees don't follow our directions, or we lose our cool when the CEO ignores changes that we feel are critical to the well-being of the company.

This leads to arguments, even shouting, and our effectiveness as independent counsel evaporates. Instead of using effective client relations techniques to build goodwill that could lead to additional work, we have created antagonism and suspicion that only leads downhill.

This type of emotional involvement is deadly to our success as well as to the client's well-being. Yet we all do it on occasion.

Q. But how do we maintain our objectivity when the battle heats up and we know we're right?

A. By never forgetting that we are actors on a stage. As we discussed previously, effective client relations demands a certain amount of role playing. The role we take depends on the circumstances. The client's facility is the stage. While on that stage we stay in the role we have chosen. Playing a role provides a barricade against believing that we are so important or so right that we become emotionally involved.

Although the need for objectivity is so obvious it hardly needs elaboration, it is also so important that I'd like to tell you about how an associate lost it.

Steve was one of the best troubled-company consultants I have known. He had a knack for untangling the web of misinformation, confusion, and outright misrepresentations that go along with this type of engagement. The CEO asked Steve to manage all internal activities of the company while the CEO took care of sales.

When the assignment ended with Steve bringing in new financing, he couldn't let go. For three months he tried to convince the CEO that when he was not on the premises the employees reverted to their old ways, and that spelled doom for the company. Several meetings ended with Steve shouting his despair at the CEO, who fortunately remained calm.

Finally, an executive from the company's new bank suggested that the company couldn't afford to pay for Steve's services any more and the CEO terminated the engagement. Steve was furious and let it be known that the company would be bankrupt in six months.

Two years later, Steve's client had recovered and added another facility. Steve was bidding on another turnaround job and needed references. He asked the CEO for a reference letter. The CEO told Steve to take a hike.

No matter how good we think we are, we are never right 100 percent of the time. And, as I mentioned much earlier, the worst trap we can fall into is to lose our objectivity to the point that we think we can run a company better than its top management. It just doesn't work that way. Client personnel always know more about the company than we do.

STOPPING WORK, FOLLOW-UP, ETC.

Q. How do I deal with unforseen problems such as a serious illness in my family or among key employees and still maintain solid client relations?

A. A serious illness or accident can happen to anyone. The longer the engagement takes, the higher the probability of something unforeseen occurring to slow you down or to abort the entire engagement.

Such unrelated roadblocks cannot be forecast, yet they happen to all of us. Most clients readily accept a delay or postponement in the assignment until the crisis passes.

On the other hand, there are those who won't give an inch. This type of problem gets very sticky. If you really cannot continue with the engagement, regardless of the reason, there is only one thing to do. Tell the client you must stop work.

Q. Does that mean I have to return the payments the client has made to date?
A. Possibly, if you can't negotiate a way out.

If the reason for stopping work is on your side—your illness, a serious accident, or whatever—and the work hasn't progressed too far, good client relations dictate returning the fees already paid and taking the beating. With the client's permission, another consultant could be brought in to finish up, of course.

If the reason emanates from the client's side, I don't see any reason why you should give up the fees you have already earned. If the CEO or a key employee dies, gets sick, or has an accident, that isn't your fault. Nor is a "force majeure" reason such as a strike, a flood, or a fire.

Q. What should I do if an engagement turns out to be much longer or much more difficult than I had originally envisioned?
A. This happens to all of us at one time or another. It's easy to misjudge time when negotiating a scope contract. That's why not-to-exceed or flat quotes are dangerous.

When a situation develops that clearly entails more work or different skills than you envisioned in the beginning, the only ethical thing to do is tell the boss you blew it. Once again, most clients will swing with the punches and agree to an extension of time and a corresponding increase in fees, as long as it isn't too much.

Without such an agreement, there are only two choices: stop work, or swallow the loss. I definitely do not recommend stopping work. Then the client is lost forever. Pragmatically, to maintain any semblance of good client relationships you have no choice but to complete the engagement as soon as you can. There might be additional work in the future to make up part of it.

Q. What tips can you give me for good client relations techniques after the engagement ends?

A. I presume you are referring to follow-up techniques.

This is another area in which many of us drop the ball. We think that because we have finished an engagement, written and delivered the final report, and bid the client adieu, the game is over.

Not so. Earlier, we spoke of client relations techniques applied to ex-clients. Similar although not as elaborate approaches can be used during the follow-up period.

Depending on the engagement, this follow-up period might be a month, six months, or even a year. In the case of business acquisitions, it's frequently nine to twelve months.

I make it a practice to schedule a follow-up call in not more than thirty days after completing an assignment. I either telephone or stop in for a short meeting or lunch. This is an important final step in an engagement. It gives clients a good feeling to know that you are conscientious enough to find out if your recommendations are working. Sometimes they don't get implemented right away and this follow-up tells the CEO to get moving.

In business acquisition engagements, I always follow up in less than thirty days to make sure the transition is proceeding smoothly. Then in about six to eight months I follow up again. By this time the bugs should have been worked out. If they haven't, I ask if I can help, and I usually pick up some short-term work.

Regardless of the time span or the techniques used, I have found that following up usually brings additional work. At a minimum, it's good client relations. And it's the ethical way to end an engagement.

Chapter 11

PAINLESS PAYING

How to Bill Clients and Get Them to Pay

Q. I'd like to know about alternative billing procedures. Where, when, and how do other consultants handle billings?
A. Four elements are involved in the billing cycle:

1. Fee structure
2. Terms of payment
3. Invoicing
4. Collecting

We have discussed commonly used fee structures: hourly rates, not-to-exceed prices, min-max ranges, and Lehman scale fees for M&A work.

We also covered terms of payment: in advance, weekly, monthly, at the end of the job.

Invoicing is merely the preparation and delivery of an invoice. Collecting means getting the client to pay it. That's all there is to it. Nothing very complicated.

BILLING FORMATS

Q. Could you simplify the billing/collection cycle?
A. Let's talk about some options for preparing invoices.

To avoid confusing already argumentative clients, and hence creating a longer paying cycle than necessary, try to match the wording of the invoice with the payment terms stipulated in the scope contract. Although consultants use a variety of terms to suit specific client needs, the three most common are:

1. On receipt of weekly or monthly invoice for work accomplished to date
2. A flat weekly or monthly advance payment
3. Total payment upon completion of the work

Here is a sample of the invoice wording for the first situation.

Fig.11-1

INVOICE

For services rendered based on our scope contract executed April 2, 1998.
Cumulative through prior invoice dated June 1, 1998:

43 hours @$150 per hour	$6,450

For the week ended June 7, 1998
June 4:

Meeting with warehouse employees for inventory control training	5 hours
Meeting with Mr. Brown re: filling out bank inventory report	2 hours
Designing form for controller's daily cash report	2 hours

June 5:

Supervising physical inventory of supplies storeroom	8 hours

June 7:

Meeting with bank auditors to explain inventory variances	3 hours
Instructing Ms. Horner re: new inventory control software	4 hours

TOTAL FOR THE WEEK	24 hours
Hourly billing rate	$150
Total this week	$3,600
Total billed to date	$10,050
Paid to date	($6,450)
NET DUE THIS INVOICE	$3,600

Some consultants disagree with this approach, arguing that showing the client a cumulative-to-date fee has a negative impact. They claim that company records show the total billed. They ask, why keep bringing it up, especially on weekly invoices?

They could be right, but I believe the client has a right to know how much my work is costing whether the company keeps accurate records or not. I would rather know immediately if the CEO believes that the job is costing too much. I can then suggest tapering off, withdrawing for a while, or stopping completely. I'd much rather stop a job than get to the end and not be paid.

In addition, many consultants disagree with the practice of listing hours by specific task. They argue that it's too much work to keep track of every hour on the job.

I strongly disagree with this argument. Once again, I believe the client has a right to know how much time it took me to accomplish a given task or to attend a meeting. That's just good control.

Lawyers are famous for sending summary invoices without any indication of the detailed work. How many times have you received or seen a lawyer's invoice that reads, "For services rendered— $2,000"? When I get invoices like that I throw them away. I don't pay anything unless it's itemized.

Q. What should the wording be for a flat weekly or monthly advance payment?
A. The complexity of these invoices depends on the caveats attached to the advance payment: that is, how the advance payment is to be applied. The most common caveats apply advance payments against:

- Days to be worked in a given period.
- Hours to be worked in a given period.
- Total project fee contingent on completion.
- Total fixed price.

Here is a sample of a format used for billing advance payments against days worked.

Fig. 11-2

November 22, 1998
INVOICE

For services rendered re: scope contract dated October 5, 1998:

Days worked prior to this invoice	10
Daily rate	$1,200
Total earned prior to this week	$12,000
Total advance payments through November 21, 1998	$10,800
Amount due from prior invoices	$1,800
Days to be worked week ending November 28, 1998	3
Daily rate	$1,200
Payment due for this week	$3,600
Amounts due from prior weeks	$1,800
Total due upon receipt of this invoice	$5,400

An identical format should be used for advance payments against hours to be worked.

Consultants seem to be divided about the advisability of showing this much detail, just as they are for showing unpaid hours. As far as I am concerned, the more detail you give the client the less chance for an argument. I very seldom have collection problems regardless of the terms of payment. Perhaps being completely candid in my invoices has something to do with it.

Q. How would you handle the other two caveats?

A. Invoices for advance payments applied on completion against a contingency fee are straightforward, as in this sample.

Fig. 11-3

INVOICE

For services rendered re: scope contract dated October 4, 1998

Monthly retainer per contract		$3,000
Amounts billed to date	$20,500	
Paid to date	($20,500)	
Amounts due from prior invoices		—0—
Total amount this invoice		$3,000

Here is an example of the language to use at the completion of the job.

Fig. 11-4

INVOICE

For services rendered re: scope contract dated XXXX

Total project fee per contract	$150,000
Paid to date on retainer invoices	($45,000)
Total due upon receipt of this invoice	$105,000

Q. What about billing the entire job at one time?
A. This is seldom done. I have never waited until the end of a job for payment in full, and have known only one consultant in my entire career who agreed to such terms.

BILLING FREE TIME AND EXPENSES

Q. It seems that I am consistently giving away free time to clients either because I think the hours are extraneous to the job or because I goof up and take longer to do something than I should. Is there any way I can get client relations mileage out of these hours?

A. Positively! If you can't charge for hours, you might as well try for other benefits, as long as you are not at fault. This is one of the truly great promotion devices that very few consultants use to the fullest.

In one sense, freebie promotional hours don't cost a penny. They are incurred without laying out any cash. In another sense, they do cost. Lost hours could have been billed on another job at the standard rate. Perhaps.

In any event, we all incur unbillable production hours for one reason or another. That being the case, we should use lost time to develop client goodwill; which is why most lost hours occur anyway. But we can't get the full benefit unless we tell the client how many hours, and hence lost billings, we have donated to the company.

One way is to tell the CEO verbally how many hours were lost on the job, but this sounds like sour grapes. It gives the impression that you feel the company has cheated you out of fees that have been rightfully earned.

A much easier and far more beneficial way is to include free hours in weekly or monthly invoices. That way you can blow your own horn without sounding pompous.

A refinancing job was taking far more time that I had expected, due primarily to promised meetings aborted by bankers. For every billable hour, I lost an hour. I decided that matters had to change and on my next invoice I concocted this formula.

This accomplished two objectives: (1) it created the impression that I was conscientious about not charging the company for hours without benefit (which contributed a lot toward building goodwill), and (2) it succinctly illustrated to the CEO that he should take action to get the bankers moving. The goodwill resulted in additional work. The CEO began accompanying me to bank meetings, showing the bankers he demanded their attention.

Fig. 11-5

INVOICE

For services rendered re: scope contract dated May 4, 1998

Cumulative through prior invoice dated July 10, 1998
64 hours @$175 per hour $11,200

For the week ended July 17, 1998

July 18:
    Meeting with Chase Manhattan representatives in New York,   7 hours
    bankers did not show up (1)

July 19:
    Meeting with Mr. Brown, First Bank of New Jersey   3 hours

July 21:
    Assisted company controller with financing plan   6 hours

Total for the week	16 hours
Hourly billing rate	$175
Total this week	$2,800
Less: July 18 hours not benefiting company (1)	7 hours
Hourly rate	$175
Amount deducted from this invoice	($1,225)
Total billed to date	$12,775
Paid to date	($11,200)
Net due this invoice	$1,575

Q. How about lost hours resulting from my errors?

A. That's a different matter. It would be unethical to claim that external events or people were at fault. Better to eat the loss and try to beat your schedule at the next step.

Q. How should I deal with out-of-pocket expenses?

A. Some clients complain about any expense they have to pay for. I can offer a few tips, however, that might smooth the way.

Most larger companies prefer to reimburse expenses from their standard employee expense report form. Smaller clients seem less fussy about the form as long as supporting documents are attached.

The biggest problem I face with expense reimbursements is remembering to get client approval before I incur the expense. Some expenses are easy to remember: air fares, meeting expenses, auto mileage, and so on. Reimbursable expenses incurred in my office are another matter. Long distance or fax charges, postage for special mailings, overnight delivery service, and so on are easy to track after the fact, but getting approval ahead of time is a nuisance.

Clearly, if a client authorizes you to incur certain expenses there shouldn't be any gripe when a billing is submitted. Unauthorized expenses are the primary reason for client complaints.

Here are a few tips to avoid client confrontations over out-of-pocket expenses:

1. Specifically identify in the scope contract the types of expenses likely to be incurred. Then make sure the client understands that the contract itself authorizes you to incur these expenses.
2. Submit expense reports currently. Don't bill two months after the fact.
3. Enter out-of-pocket expenses on a normal invoice. This is a good reminder to bill expenses currently.
4. Get verbal approval, at least, before incurring expenses not covered by the scope contract.
5. Keep meticulous bookkeeping records to support any and all reimbursable expenditures.
6. When given a choice, such as with airline fares or car rentals, always choose the least expensive available, and tell the client when you do this.
7. Attach supporting receipts for *all* expenses. Explain on the expense form or invoice specifically why each expense was incurred.

Q. Does the method I use to deliver my invoice make any difference in getting paid promptly?

A. The longer we stay in consulting the more lax we become. As the years roll by, as we become more confident of our business survival, as we get to know our clients better, it becomes easier and easier to procrastinate, to put off administrative drudgery until evenings or weekends.

For three years in a row, I prepared all my billings on weekends, provided nothing more interesting came up. I became further behind in billings and collections as the months wore on. At one stage, I was three months behind in billing clients and was startled to see my cash flow dry up! I immediately set to work to catch up and, needing the cash quickly, faxed the invoices to three out of four clients.

To my chagrin, faxing didn't speed up collections even by one day. On the contrary, several clients told me later that faxing invoices was a sleazy way to do business and expected better of an experienced consultant. That cured me.

If your choices are (1) hand carry, (2) mail, or (3) fax, the most courteous method is to hand carry the invoice and sit down with the CEO to go over it. If that's not practical, mail is second best. When the billing covers advance payments, personal delivery is the only way to be assured of getting paid promptly.

I don't like to use courier services either. That may suggest that I am either extravagant or too desperate to wait for the mail.

GETTING PAID

Q. How do I speed up collections without aggravating a client?
A. I am convinced that consultants remain the most inept of any group of business people when it comes to collecting bills. For some unexplained reason we can be tough as nails when doing a job or beating competition, yet soft as a feather when it comes to collections. Lawyers are almost as bad; but I believe consultants take the blue ribbon. I am not sure why.

It could be because we're afraid of being too pushy and losing a client. We struggle so long and hard to get clients in the first place that we are willing to do almost anything to keep them—even wait months to collect fees. As business advisors, we should know how important cash flow is to the health of a business, but, just like the accountant who can't balance his own checkbook, we don't practice what we preach.

A second reason might be that without a national organization to conduct practical "how to run your business" seminars for consultants and virtually no help from consulting books and articles, we learn collecting techniques through trial and error. Very often, we learn methods that don't work.

Q. What are some general rules to follow?

A. It took me nearly four years to realize that if I couldn't stimulate my clients to pay on time, I would soon be out of business. The timing for this revelation was all wrong. The country was in the midst a recession and every client was strapped for cash. Experimenting with several tactics that didn't work, I eventually settled into the following routine that did work.

Although each client required variations depending on the personality of the chief executive and the company's needs, these were the general rules that formed the foundation for my collection program:

1. Recognize that I did not have the resources to finance other companies—not even for 30 days.
2. Insist on definitive clauses in the scope contract specifying exactly when payment would be made on each invoice.
3. If you don't negotiate for weekly or monthly advance payments, conduct a thorough credit search, including bank references, before executing the scope contract.
4. Never grant delayed terms. Insist on payment before leaving the premises.
5. Avoid billing disputes by itemizing on the invoice all work performed.
6. Present each invoice to the CEO in person, even if this means tracking him or her down outside the company facilities. (Once I located a CEO in his boat anchored off the Jersey shore.)
7. Do not be afraid to insist on payment before continuing work. If billings are lost because of this, the client wasn't worth keeping in the first place.

8. Hold back important information or implementation steps until the invoice is paid.

Q. Can you comment on the reception you get from taking the first four steps?
A. At least half of the problems in collections begin with the initial negotiations that lead to the scope contract. Doing your homework at this stage makes collecting during the job a lot easier.

Take the first rule, not financing a company, which is probably the most important of all. Nearly all small business entrepreneurs pay lip service to this concept, but very few have the guts to practice it, much less come right out and tell a customer to get financing elsewhere.

The larger the client, the more likely the company is to take advantage of small suppliers. Corporate executives call it good business. I call it thievery.

Certain industries are worse than others. Hospitals, schools, foundations, government agencies, and other not-for-profit businesses head the offender list. Publishing companies and foreign-owned subsidiaries rank right up there too. At the other end of the spectrum, automotive companies, aerospace giants, and computer manufacturers have generally treated me fairly.

I would rather lose a client, or not land a new account, than finance a company for thirty or sixty days. Therefore, I now make it a practice to clarify this point during scope contract negotiations. If the CEO doesn't like my approach, I pack my bags and go elsewhere.

I also insist that the scope contract include one or more clauses relating to payment upon receipt of invoice. The best way, of course, is to get advance payments. Then it's very simple to stop work until the invoice is paid.

Helen and I attend the same church. Laid off from Arco Chemical in suburban Philadelphia, she started a consulting business concentrating on small health care suppliers. During her second year, with cash flow drying up, she asked for my help. She couldn't bring herself to be tough about negotiating advance payments and found her receivables piling up.

I accompanied her on a few marketing sojourns and when a prospect agreed to hire her to solve a distribution problem I sat in on the scope negotiations, insisting that the client provide weekly advance payments against her commitment of two days per week. The CEO threw us out. In two weeks he called Helen and agreed to advance payments.

Today, she not only survives but is one of the most successful consultants in her area, and she still does work for the obstreperous client—with advance payments.

Q. How about your last point, holding back information?

A. Yes, we've talked about delivering invoices, but I'd like to go one step further.

Hand delivering an invoice to the CEO, rather than the accounts payable department or the controller, puts the top dog on the spot. Very few top executives have the courage to play hardball about paying bills; they pawn this task off on the accounting department. By going to the top, the probability of getting paid right away increases dramatically.

This also provides the opportunity to threaten to stop work, if that becomes necessary. That's impossible to achieve with a mailed invoice. A controller or an accounts payable clerk can't react either. Only the CEO or other executive who signed the scope contract cares about whether we continue or not.

Clearly, if the CEO doesn't want the job completed, this tactic won't work, but that seldom happens.

None of us like to confront a client with a threat to stop work. It hurts our pride. It can damage our reputation. It will probably harm the client, assuming the project was worthwhile to begin with. On the other hand, it's better to go on to other clients than to continue working without pay.

With a little finesse, you should be able to get your point across without a direct stop-work threat, provided the invoice gets to a decision-maker.

Q. How about rule number eight?

A. This is the "coup de grâce."

Nine times out of ten it works, with one proviso: if you don't get paid on time you must be prepared to back off the job until the check arrives.

All service businesses use this tack. Have you ever tried to get a doctor, CPA, or lawyer to perform additional services when you owe them money from the last time? How about getting your car repaired by a mechanic that hasn't been paid for the last go-around?

Management consultants are in a better position to use this tactic than most service businesses, because our engagements normally entail a series of actions or recommendations over a period of time. They are not one-visit projects. Therefore, progress (or interim) billings are the norm, not the exception.

Q. But what type of information or steps can I hold back, and how do I do this without making it sound like a threat to stop work?

A. We come now to the fine art of not only getting the client to pay up, but getting him to be enthusiastic about paying. I can't provide a set of rules that guarantee this happening. It's an art, not a science. However, I can discuss a few broad concepts that apply in most cases.

In general, the holdback process works best when the billing cycle is weekly or biweekly—preferably weekly. The shorter the time frame between billings, the more critical your work in the subsequent period, and consequently, the more eager a client is to see you keep moving.

The invoice must be personally delivered to a top executive. After the first couple of times, adroitly implying that without a check you can't afford to meet with that banker next week, or negotiate a contract with a supplier, or continue employee training sessions already started, the executive catches on that he had better have a check ready and waiting when you arrive, or at least alert the accounting department to get one prepared for his signature.

The process also works in reverse. On some jobs it's the employees who benefit most from our efforts and they want to see us finish the engagement. More often than not the assignment entails at least some contact with the controller or the accounting department. By dropping a tactful word here and there about how you must have immediate payment to afford to carry out the scheduled steps next week, or next month, you can be assured that the controller will get the message to the CEO.

The same reverse technique works with bankers, a company's external lawyer or public accountant, or other outsider that the CEO relies upon. Much of my work involves contact with bankers. If I let the company's banker know that payments must be kept current (which in most cases means weekly) I can be certain that word will quickly filter back to the CEO.

It's important to understand the nuance that separates this approach from announcing that you will stop work if not paid. The latter case is far more confrontational, dramatic, and can in the end create animosity, unless a person is extremely diplomatic.

By tactfully implying that we cannot accomplish a specific task *next week*, the impression should be that that we will have to postpone next week's events, not that we are threatening to stop work. The difference in an executive's eyes can be enormous.

THE POOR BOY ROLE

Q. Doesn't this approach sometimes give the client the wrong impression, that your business is on the brink, and therefore that you are not financially viable?

A. It can. But it shouldn't, if handled properly.

When we talked about client relations, we explored role playing as a major tactic for successfully accomplishing an engagement. We discussed how crucial it is to adapt our personalities and work habits to the demeanor of client personnel.

I attach the same role-playing importance to getting paid. This is where a sole practitioner has it all over a larger consulting firm. The larger the firm, the more a client expects payment concessions.

It's difficult to justify the need for immediate payment when you maintain a high-rent office with several partners and a bevy of administrative personnel. Keeping the cash flow rolling may be just as crucial for a large firm, but clients will never believe it.

The "poor boy" role is ideally suited to sole practitioners. Because consulting is such a personal business, it's unusual not to be on a first-name basis with the CEO and other top executives. Not infrequently, both consultant and client personnel know who has how many kids in college, where each other's homes are located, and a myriad of other personal matters.

With a minimum of socializing, it's easy to get the point across that you don't have the resources to support a thirty- to sixty-day receivable. The poor boy approach emphasizes a sound business practice—that cash flow must be kept current to pay bills. Nothing wrong with that.

Most executives would feel the same way if they were in your shoes. As long as I maintain a "professional" air about my personal demeanor and my work, I never suffer from playing the poor boy role.

Q. Wouldn't I be better off playing a financially viable role?
A. Here's a story related to me by a consultant I met at a seminar. His modus operandi was to play the "wealthy executive role," driving a Cadillac to client offices, consistently picking up lunch tabs, flying first class, and generally presenting the impression that he was very well-off.

This approach didn't seem to be working, however. As he picked up our lunch tab, he complained that he couldn't get clients to pay up, and didn't know why. He certainly had a big ego, however. Maybe feeding it by financing clients was a good trade-off for him.

Which role works best? The choice is yours.

WHEN THE CLIENT CAN'T PAY

Q. How do I get a client to pay when there isn't any money in the bank?
A. If you believe that a company still in business has no money in the bank you are either very gullible or don't understand business. As long as a company produces and sells, meets payroll, and pays utilities, it has cash—even if it's borrowed.

One of my market niches is consulting to troubled companies. I've been doing it for years. Troubled companies, by definition, are cash poor. Many can't meet debt service payments. They call on me to help find a solution to keep them in business, or to liquidate assets. I refuse to take one of these jobs without weekly advance payments. In theory, these companies have substantially less cash to pay bills than profitable companies. Yet they come up with enough cash to pay consulting fees. If they can do it, any company can.

If the scope contract calls for advance payments but you don't believe the company has the cash don't take the job.

Q. What should I do if the company's bank is taken over by a governmental entity and loans are called?

A. OK. Exceptions do exist. But they are very rare.

If there really isn't any money, the choices become very limited. To a large extent, your perception of the long-term viability of the company influences which way to go.

As I see it, ethical consultants have a moral obligation to see a client through the tough times as well as the good. I don't mean that we should work free. Too much free work is a sure way to bankrupt our own businesses.

On the other hand, if we contract to do a job in good faith, the client executes the agreement in good faith, and an extraneous event occurs at a later date making it difficult for the client to pay us on schedule, I believe we should try to make other compensation arrangements that permit us to finish the job. In severe cases, when other arrangements cannot be negotiated, we can either continue working for free or walk off the job.

To the extent that you believe the client's cash shortage will be short-lived and good long-term potential exists for additional assignments, working free for a limited period might be a good trade-off. Chalk it up to client relations.

Q. What do you mean by "other compensation arrangements"?

A. Other compensation could be a variety of things. Perhaps a promissory note from the company bearing a decent interest rate.

With small companies, a personal note from the owner might be more secure.

An out-of-town hotel client faced foreclosure. Creditors placed liens on its major receivables. With two weeks remaining on my engagement, I negotiated free rooms and meals and the use of a hotel car for the period.

Free use of a company's fishing lodge, boat, or airplane might work as alternate compensation. So might free use of company memberships in golf, tennis, or hunting clubs.

One of the best deals I ever negotiated with a cash-poor client was the use of the company's American Express credit card for the term of my engagement.

If none of these ideas work, there is always the possibility of a barter arrangement. Bartering is fast becoming an accepted medium in many business circles. It has many advantages, providing the received goods have value to you.

Q. How do you feel about using collection bureaus?
A. I think the idea is a bad one! I would rather take a beating on my fees than pay a collection bureau to harass a client. If you go this route, be assured your relationship with the client has ended forever. A collection bureau can't do anything that you can't do yourself. Why pay a high price for nothing?

Q. How about suing a client or bringing other legal action?
A. Only as a last resort. Of course, a lawsuit eliminates any potential for future business or references.

I have never brought legal action against a client, but I've known consultants who have. They tell me it's an expensive proposition if the amount isn't large. Nine out of ten times an out-of-court settlement is reached for a lesser amount. Legal fees can easily eat it up.

In addition, depositions and production of documents for a lawsuit take a lot of time that can't be billed. Unless the amount is very large, I would rather write off the account as a tax-deductible bad debt than incur the cost and effort of bringing suit. But then I am not litigious. Some consultants are.

Q. What if I haven't been paid and a client files a chapter 11 bankruptcy?

A. Under bankruptcy law, consulting fees owed by a corporation fall into the same category as any other vendor liability; the consultant becomes just one more unsecured creditor. If the company can be saved, it eventually negotiates a reorganization plan with a committee of unsecured creditors. In most cases all creditors agree to take a small percentage of their receivable—for instance 10 cents on the dollar—which usually gets paid when the court authorizes the company to come out of bankruptcy.

As an alternative to such a huge discount, a long-term payout plan might be negotiated with creditors over five to ten years. All creditors must agree to the plan, however, you can't go one way while other creditors go another.

When my last client filed chapter 11, in addition to working with the other creditors, I worked out an alternative scheme. After the filing, the CEO agreed that my consulting help would be necessary to structure a reorganization plan. He petitioned the bankruptcy court to permit the company to engage my services for four months. My fees for the post-filing period were considered an "administrative expense" under bankruptcy law, allowing the company to pay me currently along with rent, utilities, payroll, and so on.

As it turned out, the creditors negotiated an 80 percent discount in the reorganization plan. With four months' work under my belt plus 20 percent of old billings, I ended up doing better than if the company had not gone bankrupt.

As a final comment on the collections topic, I must add that collections are as important a part of consulting as getting clients or performing engagements. This is not the time to be shy. Too many consultants are terrific sales people and highly qualified management advisors but fall flat when it comes to getting paid. I hope you won't be counted among that number.

Chapter 12

TURNING DRUDGERY INTO CASH
How to Handle Administrative Chores Profitably

Q. Can you give me some ideas about running an efficient consulting office?

A. As much as we may dislike it, administrative work is an integral part of any business, including consulting. We must deal with it.

Consultants strive for two primary objectives in the administrative area: (1) methods and procedures that minimize the amount of time and effort needed to manage administrative tasks, and, (2) an office configuration that minimizes both fixed costs and administrative personnel. Optimum offices are the easiest to define, so let's begin there.

Consultants have a unique advantage over many other service businesses: we seldom invite clients or prospective clients to our office. Marketing meetings are more conveniently held in a prospect's office or neutral territory such as restaurants, hotels, sporting events or the offices of lawyers, public accountants, bankers, and so on. Production nearly always occurs at a client's facility or other field location. During my fifteen years in the consulting business, clients or prospects haven't been in my office more than a dozen times.

Since we seldom use our office as a meeting location, it doesn't contribute to our ability to get or keep clients. Therefore, an office doesn't have to be showy. It can be structured along purely utilitarian lines. We don't need a prestigious address or fancy furniture and appointments. The only criteria is to arrange an office to keep costs down and provide the most convenience for handling administrative tasks, including telephoning.

OFFICE LOCATION

Q. What do you consider the optimum office location for consultants—a center city office building or a suburban building?

A. Most consultants, especially single practitioners, don't need either one. I'll get to space alternatives shortly, but first let's look at location criteria. Through trial and error, I have found that the optimum office location should permit:

- Easy and rapid access to your home. There's no sense wasting hours commuting.
- The most efficient telephone service available in your area. We seem to spend more time on the telephone than doing anything else.
- Dependable electricity, heat, air conditioning, and water. If the temperature is uncomfortable, we can't work efficiently. If the electricity fluctuates, we spend time repairing computers and other office equipment.
- Easy and rapid access to public transportation (in metropolitan areas) and airports. For international work it's important to have ready access to an international terminal.

Q. What do you think of someone with an office in midtown Manhattan?

A. Unless the consultant also lives near his office he could probably find less expensive and more comfortable space in the suburbs. With adequate public transportation, I can't see any benefit in commuting to an office every day. I would rather spend commuting time getting to client offices.

OFFICE SPACE

Q. Would I get any mileage out of locating at a prestigious address?

A. High rents for a consulting office are a waste of money. A prestigious address might boost your ego but it won't bring in clients. It makes a lot more sense to use the dollars for advertising or promotion campaigns that can make a difference.

The choice of office space is such a personal matter that it's hard to generalize. If you feel more comfortable in a fancy office with a prestigious address and can afford it, why not splurge? Some people feel better with a new car every year, or dressing in designer clothes. If your tastes lean toward fancy offices, be my guest.

All I'm saying is that as far as the success of a consulting business is concerned, office space or address won't bring any more business or higher fees.

So-called "executive suite" offices have become very popular with single consultants. This is usually a less expensive way to go than to rent a complete office. Plus you normally get telephone answering, secretarial help, filing cabinets, access to copying machines and faxes, and in some cases, computers. This saves a bundle, and for beginning consultants, it can add to their staying power.

Executive suites also function well for smaller partnerships with two or three partners. Such a small amount of our time is spent in the office that the less we spend on rent and office appointments the better. This is precisely why so many single consultants choose to work out of their homes.

Q. What is your opinion of home offices?

A. Any time we can cut overhead expenses, we're ahead of the game. We can't do much about travel, promotions, advertising, telephone, and office supplies. Those are the tools of our trade. But we can certainly do something about office rent and utilities.

Most of the single consultants in our consortium work out of their homes. Nearly all my consulting friends from different parts of the country also do. The two exceptions seem to be those located in small towns where office rents are very low, and those who live in small apartments without adequate space for an office.

For fifteen years, I have operated my business out of my home. I built an office in the basement with all the niceties I would want in a rented space. I never commute, except to client offices or meetings. My overhead expenses are at rock bottom. Granted, building the office cost a few dollars and I spend money redecorating periodically, but these are nominal amounts.

In addition to providing comfortable space, avoiding the commuting hassle, and eliminating rent expense, an office in your home permits a sizable expense deduction for tax purposes. Instead of you paying a landlord, the Internal Revenue Service essentially pays you for staying at home.

As a consulting business grows, administrative personnel will likely be added, either on a full- or part-time basis. When planning an office, it makes sense to look to the future in terms of space requirements. Instead of moving to larger quarters as the business grows, it's cheaper and easier to acquire enough space in the beginning to handle one or two additional people.

A good rule of thumb states that you need about 300–400 square feet for a desk, files, office equipment, and yourself. Each full-time employee or partner needs another 100 square feet. Part-timers can be squeezed in.

Obviously, these rules don't apply for an office in an apartment. When I started out, the corner of a spare bedroom (about 50 square feet) proved more than adequate. Office equipment takes space, however, so apartment dwellers usually locate elsewhere.

Q. What is your opinion about opening branch offices as the business grows?

A. Depends on the market niche. Some consulting specialties such as M&A work can be adequately managed from one office, provided it is handy to airports. One of my consortium members does nothing but M&A consulting all over the world from one 400-square-foot office.

It also depends on the location of clients relative to the principal office. For example, some consultants serving clients in large metropolitan areas maintain their principal office in a suburban location and a branch in town. Usually, this proves economical only when the firm consists of several partners, each responsible for specific clients.

I don't see the need for single practitioners to maintain multiple offices. One of my associates disagrees, however. With his principal office in his home in suburban Philadelphia, he opened a branch in Baltimore to serve clients in the Greater Baltimore-Washington area. This also forced him to hire a full-time assistant to staff the branch. He claims it pays off. I'm doubtful.

TAX-SAVING TIPS

Q. How does the IRS stand on the deductibility of home office expenses?

A. In addition to being convenient, using a home office is a terrific way to charge off a variety of expenses as business deductions that are non-deductible as personal expenses.

Every so often, the IRS attempts to restrict deductions by issuing new home-office regulations. As with most unpopular tax laws, these restrictions never seem to accomplish what the IRS intends. So far, at least, the IRS has been unable to win when challenged with legitimate reasons for a home office.

Currently, the tax code states that expenses of maintaining a business office in a person's home are deductible as business expenses providing the office is "exclusively used on a regular basis" as (1) the taxpayer's principal place of business or (2) a place for meeting with the taxpayer's patients, clients, or customers.

In recent years the Tax Court further tightened the noose by applying a "focal point of a taxpayer's activities" test. This defined the principal place of business as the place where goods and services were provided to customers, and revenues were generated.

Recent Tax Court decisions, however, have relaxed this "focal point" test. I used the following case descriptions to clarify this point in my recent book, *Tap the Hidden Wealth in Your Business.*

A landmark case involved an anesthesiologist (N.S.Soliman, 94 TC 3) who worked at several hospitals but had no office in any of them. He used one room in his apartment as an office. Each day he worked on administrative matters for two to three hours. The IRS disallowed business deductions on the basis that since hospitals were where the doctor provided services to his patients (similar to the client's facilities for a consultant), this was the "focal point" of his business, not his office-in-home.

The Tax Court disagreed. Even if it isn't the "focal point," office-in-home deductions will be allowed where:

- It is essential in the taxpayer's business.
- The taxpayer spends a substantial amount of time there. In this case the court ruled that 30 percent of the taxpayer's time was substantial.
- No other office is available to perform management functions. In this case, the court ruled that the place where a business is managed and administered can be the principal place of business.

The doctor's driving expenses to and from the hospitals were also allowed. The IRS is appealing.

Three other landmark decisions by the Court of Appeals are worthy of mention:

1. In Ernest Drucker (715 F2nd 67 (_Cir. 19__)) the Court of Appeals ruled that a professional musician was allowed office-in-home deductions. Even though he performed in music halls, he needed his home for practicing. This case seems to authenticate the deduction for writers, salespersons, management consultants, and others who spend a considerable amount of time working in their home office.

2. In John and Sally Meiers (CA-7, No. 85-1209) the Court of Appeals ruled the deduction allowable because Mrs. Meiers spent more time working at home than in her laundromat—two hours per day doing administrative work at home versus one hour per day at the laundromat. In this case the proportion of time spent at a location determined the principal place of business.

3. In David J. Weissman (CA-2, 751 F2nd 512 (_Cir. 19__))
    the Court of Appeals ruled the deduction allowable because
    Weissman, a college professor who spent 80 percent of his
    time doing research and writing in his home office, did not
    have a suitable office at the university to perform such
    scholarly work. In this case, the type of work performed
    determined the principal place of business.

Q. Specifically, what types of expenses are deductible?

A. Three types of expenses can be deducted: direct expenses,
allocated expenses, and depreciation of your residence.

Direct expenses are self-explanatory and include all expenses
incurred directly and only to support the office or to benefit your
business.

Allocated expenses include a share of the operating, upkeep, and
maintenance costs of a home. These expenses are normally allocated based on the square footage utilized by the office. If the office
is 1,000 square feet and the total residence 3,000, then one-third of
shared expenses get allocated to the business office.

The type of expenses falling into each category are:

Direct Expenses

- Separate business telephone line
- Office supplies
- Remodeling or redecorating expenses for office
- Depreciation of office furniture and fixtures
- Electricity, gas, and water if separately metered
- Interest expense on loans to purchase office furniture and fix-
  tures or for office remodeling
- Carpets and rugs
- Personal property taxes
- Local business fees and licenses to operate a home office

Allocated Expenses

- Rent (if home is leased)
- Condo mimimum fees
- Escrow costs

- Legal fees for real estate services
- Real estate taxes
- Mortgage interest expense
- House insurance
- Electricity, gas, water, and fuel oil if separate meters are not used
- Telephone, if separate line is not installed
- Trash pick-up
- Landscaping
- Repairs to residence, furnace, electrical system, plumbing, and appointments
- Exterior painting and maintenance
- Snow removal
- Contract labor for general maintenance and upkeep

Depreciation of House

- Depreciation of the residence must be calculated according to current tax regulations and allocated on the same square footage as other expenses.
- Rental expense pertains to rented residences and, of course, depreciation is then not applicable.
- The allocation to the office-in-home is on the same square footage basis as other allocated expenses.

Home office expenses may be deducted up to the gross income of your business, less all operating expenses. In other words, office expenses can bring Schedule C income to zero (if the business is not incorporated), but cannot create a deductible loss. To the extent that the full application of these expenses results in a net business loss, the loss can be carried over to future years as a business deduction.

Q. A friend was talking about some type of IRS trap if I tried to deduct these expenses. Do you know anything about that?

A. Aside from non-compliance with the rules we have already covered, the only trap I'm aware of concerns the sale of your residence.

If you deduct home office expenses (allocated, not direct) during the year the residence was sold, any gain on the sale must be allocated between the residence and business portions of the home. The business portion must be reported as taxable income in the year of sale. Obviously, residence gain can be deferred by purchasing another residence.

One possibility exists to avoid this trap. If home-office expenses were deducted in prior years but not in the year the residence was sold, the entire gain can be rolled into the cost of a new residence without reporting any part of it as taxable income.

Q. Is it true that consultants can save big tax bucks by incorporating rather than operating as a sole proprietor?

A. It's true that running your business as a corporation permits tax planning flexibility not available to sole proprietors (also called self-employed by the IRS). Corporations also provide a measure of legal protection in the event of a lawsuit, although recently the IRS has been increasingly successful in penetrating corporate shields of one-person businesses.

Incorporating a business is easy and inexpensive. Both Delaware and Nevada have very lenient incorporation laws. Companies in these states that specialize in doing incorporations advertise in the *Wall Street Journal* and many other publications.

I have formed thirteen corporations myself through these services and have formed many more for clients. The cost runs between $150 and $200, including a minute book, stock certificate, corporate stamp, and first-year registration fees. It doesn't make any difference where you are located or in which state you conduct business. A Delaware or Nevada corporation can be used in all fifty states.

Although space won't permit a detailed comparison of the pros and cons of incorporating, I cover the topic at length in *Tap the Hidden Wealth in Your Business*. In summary, the major advantages of using a corporation are that it:

1. Limits personal liability for business debts.
2. Facilitates multiple business investment vehicles—especially important when and if you sell the business.
3. Provides retirement income options.
4. Enables multiple succession alternatives.

5. Segregates businesses operating in different locations or different types of businesses.
6. Increases the options for estate planning.
7. Facilitates the sale of the entire business upon retirement.
8. Makes borrowing money easier.
9. Enables the use of family member ownership to spread taxable income vis-à-vis the S corporation election.
10. Reduces estate taxes.
11. Permits a greater variety of IRS-approved benefit and retirement programs.
12. Makes selling the business easier.
13. Permits easy entrance and exit of partners.

A few disadvantages should also be noted. The major ones are:

1. Potential for double taxation (if S corporation is not used).
2. Initial costs to set up the corporation.
3. Additional state income taxes might be due even though the corporation reports a loss.
4. Annual agent fees and state registration fees.
5. Additional bookkeeping requirements.
6. Maintenance of corporate records such as stock transfer records, board of directors minutes, and stock certificates.
7. Limited liability might not apply if a court breaks the corporate shield.

Q. What do you mean by double taxation and how does an S corporation eliminate this threat?
A. Double taxation remains the major drawback to incorporating any small business, including a consulting business. When you withdraw cash from the business in excess of what the IRS determines to be reasonable compensation, the service has the option of reclassifying the withdrawals as dividends rather than compensation. The corporation pays a tax on income and you pay tax on withdrawals of the same income in the form of dividends. Ergo, double taxation.

Electing to have the corporation taxed as an S corporation eliminates this problem. Then all corporation income passes through to shareholders and is reported on their personal tax returns. Double taxation cannot happen.

Shareholders report income in the years the corporation earns it, regardless of the amount of cash distributed. Cash distributions are not taxable, only the corporation's income.

Making family members shareholders enables a splitting of income, conceivably reducing the total family tax bite to 15 percent rather than 28 or 33 percent. S corporation rules keep changing, however, which is another reason for staying in close contact with a competent tax advisor.

THE HIGH-TECH OFFICE

Q. What office equipment configuration do you recommend?

A. Well, the information age is upon us and we can't change that. If we don't adapt to meet client needs, we won't stay in business very long. And one of those adaptations is a high-tech office.

State-of-the-art office equipment improves our production efficiency by speeding-up the preparation and transmission of client reports. It also helps to keep costs in line by reducing the number of full-time or part-time employees needed to manage administrative tasks. Some consultants create extra income by selling office services to other small businesses.

Q. So what equipment do you recommend and what does it cost?

A. I find it helpful to think of office equipment, and specifically computers and related software, as serving four primary purposes: records management, communications, marketing and reports, and information retrieval.

As far as costs are concerned, the technology in this field is advancing so rapidly that the price curves of practically any office equipment, as well as computer software, are declining steeply.

Q. Can we begin with equipment that can increase the efficiency of records management?

A. As we all know, it doesn't take long to get buried in paper—client files, correspondence, report drafts, canceled checks, tax returns, supporting documentation, bookkeeping records, and so on. And paper takes up valuable space. The high-tech office does away with most paper files. A high-quality personal computer replaces manual records with electronic files.

A personal computer capable of doing everything necessary for a consulting office can be purchased new for under $3,000. A high-speed printer runs an additional $400 to $800. My preference leans toward IBM or Compaq computers, and Epson, NEC, or Hewlett-Packard for printers.

Several excellent software packages exist for nearly every conceivable application, with wide price ranges. Once again, I prefer the name brands and basic, workhorse software.

Software packages to handle accounting, word processing, financial forecasting and analysis, database storage, desktop publishing, and telecommunications provide sufficient breadth to handle virtually any administrative or client need. The first four apply to records management.

Q. How do I know what brands to choose?

A. Start by picking up a copy of a consumer computer magazine. They do a good job analyzing the advantages and disadvantages of new programs. It also carries a wide variety of advertisements for the old standards as well as new innovations.

The following configuration is very basic but allows you to get up and running without spending a lot of learning time. These are the easiest to learn yet the most comprehensive of basic records management software:

Accounting—One-Write Plus
Word processing—Corel Wordperfect
Financial forecasting and analysis—Lotus 1-2-3
Database storage—Approach, Access, or Filemaker Pro.

Q. Can I also do my own tax returns on this software?

A. Not easily, although the accounting and spreadsheet package can be used to analyze tax alternatives.

Several good software packages are available to prepare entire tax returns by computer. Prices are high, however, ranging from $1,000 to $8,000. The package must be updated annually as tax laws and return formats change. Personally, I let my CPA spend the money.

The data base program is very helpful as a substitute for file cabinets. It holds all supporting documentation for tax returns, accounting records, copies of correspondence, client reports and virtually anything that was previously kept on paper and stored in filing cabinets. Of course, backup copies should be kept in safe storage as a precaution.

Q. Why do I need communications software?

A. For two reasons: (1) to transfer data between your office and client offices, (2) to access vast electronic storehouses of information commonly referred to as databases, and (3) to access the Internet.

The technology in communications equipment and software is moving so rapidly that the information I give you now will probably be out of date within weeks.

Let's begin with a compatible telecommunications software package and reliable modem. With this capability, you can tie directly into a client's computer system to download data and reports. Conversely, you can forward data, reports, analyses, forecasts, and a variety of other information direct to a client.

Internet capability also allows direct communication with airlines reservation systems, hotel bookings systems, current news announcements, financial market trends, the Securities and Exchange Commission, market intelligence data bases, and a variety of other national and regional computer systems. It costs money to access some of these systems, but the time saved compared to manual research usually is a good trade-off.

International consultants must have telecommunications capability. Not only does it permit direct access to their home office, it provides another valuable tool for obtaining data and reports from local government and financial circles. Quick and easy access to information makes the difference between winning and losing in international circles.

Q. Would a computer network be applicable to a consulting business?

A. For firms with employees, partners, or more than one office, computer networks can be a lifesaver. Each desktop computer feeds into a central processing unit (a "server") with significantly higher processing speed and storage capability than an individual PC. Several people in different locations can use the same files or download the same reports whenever they need them.

Remote offices can be tied into the same server and data accessed at will. File security is maintained with private entry codes that limit access to those with the proper password.

Q. How about a fax machine?

A. A fax machine is crucial for a modern consulting office.

Not long ago, a reliable fax machine cost between $700 and $1,500. The technology has now advanced to the point where a satisfactory model can be purchased for less than $500. Also, transmission speed has doubled, and for some machines tripled.

There is no way to avoid a fax machine if you get into international consulting. Fax machines are replacing outmoded telex equipment all over the world—even in lesser developed countries. Most foreign government agencies have them. Because it is often difficult to speak through overseas telephone connections, a fax is usually the only way to communicate.

Whether you use the Internet or a fax machine, both are subject to the same limiting factor: sending and receiving locations must each have reliable electrical service and dependable telephone systems.

Neither dependable electricity nor telephone service is available in some of the lesser developed countries. This continues to make communications difficult and is a problem for which I have not found a solution. Regardless of this limitation, it is safe to say that high-speed, inexpensive telecommunications is here to stay.

Q. How do you feel about advancing technologies in mobile phones?

A. Personally, that's where I draw the line. I flatly refuse to purchase a mobile phone either for my car or for any other location. Most consultants think I'm nuts, but I value my privacy too much to be constantly interrupted by mostly inconsequential phone calls.

Nevertheless, no truly modern office is complete without a mobile phone. Recently, digital telephones have come along to replace cellular models. Pocket phones are a timesaver when traveling or working off-site. Although the cost is generally higher than conventional service, technology and competition will make them more affordable in the near future.

Q. What equipment or software do you recommend for report generations?

A. In the age of computer technology it's hard to believe that some consulting firms continue to issue manually prepared reports. To go one step further, they get reports printed and bound by a professional printer—a very costly exercise.

Desktop publishing software is the solution. This easy-to-learn type of program brings professional layout, printing, and report production capability to the modern office. With a first-class laser printer, reports can be generated in full color, with pictures, logos, diagrams, and graphs.

Advertising costs can also be trimmed substantially with desktop publishing. Full-page color ads, brochures, client flyers, newsletters, even letterhead and envelopes complete with logo can be produced in your office. Many consultants, including myself, have completely abandoned advertising agencies and print shops except for very complex jobs.

To expand report generation capability, purchase a small laminating machine to plastic-coat report covers, and a punching machine to install plastic binders. Now you can prepare complete reports and production copy for media advertising as well as snappy client reports.

A high-speed copying machine is another essential piece of equipment. I prefer Xerox, but Ricoh, Canon, and a number of other manufacturers now offer very high-quality equipment. I suggest a copier with collating capability to save additional time. The machine should produce copies on both sides of a sheet of paper. This cuts paper costs in half.

I haven't gone this far, but other consultants in our consortium find camcorders useful for videotaping promotion pieces. These videos are great for advertising spots on local television channels. Quality camcorders run under $1,000. That is much less expensive than making a TV spot in a studio.

Video conferencing equipment has been available for several years and is used for conference calls with clients in remote offices. New hardware is smaller and easier to use.

Q. What do you recommend in the way of data retrieval?

A. Data retrieval refers to accessing large sources of information about markets, companies, products, and a variety of other subjects. Research is something we cannot avoid. More than one consultant has been deterred from specializing in a market niche that depends on extensive research.

Searching for acquisition or divestiture targets, uncovering likely customers in foreign markets, isolating financing sources, identifying joint venture partners, and evaluating market and product demand can be time-consuming and many times unbillable. Identifying potential new clients very often requires extensive research. Now, Internet search engines and other sophisticated retrieval software reduce these efforts to a manageable level.

Database searches are especially helpful in the M&A business and in international consulting engagements. In fact, it's nearly impossible to penetrate these markets without the use of at least one database. The Department of Commerce, Digilog, Dun & Bradstreet, and many others have compiled enormous databases of information about everything imaginable. Some federal government data bases can be accessed directly from your computer at very little cost. Private company data bases cost more.

GETTING HELP

Q. Do you have any tips for hiring either full- or part-time help?
A. What type of help do you have in mind?

Q. Right now I need typing, filing, and telephone answering help. I guess I should consider hiring a secretary, right?
A. Wrong!

If you have made it this far on your own, I can't see any reason to be saddled with the additional costs of an employee, whether it be a secretary, file clerk, or bookkeeper. A multi-partner firm is different. If you have suddenly taken on two or three very large accounts, that's different. Multiple office firms are different. For the normal single practitioner, however, other options are more attractive.

Q. What other options?
A. For example, at least in metropolitan areas, telephone answering services have become quite sophisticated. It's nearly impossible to tell whether the person answering the phone is an employee or an answering service.

Many telephone companies now offer an answering service that takes the place of a recorder on your office phone. My local Baby Bell's service costs a mere five dollars per month, and I can access messages from anywhere in the world.

I know that some people still object to leaving messages either with an answering service or on an answering machine, but that number is shrinking very rapidly. Either recorded or live answering services are the wave of the future and before long everyone will use one or the other to filter out unwanted calls, if nothing else. Many large companies already use a "cafeteria" recording—"Push 1 if you want this, push 2 for that," and so on.

Typing and administrative help is a different story. If you can't find time to handle administration, and most of us who have been in business for a while cannot, try part-time help. It takes a very large consulting business to require typing or administrative assistance eight hours a day, five days a week. The office configurations we just talked about should cut this time down to one or two days a week maximum.

The best part about hiring part-time help is that you can usually justify treating the person as an independent contractor rather than an employee.

Q. What is the advantage in that?
A. Personnel costs can be significantly reduced. Independent contractors are not included in group health insurance or pension programs. No Social Security taxes are payable (nearly 8 percent of salary). Neither are unemployment taxes (up to 12 percent in some states) or worker's compensation (between 2 and 8 percent of payroll dollars). In some states these taxes and benefits easily add another 30 to 50 percent to salary costs.

Avoiding employee taxes and fringes saves significant out-of-pocket expenses. It also eliminates reams of forms for federal and state government agencies and insurance companies. That in itself can make independent contractors the way to go.

The only caveat is to be certain to follow IRS guidelines for independent contractors. Generally, an independent contractor sets his or her own schedule, works for more than one company, and doesn't require immediate supervision. Check with a tax expert for the full details.

Q. What do you think of subcontracting out work that I don't have time or the skills to do?
A. Subcontracting client production work was covered when we talked about informal partnerships and networks. As we discussed then, as long as you retain responsibility for the accurate, timely completion of the engagement and each of its segments, subcontracting work out to other consultants or specialists in a technical area is a convenient way to get over these hurdles.

The downside is that it can be an expensive proposition. Some subcontractors will take reduced fees for short jobs or in exchange for other favors. Generally, however, expect to pay their full rate.

Subcontracting out administrative work is a slightly different matter. Now the work is for our benefit, not a client's. Paying someone else to do it is our prerogative. I usually let a CPA prepare my tax returns. An associate of mine subcontracts out all his bookkeeping. Another friend subcontracts her entire billing function.

Subcontracting administrative chores is practically the same as hiring independent contractors to come to the office as part-time workers.

In many parts of the country, outside tax, bookkeeping, billing, and other administrative services can be so inexpensive that it doesn't pay to waste time doing these chores yourself. In other areas, it's much too expensive.

I generally prefer to keep as many administrative functions as possible in-house. It gives me better control and costs less. The one exception is my own tax return. Also, during periods when I'm swamped with work, I have no other choice but to subcontract.

EXTRA INCOME

Q. Assuming I have my office up and running, is there any way to utilize my office equipment to generate extra income?

A. Yes. Office location dictates the market. In smaller communities, with fewer up-to-date offices around, the market for office services can be substantial.

For instance, I set up an office in the Virgin Islands to handle FSC accounts. At that time, computers were just finding their way to the islands. Hardly any law firms or public accounting firms had them yet, and those who did lacked experience and appropriate software.

I hired an independent contractor and taught her how to use the word processing and bookkeeping software. We took in so many jobs that she ended up working full time. After deducting her wages, the extra income covered all office expenses, including rent, plus a reasonable profit.

A consultant in my area has a high-speed copier. He charges 5 cents a copy—less than the quick-print shops—and claims he makes a handsome profit over and above the rental of the machine.

Two partners in California went one step further. They purchased a used offset press and, with their normal office equipment, have an office services business as active as any small print shop. They sell fax time, copying, small print runs, and desktop publishing services. In addition, they recently began teaching computer courses in their office on weekends. All this in addition to their regular consulting business!

Q. If I do hire a bookkeeper, for instance, what do you think of bringing in outside bookkeeping work to make the job full time?

A. I think it's a great idea, provided it doesn't interfere with your consulting business.

Actually, any office function that is not fully utilized can be sold as a sideline. This works especially well in distant suburbs or small communities. Competition in high-tech office services usually isn't very pronounced in these areas. You might also consider handling UPS packages or setting up a mail box facility, although these activities are a far cry from normal administrative functions. In the beginning, I tried to sell a variety of office services and found that the distractions were so great that in the end I dropped everything except computer instruction classes.

Q. Is there any potential image conflict between a consulting business and selling office services?

A. Yes. The image of a first-class management consultant can be easily tarnished if these extraneous grow to be too visible to clients. An occasional sale won't make any difference, but if an office services sideline gets to be a major income generator, clients could view this as your prime business rather than management consulting.

Q. How do I get around this problem?

A. We have to assume that if office services do become a major income generator, the marketing and production effort will be done by an administrative assistant or office manager, not yourself.

Developing a growing consulting business won't allow you the spare time needed to develop an office services business as well.

The second step to ensure that this sideline doesn't interfere with the consulting business is to set up a separate corporation for office services. This way the marketing, production, personnel, expenses, and billing activities are divorced from consulting. Many organizations run two or more businesses from the same location, so operating out of the same address shouldn't be a problem.

A separate corporation also presents some interesting possibilities for tax savings. Expense allocations and splitting income between the two companies provide additional opportunities for strategic tax planning. Consult a qualified tax advisor for the best approaches for your situation.

BOOKKEEPING

Q. I am not an accountant, yet I know bookkeeping records must be maintained for tax purposes. Can you give me some tips on the types of recordkeeping consultants use to satisfy IRS requirements?

A. Second only to research, accounting (or bookkeeping if you prefer), is the biggest pain for consultants. I don't mind it too much, because I am a CPA and have extensive accounting experience. No other consultant in our consortium, however, has this training and they all hate keeping records. So you are not alone.

Earlier I suggested a very simple bookkeeping software package called "One-Write Plus." This program leaves a lot to be desired as far as sophisticated accounting techniques are concerned, but it is the easiest bookkeeping program I have seen. Anyone can learn to keep a set of books with this software in a matter of hours. I strongly suggest the One-Write program or other equally simple software rather than trying to maintain a manual set of books.

The following types of detailed records are needed to satisfy IRS requirements:

1. A business bank account separate from your personal accounts.

2. Receipts for all business expenditures.
3. Bank deposit slips for all income.
4. Bank account statements.
5. List of office furniture and equipment showing the date purchased and the purchase price.
6. Depreciation schedules for all depreciable assets.
7. Automobile mileage driven for business purposes. Also, receipts for tolls and parking.
8. Explanations of business purpose for all entertainment and travel expenses not reimbursed by client.
9. Receipts for all expenditures relating to your home, if your office is located there.

In addition to these detailed records, summary records are necessary to prepare tax returns and to show IRS auditors, if necessary. These summary records do not need to be elaborate. If you use a bookkeeping software package they are generated automatically. All businesses require the same summary records. They are:

- Check register and cash expenditures journal
- Deposit register and cash receipts journal
- General journal for non-cash entries such as depreciation
- General ledger which records the monthly total from each of the journals.

With this set of summary accounting records and supporting detail, tax return preparation and later verification is a snap. Any business of any size uses these same basic records. Bookkeeping systems for large corporations add a lot of bells and whistles, but these are the basic records they also must have to comply with IRS and SEC regulations.

Of course, you should speak with a qualified tax advisor to determine all the IRS requirements your business will have to meet.

Chapter 13

FINANCING A CONSULTING BUSINESS
How to Raise Cash to Grow Your Business

Q. Is there a way to borrow money to finance important purchases and see me through a cash crunch?

A. As I mentioned earlier, few banks lend money without collateral. I assume that you don't have any more assets in your business than the normal consulting firm.

Office equipment generally qualifies as loan collateral. Accounts receivable could also be used. In both cases, however, a bank also will likely require a personal guarantee. Acceptable personal guarantees must be backed up with assets that the bank can seize upon default, such as your house, car, personal bank accounts, antiques, investments, and so on.

As a financial expert, I have counseled hundreds of business owners about the hazards of personal guarantees. In most cases I strongly recommend staying away from both guarantees and banks that require them.

Bankers are extremely difficult to do business with. The odds are very high that they will simply never understand your business. Also, all bank loan agreements are unilateral, meaning, a bank may call the loan (make you repay the entire loan amount) at any time, even though all principal and interest payments have been made on schedule.

Even though they recognize the potential danger of borrowing from a bank, many small businesses still do it. If you do decide to borrow, you will need to know how the process works.

Some of the following must be tempered to fit a given situation. Most of what I have to say, however, applies to financing any small business.

First, we need to distinguish between debt and equity financing. Within the debt category, banks make long-term loans—usually secured by hard assets such as equipment or buildings—and short-term loans secured by receivables and inventory. Short-term loans may be payable on a certain date, or they may fluctuate with the level of receivables and inventory. "Revolver" or "revolving loan" are terms commonly used to describe the latter.

A great many financial organizations other than commercial banks make business loans. Finance companies (also called asset-based lenders), the Small Business Administration and other government agencies, investment banks, brokerage houses, equipment manufacturers, and non-bank financing organizations (principally for export/import transactions) are a few of the more common ones.

In addition to straight debt financing, leasing continues to be a popular method for financing hard asset acquisitions. Thousands of leasing companies exist throughout the country.

Equity financing involves selling an equity share in your business. Buyers might be partners, limited partners, friends, neighbors, and relatives, suppliers, employees, investment banks and venture capital firms, or clients.

I should add that if you need more information, or if you need help arranging financing for a client, you might want to review my book *Financing the Small Business* (Simon & Schuster).

DEBT FINANCING

Q. How should I go about getting a loan?
A. The starting point for any loan application is a financing package. A financing package contains all the information necessary for a lender to make a decision. It consists of two broad sections and several detailed segments within each section.

The first section covers personal material relating to you as a business owner. It includes four sub-headings:

- Personal background
- Business experience
- Financial status
- Reference letters

The second section includes four segments that provide information about the business:

- Company structure and history
- Product/service characteristics
- Market status
- Financial performance

Q. What should be included in the personal section?

A. Lenders rank management ability at or near the top of the priority ladder, especially for service companies that depend on the owner's ability to sustain and grow the business.

The first segment gives your personal statistics: residence address and phone number, education (including any academic awards), family status, health, and, even though it smacks of discrimination, age.

The financial community continues to harbor traditional misconceptions about age that must be addressed at the first meeting, anti-discrimination laws notwithstanding. For older applicants, I usually suggest doing research first to learn about a specific bank's prejudices. There's no sense wasting time and effort where you can't win.

The second segment outlines your business experience prior to starting the consulting business. It also includes experience gained since entering consulting. Lenders look at work experience from two vantage points—management experience and technical experience—and both should be covered in this section.

A statement of business objectives is always necessary: growth strategy, specialization, continuing training, and so on. This should reflect a clear long-term commitment to the business. Lenders frown on short-term goals.

Lenders are keenly interested in an applicant's personal financial status independent of the business. They want to know how much capital has been contributed to the business, what personal assets you own, and what liabilities you owe. This tells them how much outside collateral could be pledged against a personal guarantee. And the more capital in the business, the less likely the owner is to abscond with the loan.

Two types of documentation substantiate financial commitment: a personal statement of financial condition, and personal tax returns. A personal statement of financial condition lists all personal assets at current market value, and all debts and obligations owed to non-family creditors.

If you have not prepared one before, here is an example of a typical format. This statement shows personal assets and liabilities only, not those of the business. Business financial statements appear in the second section of the package.

Fig. 15-1

STATEMENT OF FINANCIAL CONDITION
As of date _____

A. ASSETS
a. Cash in checking and savings accounts
b. Cash equivalent investments—CDs, money market accounts, etc.
c. IRAs, Keogh plan accounts, SEPs, and other retirement accounts
d. Marketable securities—publicly traded stocks, bonds, mutual funds, etc. (at current market value)
e. Cash surrender value of life insurance policies

TOTAL CASH AND CASH EQUIVALENTS _____

g. Investments in privately held companies or public companies whose stock is not traded
h. Investment in limited partnerships
I. Investments in commercial or rental real estate (current market value)
j. Collectibles—stamps, coins, antiques, jewelry, art, etc. (current market value)
k. Investment in land (current market value)
l. Other non-liquid investments

TOTAL NON-LIQUID INVESTMENTS _____

m. Residence (current market value)
n. Second or vacation home, (current market value)
o. Automobiles (current market value)
p. Personal property at estimated market value:
    Furniture
    Hobby equipment
    Library
    Boat
    Airplane
    Other personal property

    TOTAL PERSONAL PROPERTY   _____

Q. Other assets

    TOTAL ASSETS   _____

B. LIABILITIES

aa. Notes and other loans payable to banks (list bank and amount):

    #1 _____

    #2 _____

    #3 _____

bb. Loans against cash surrender value of life insurance
cc. Current credit card balances
dd. Other bills payable

    TOTAL CURRENT DEBT   _____

ee. Mortgage on residence (current balance and monthly payment amount)
ff. Mortgage on other property (current balance and monthly payment amount)
gg. Loans from family members, friends, etc. (balance and due date)
hh. Other loans, debts, and obligations (list)

    TOTAL LIABILITIES   _____

C. NET WORTH (subtract total liabilities from total assets)

D. INCOME

	Monthly	Annual
1. Interest		
2. Dividends		
3. Pension		
4. Annuities		
5. Rentals		
6. Other investment income		
7. Spouse's wages		
8. Other income		
TOTAL INCOME		

Tax returns will show the bank how much income was earned during the prior three years. I have never understood how this actually benefits lenders, but it gives them comfort to see that you have paid taxes. Although it may seem superfluous, it's what they want.

Q. How about references? Can I use the same ones as in my marketing program?

A. Why not? If they satisfy clients, they should satisfy banks.

In addition, lenders like to see reference letters from banks or other financial institutions. If you have had prior loans, a letter verifying compliance with loan terms and repayment schedules is a big help.

THE FINANCING PLAN

Q. What is included in the section relating to my business?

A. This section of the business plan is typically called a "financing plan."

Financing plans consist of four parts: a history of the company, a description of the consulting specialties you offer and the market niches you serve, and the company's financial statements.

Begin with a preamble, describing how much money you need and what it will be used for. Include one-sentence statements relating to the types of services offered, market niches, how the borrowed money will be used, and when and how the loan will be repaid. Short and succinct, the preamble gives lenders a synopsis of the rest of the plan.

The history segment describes the ownership of the business (yourself, spouse, partners, etc.) and capitalization (how much money you and the other partners have put in). If an S corporation election has been made, include the names, relationships, and ownership percentage for each of the shareholders.

Describe any company name changes and variations in ownership percentages of the business that have occurred since the beginning. Identify any outstanding debts to banks, to other institutions, or to individuals (other than family members).

The next segment provides a detailed description of the skills or specialities offered clients. Don't be too elaborate or technical: lenders won't understand what you're talking about. For highly technical or unusual specialties, include a few market statistics to prove that demand does, in fact, exist for these services.

The most important item in this segment is a persuasive argument to explain why your skills are unique: why your consulting services are better than your competitors'. Lenders theorize that if you can't come up with a better mousetrap, you shouldn't borrow money to bring it to market.

Segments covering markets and competition need special attention. Most lenders have no idea how consultants stay in business. Since they haven't hired a consultant, they can't understand why any other business would. A description of market niches must include sufficient evidence of demand for consultants to convince a skeptic. Pointing out the names of competitors, especially if they are well-known, adds strength to these arguments.

Explaining competition is vitally important. Which consultants sell into your market niches? Do any non-consulting firms compete, such as law firms, public accountants, financial planners, or export management companies? How big are they and how long have they been in the market? Can you compete with price, or must you rely on service or superior quality? What is the potential for new entrants over the succeeding five years?

Here's a tip that I find works every time. I have never met a lender who doesn't get excited when you mention international business. Most don't know anything about exporting, importing, or direct investment overseas, but they pretend to, and they love to hear about accomplishments and expansion plans in this area. International consulting just plain looks good in a financing plan.

The final segment includes historical and projected financial data about the business. This is the one part that lenders should be able to grasp completely. If the business has been operating for at least two years, include annual balance sheets and income statements for each year. If you don't have financial statements, and most of us don't, get a CPA to put one together from tax returns.

Business tax returns for a corporation or partnership should be included to substantiate financial statements.

The pro forma, or projected financial statements for the next five years, is the most important segment of the entire financial plan. This proves to a lender that the business can generate sufficient cash to repay the loan. Once again, if you don't know how to do this, latch on to your favorite CPA. (You might be able to barter for the services.)

Q. How should I present my application?

A. Putting the financing package in the right wrapper and then presenting it properly can be as important as what it contains.

As we know from our marketing efforts, showmanship is the essence of any successful sales campaign. Getting a loan requires the same theatrics as landing new clients. The "look right" goes a long way toward capturing the attention of even the most jaundiced banker.

This financing plan forms an integral part of the total presentation, but it should be packaged separately. Most financing plans should not be more than twenty or twenty-five pages. I find a spiral plastic binder the easiest, least expensive, and most acceptable way to bind the plan. The cover and back should be laminated.

First-class quick-print shops have the capability to do all this for a nominal price.

Regardless of the specific packaging technique, if the financing plan looks professional, it will be regarded with professional interest. This adds immeasurably to the reception from lenders. Time and again, I have seen bankers peruse a professionally prepared plan cover to cover, whereas one that is sloppily prepared or poorly presented gets tossed in the trash barrel.

SOURCES OF FINANCING

Q. Where can I get the money?

A. Creativity is the name of the game here. The trick is to locate a financing source willing to gamble on your ability to grow the business and at the same time not charge exorbitant interest or fees.

The six primary sources of short-term working capital are:

- Commercial banks
- Small Business Administration
- Foreign banks
- Finance companies
- Venture funds
- Small investment banks

I have never raised financing for a consulting business or any other small service business through venture funds or small investment banks, but other consultants tell me it is possible. I have used both for financing manufacturing, retail and distribution companies, but never a service client. To save time, I'll ignore these two in this discussion. If you are interested, see my book *Financing the Small Business* for a complete description.

If your market niches involves rapid growth industries—health care diagnosis and treatment, services for the elderly, top-of-the-line travel and leisure activities, advanced telecommunications, the Internet, or environmental services for example—try a commercial bank first.

Banks will probably want personal assets as security, but they usually charge less interest than other sources. They love to get into what they perceive to be rapid growth industries.

Q. Most of my clients are not in those industries. They are local companies in fairly stable markets. Will banks also work in that case?

A. That depends on how well you know your banker. If the relationship is on solid ground, a commerical bank is a good place to begin. Small banks concentrating on purely local markets are the best bet. It's entirely possible that many of your clients bank at the same place. In that case, borrowing against their unpaid invoices may be a snap.

The Small Business Administration might work, although it is becoming increasingly difficult to interest the SBA in lending to personal service businesses. The most likely result from this source is an SBA bank guarantee. A bank must do the actual lending and carry 10 percent of the risk. In some parts of the country, it can be difficult to find one willing to do that.

All medium-sized and large cities have SBA offices. If you are interested in trying for funding help there, simply contact the office for an application, prepare the financing package, find out which banks handle SBA loans, and submit an application. The chances for success increase if you submit the application through a bank rather than direct to the SBA.

The SBA also has the authority to grant direct loans. A business must be turned down by at least two banks before applying, however. Bear in mind that congressional allocations to SBA offices vary by district. You may be located in one that has no funds available.

Non-SBA loans are also possible through a variety of federal and state agencies. The local SBA office is usually a good starting point for accumulating information on which government agencies are currently in the loan business.

Chamber of Commerce offices might also help. Occasionally they can identify trade groups, state bureaus, or city or county programs that have funds. Don't count on these sources, however. Once again, consultants are not their favorite customers.

Q. Are my chances improved if I have international customers?

A. Yes, much better, especially if a foreign bank has a branch in your area. Although Japanese banks usually ignore smaller accounts, British and French banks tend to be receptive. British and Canadian banks finance receivables from clients in the Caribbean, for example. County NatWest, Barclays, Lloyd's, and the Bank of Nova Scotia are good possibilities.

Receivables from clients in the Pacific region could be financed through a branch of the Hong Kong and Shanghai Bank. The main idea when approaching foreign banks for loans is to contact the ones that represent the countries of origin of your clients.

Q. I've heard that no one should borrow from finance companies it they can avoid it. Is that true?

A. Finance companies fill a market niche that commercial lenders shun—companies in financial trouble, low-equity business acquisitions with substantial hard assets, risky receivables, and so on.

Because they incur higher risks than banks, finance companies demand and get substantially higher interest rates—as much as 6 percentage points higher. In addition, they charge a commitment fee that easily exceeds $25,000. Finally, finance companies are difficult to work with, stepping into decision-making roles at the slightest indication of trouble.

I have never heard of a consulting firm borrowing from a finance company, although I'm sure some do. I recommend that you stay away from this source.

WORKING CAPITAL LOANS

Q. How do I borrow against my accounts receivable?

A. Although as a prudent financing expert I do not recommend it, I can give you an outline of how this works. Remember, management consultants need all the marketing flexibility they can get. Commitments to loan repayment schedules severely limit this flexibility. In addition, borrowing can become habit-forming. Once you've started, it's hard to stop; the deeper you go into debt the less flexibility and independence you have. I feel very strongly that taking on debt is a bad practice for consultants, as well as many other small businesses. But, if you insist . . .

Most banks and finance companies consider accounts receivable from quality customers prime collateral. I won't get into the details of the variations in structuring accounts receivable loans: there are too many. Generally, however, a bank lends an amount equal to 80 to 85 percent of receivables less than 90 days old. Under a revolving loan agreement, collections flow directly to the bank and reduce the outstanding loan balance. As new receivables are created, additional loans are made.

Given a choice between borrowing against receivables on a revolving loan and taking a term loan, I always recommend choosing the latter. It's easier to pay off, less habit-forming, and keeps the lender out of your business.

Here is an example of how a term loan works for a small consulting business with salaried employees and a rented office.

Fig. 15-2

JONES ASSOCIATES, INC.
STATEMENT OF CASH FLOW
For the four months ended September 30 , 19XX

	June	July	August	Sept.	Total
Billings	-0-	25	30	60	115
CASH RECEIPTS					
Collections from sales	-0-	-0-	25	30	55
Bank loans	150	-0-	-0-	-0-	150
Total receipts	150	-0-	25	30	205
CASH EXPENDITURES					
Interest on bank loans	1	1	1	1	4
Payroll and payroll taxes	8	8	8	8	32
Employee health insurance					
and worker's compensation	2	2	2	2	8
Building rent	1	1	1	1	4
Electricity	1	-0-	1	-0-	2
Fuel	-0-	1	-0-	1	2
Telephone	6	6	6	6	24
Business insurance	3	3	3	3	12
Office supplies	8	8	8	8	32
Lease payments	2	2	2	2	8
Transportation (auto.)	3	3	3	3	12
Advertising and sales promotion	10	10	10	10	40
Market research	3	3	3	3	12
Other operating expenses	2	2	2	2	8
Total expenditures	50	50	50	50	200
CASH SURPLUS (SHORTFALL)	100	(50)	(25)	(20)	5
Less: Owner's salary/draw	4	4	4	4	16
NET CASH SURPLUS (SHORTFALL)	96	(54)	(29)	(24)	(11)
Beginning bank balance	5	101	47	18	5
Net cash surplus (shortfall)	96	(54)	(29)	(24)	(11)
Ending bank balance	101	47	18	(6)	(6)
BANK LOANS					
Term loan balance	150	150	150	150	150

Eventually, of course, the loan must be repaid. It could be structured with monthly or quarterly payments, it could be repayable at the end of its term, say 12 months, or it could have low monthly principal payments with a balloon payment at the end.

Naturally, a pro forma schedule similarly constructed should appear in the financing plan when applying for the loan.

Q. Should I consider borrowing from clients?

A. In extreme emergencies, you might be able to get a short-term loan from a client or get an advance on your fees, providing you know the CEO well enough and have a strong working relationship. This is a very bad practice, however, and will create all kinds of problems down the road.

It's impossible to remain independent if you owe a client money. In this respect even an advance on fees compromises your position. I have never even considered asking a client for either a loan or an advance, but I know of consultants who have done so without a second thought.

While participating as a panel speaker at a conference on raising capital, a consultant from Seattle I'll call Beth related the following experience. Beth was in her second year as a practicing consultant. She ran up over $30,000 in receivables and couldn't find a bank willing to make her a short-term loan. Beth's ex-employee contracted with her to develop a management incentive program.

Two weeks into the engagement, Beth convinced the company's CEO to advance her $10,000 against her fees. She agreed to pay 9 percent interest. Within hours, word spread throughout the company that Beth was not making it in her own business. Key managers snubbed her and withheld suggestions. Even the CEO questioned her competency to complete the assignment. This had a material impact on her independent judgment of which incentive program was best for the client.

She submitted her final report, liquidated the advance, and arranged an exit interview with the CEO. He offered to loan her additional money, for old times sake, but casually mentioned that they would not be needing her services again.

Borrowing from a client is a very risky business. I definitely recommend you avoid this course.

FINANCING OFFICE EQUIPMENT

Q. How about financing office equipment purchases?
A. As we have seen, there are significant disadvantages to borrowing for working capital. Still, few of us have excess cash to lay out for relatively large purchases like equipment.

Loans collateralized by equipment (hard assets) are considered long-term. They usually extend over three to five years. Frequently, either a bank or finance company will structure it as an "installment loan." Installment loans always cost more than a simple-interest term loan, so if possible, negotiate the latter.

The same financing package previously discussed should be presented with the loan application.

Increasingly, equipment manufacturers or dealers provide financing as a selling tool. They either finance the purchase themselves or are tied in with one of the large finance companies, such as GE Capital Corp. Be prepared to pay a high interest rate; however, many manufacturers will sell equipment with full financing, foregoing a down payment completely.

Leasing is a viable alternative to borrowing, and for certain types of equipment makes a lot more sense.

Q. Some people claim that lease payments give bigger tax deductions than owning assets and that leases are cheaper than loans. Their philosophy is that one should never buy a piece of equipment or a car for one's business. Do you agree?
A. No. People frequently have a misconception about the tax advantages of leasing. Many clients have told me that they lease rather than buy automobiles because they get more tax deductions. This is dead wrong. The IRS applies the same deductibility definitions to lease payments as to depreciation and interest payments for purchased assets.

Anyone who believes that leases are cheaper than buying doesn't understand how lease payments are calculated. The subject is treated in depth in my book *Financing the Small Business*.

The fact is that the sum of the payments over the life of a lease cannot be less than the original purchase price of the asset. The lessor must buy the asset first, cover interest and fees on loans used to make the purchase, and then make a profit on the lease. In leasing parlance, a lessor's cost is the price paid for the asset, plus administrative costs, less the residual value of the asset.

Perhaps a lessor can borrow money at a lower interest rate, which should result in a lower cost. On the other hand, by paying a lessor for administrative costs and profit, it seems unlikely that a person couldn't do better buying the asset outright, even if they paid a higher interest rate.

Some people also believe that leasing is a good way to conserve cash. After all, down payments can frequently be avoided. They assume that the sum of the lease payments will be less than the combined principal and interest payments on a term loan. If the residual value is very high relative to the original cost, this argument may have some merit. The lessor takes less rent but ultimately sells the asset to recoup investment and profit. But if the lessor can sell the asset, so can you!

Considering residual value on both sides, it's hard to see how lease payments that include a lessor's costs and profit can be less than principal and interest on a term loan.

Q. What are the pros and cons of leasing versus borrowing?
A. I wish there was a straightforward method for arriving at a lease or buy decision. Unfortunately, there isn't. If there was, either leasing companies would be out of business or banks would no longer make hard asset loans.

Leasing makes sense for some companies but not for others. With all the variations of lease agreements, the number of influencing factors may very well be limitless. Nevertheless, certain circumstances seem to favor a lease decision, while others quite clearly point to buying.

In general leasing is the way to go when:

1. You do not have the capital to make a downpayment.
2. The asset will probably become obsolete before the end of its useful life, as in the case of computers and perhaps copiers.

3. You have a poor credit rating and financial institutions insist on very high interest rates. This is not always a good reason, however, because a lessor takes this into consideration when evaluating credit risk for establishing rental payments.

4. Implicit lease rates are similar to borrowing rates but a loan imposes other costs or restrictions, such as commitment or application fees, compensating balances, non-business collateral, or personal guarantees.

5. The equipment has unusual service problems that would be costly, or even impossible, to handle internally. Copying machines certainly fall into this category.

6. The equipment will probably be difficult to dispose of or has a very low resale value when no longer needed.

7. Equipment is needed for only a short period of time. Automobiles are often leased for this reason.

8. Collateral and borrowing power are needed for other financing.

9. A comparison of tax advantages clearly favors leasing.

Leasing should be avoided when:

1. The sum of the lease payments exceeds the cost of buying. The purchase price, of course, must be reduced by the asset's resale value.

2. It is advantageous to own the asset free and clear after the loan gets repaid.

3. Tax benefits clearly point to buying.

4. You anticipate selling the business before the expiration of the lease period.

5. The asset will likely appreciate in value. This seldom occurs with cars or office equipment.

PERSONAL GUARANTEES

Q. A short time ago you mentioned the use of personal guarantees as additional collateral to bank loans. Can you expand on that?

A. All banks and most lessors insist on a personal guarantee regardless of the amount of the loan or the value of pledged business assets. Lenders believe that a personal guarantee encourages current debt service payments and discourages walking away from the business.

When agreeing to a personal guarantee, keep in mind that if and when you get in financial difficulty, the availablity of federal bankruptcy laws make personal guarantees difficult and costly to enforce. Therefore, the likelihood of a bank actually collecting against a guarantee is relatively remote. On the other hand, personal guarantees create a heavy psychological burden.

It's also important to know that most states exempt certain personal assets from liquidation in a bankruptcy: bank accounts, investment securities, automobiles, equity in a residence, personal property, and so on.

Some states allow execution against the borrower's portion of jointly held assets, but this is even more difficult to enforce. Assets held entirely by a nondebtor spouse who has not cosigned a guarantee are excluded from any claim.

Q. Are all personal guarantees the same?

A. No, several variations are used. A lender's choice is based on the amount of the loan, the liquidity of business assets, and the type and amount of personal assets of the borrower.

Some personal guarantees cover the full amount of the initial loan balance for the entire loan period. Others decline with principal payments. Occasionally a bank limits the guarantee to the estimated liquidation value of personal assets. Some banks require co-signers—a spouse, relatives, friends, or a third-party financial institution or government agency.

Q. I don't like the concept of personal guarantees; it sounds too risky. Is there anything I can do to protect my personal assets from banks?

A. Several methods can be used to protect personal assets from banks as well as other creditors. Transferring title is the best way.

Put your share of any jointly-held assets exclusively in your spouse's name. Transfer title to an irrevocable trust with children or other relatives as beneficiaries. Set up a corporation and transfer assets to it, making sure other persons have controlling interest: a spouse, children, relatives, friends, or anyone you can trust.

I have pointed clients to another way that is not fail-safe but works in most cases. Make asset ownership so complicated that the cost of seizure by a bank or other creditor exceeds the value of the assets. Under four popular scenarios, assets can be transferred to:

1. Several corporations, each with different ownership structures
2. Several corporations located in different states
3. Revocable trusts located offshore
4. Off-shore corporations in a safe-haven country

If the judgment is large enough and the assets have a high enough value, of course, creditors will come after you even if it is difficult, time-consuming, and costly to do so. Corporate shields can be pierced by court action. Asset transfers to revocable trusts can be invalidated. Generally, however, these methods are sufficient to deter all but the most aggressive creditors.

RAISING EQUITY CAPITAL

Q. What if I want to stay away from debt completely? How would I raise equity capital?

A. Avoiding debt is a smart decision. Debt has sunk more than one small business, including consulting businesses.

If you are short of capital and have the opportunity to land big jobs, or want to add multiple offices, or decide that international consulting is the right market for you to focus on, perhaps bringing in a full-time partner makes sense. Not only does a partner bring additional skills to your business, you may have access to more capital as well.

Q. I thought we already covered partnerships earlier, except then you called them "informal" partnerships. What's different now?
A. An informal partner doesn't usually contribute capital. With a standard partnership, each partner should contribute approximately the same amount, assuming it's an equal partnership.

More consultants raise external capital by creating a partnership than by borrowing from a bank or any other lender. I realize that sharing decision-making can be traumatic at first, but we wouldn't do it unless we needed cash. We have to expect to give up something for the money. And this is certainly the most inexpensive way to go.

A partner may be either active or passive, but consultants usually end up with the former. Ideally, this person is already in the consulting business and can bring along a cadre of clients.

In addition to bringing cash, new skills, and hopefully a client base, a partner serves as a ready buyer for your share of the business when it's time to retire.

Q. Do I incur a tax liability when I bring in a partner?
A. Not if you don't sell part of your business. If you do, then a tax liability arises on the gain.

A much better way is to form a new company, using the same business name if you want. This eliminates any tax problem. Each partner contributes capital to the new company. Perhaps office equipment and client lists represent your equity contribution. Of course, you should consult a qualified tax counselor for the particulars of your situation.

Q. Do you have any recommendations about how to structure a partnership agreement?

A. A partnership agreement should be reviewed by your attorney, and should include the following items:

1. Amount of capital contributed by each party and percentage ownership
2. Percentage allocation of the company's profits, losses, and assets
3. Percentage allocation of the gain or loss if the company is sold or liquidated
4. A right of first refusal, and the price for each partner's share should either partner want to sell out
5. Conditions, price, and terms for the new partner to acquire additional interest in the company
6. Whether arbitration or other means will be used to settle major disputes between the partners
7. Conditions, price, and terms for admitting additional partners
8. State laws governing the agreement

A partnership buyout agreement should also be executed, preferably separate from the partnership agreement. It covers the steps to be taken under four possibilities:

1. One partner becomes disenchanted with the other and wants to get out.
2. One partner dies.
3. One partner becomes disabled and cannot continue to assume an active role in the company.
4. Both partners die or become disabled either simultaneously or in close proximity to each other (such as in a plane crash).

When I refer to a partnership, I don't necessarily mean a business structured in the partnership form. A corporation works just as well, with each partner owning proportionate shares of stock.

One word of caution: a partnership, in any form, is much like a marriage. It's a lot easier to get into than to get out of.

Q. What are the pros and cons of partnership?

A. Partnerships bring several advantages to a consulting business and are clearly an excellent way to raise cash without incurring debt. As I see it, the main pluses are:

1. No interest or principal payments burden future cash flow.
2. A working partner brings new expertise or energy to the business.
3. Getting out position is easy to structure.
4. Continuity of the business is ensured in case you become disabled or die.
5. It's easier to borrow money in the future with an expanded net worth and two managers.

I find that the major negatives are:

1. It can be very difficult to locate the right partner.
2. People change, and what was once a good personality fit may turn sour over time.
3. Goals and objectives of the two partners may diverge over time.

Q. Would you recommend a partnership over going it alone?

A. Not unless you have an excellent reason for entering a partnership, such as desperately needing outside capital or additional skills. I much prefer to conduct my business the way I want to do it without the necessity of getting anyone's concurrence. If you feel more comfortable with someone to work with, however, forming a partnership certainly fills the void, and it brings in cash at the same time.

Chapter 14

LEAVE YOUR CLIENTS SMILING
How to End an Engagement Gracefully

Q. Why focus on ending an engagement?

A. I wouldn't be doing my job if I didn't go over the one activity that consultants continually screw up—ending an engagement. Anyone can walk away from a job: the key is to do it in such a manner that clients believe they must rehire us in the future.

I know we have touched on this topic several times when discussing client relations, billings, reports, and marketing, but we didn't get into it very deeply. This subject is so crucial to a continuing, successful consulting business that we should look at it now in more detail.

Q. When I complete the engagement I write the final report, deliver it, get paid, and that's it, except for follow-up contacts as you described earlier. What else should I do?

A. As we have seen, company management harbors one of three possible attitudes when you tell them the work is finished. They:

- Breathe a sigh of relief that you are finally leaving.
- Are indifferent to your presence or absence.
- Are anxious to have you return for another job.

Obviously, we all want every client to opt for the latter. A graceful exit is necessary to ensure it happening.

Q. What do you mean by a "graceful exit"?

A. Regardless of difficulties or indifference encountered during an engagement, when it ends, all should be forgiven. The client should be satisfied that the money expended brought the results expected. A bond should have been created between consultant and company personnel. No one should feel disadvantaged or put upon by our presence.

In other words, client personnel who have worked with us, from the CEO down, should feel that we have done the best job we were capable of doing, and that our advice was given solely for the well-being of the company. They should believe that what we have done is right and proper, that we have done it with a sense of decency. And that we are the type of people they like to have around. Ideally, we feel the same way about company personnel. It makes for a much smoother relationship.

As for smoothing *your* ruffled feathers, that's a different story. A consultant's feelings are not crucial to being invited to further engagements, however. It is always more pleasant if good feelings are reciprocal, but certainly not necessary. Your acting ability should bridge any negative feelings you may harbor.

Q. Where do I begin?

A. That's what we are going to talk about now: the do's and don'ts leading up to this exit. Without getting too theoretical, it would probably help to review the elements of a typical consulting engagement.

THE ENGAGEMENT STRUCTURE

Q. What do you mean by the engagement structure?

A. During most engagements, about halfway through the job, top management as well as lower-echelon employees begin to become anxious about a consultant's presence. I don't understand why this happens, but it invariably does.

A consulting engagement can be compared to the structure of a novel. Both have a beginning, a middle, and an end.

An author first lays out the setting and then develops the background and roles of each major character. The sequence holds as well for a consulting engagement. The first few days on the job we get the lay of the land, try to grasp the CEO's real reasons for hiring us, perform an operations review, meet the employees, and assess the stumbling blocks. This process establishes the key players in the drama and our relationship to them.

If a novelist lays the groundwork adequately, we are intrigued enough to keep reading. If not, we put the book away and go on to something else. The same holds true on a consulting engagement. If we lay the right groundwork in the beginning, identify what role to assume, and establish working relationships with top managers and key employees, everyone is anxious to move on to the next step. Adrenalin flows. Enthusiasm abounds. If we blow it in the beginning, chances are high the job will not be successfully completed.

A consulting engagement is no different. If we cannot logically arrive at workable recommendations, if our analyses are incomplete or inaccurate, if our technical background doesn't match the client's needs, executives and lower echelon managers alike lose confidence in our ability to meet their expectations.

By fumbling either the beginning or our performance during the production phase, relationships wither and the probability of repeat business diminishes.

Two elements underlying an author's work can save the day even if the novel's beginning and middle are less than perfect: style and the method used for bringing together loose ends at the finale. If an author's style is interesting, provocative, or unique, readers tend to wade through the middle, hoping and expecting a dramatic conclusion. If they are not disappointed, both the author and the work will probably be remembered and recommended to other readers. The same two elements can save the day for consultants. Style is something we can only develop over time. It becomes an integral part of role playing. It serves as the foundation for client relations. And a self-confident, commanding yet compassionate style is a necessary ingredient for a graceful exit.

As we see the end of an engagement approaching we slowly but surely transfer the reins to client personnel. A shifting of command from consultant to employees stimulates interest in seeing recommendations implemented (which of course, is what we all strive for). If employees are eager to get on with our recommendations, chances are good the CEO will be also. This attitude practically always assures a graceful exit, regardless of the hurdles and obstacles encountered during the job. (Remember, if you can't get the employees on your side, the boss won't be on your side either.)

Q. Are there any other techniques I can use to lead up to a graceful exit?

A. Yes. Let's look at five areas that can make or break good client relations when bringing a job to a close:

- Determining when to end
- Advance notification
- Conflict resolution
- The final report
- Ending before recommendations are implemented

WHEN TO END

Q. What do you mean by determining when to end an engagement? Doesn't the engagement end when it's completed?

A. Yes. But as we all know, in many cases the ending date in our minds is not the same as that in the mind of a CEO or top executive. Unless the client has severe cash flow problems and wants us out to save money, the CEO typically wants us to continue beyond our definition of the conclusion of an assignment, especially with continuing engagements.

For instance, the CEO of a $12 million household appliances distributor hired me to locate a joint venture partner to form a local distribution outlet in one of four alternative Caribbean nations. The scope contract specified that I would present a handful of potential partners, check out the two most promising as chosen by the client, and negotiate a joint venture agreement with the winner. That was all. A typical engagement with a beginning, middle, and end. I estimated it would take about thirty days of my time, spread over five months.

It took me three days to set the stage in the beginning and 22 days to perform the search and contract negotiation. My client had a new partner in Barbados, and I wrote the final report and submitted the final invoice.

The very day that the CEO received my invoice I received a call from the company controller. Panic-stricken, he related that the CEO, upon learning that I was finished, had flown into a rage. Wouldn't I please come over for a meeting that afternoon? I did. The CEO, calmed by then, informed me that the engagement wasn't over and that he wanted me to work with his manager and the joint venture partner to be certain that the new distributorship was functioning properly. And by the way, this, according to the CEO, was what I had agreed to do (although, or course, it was not in the scope contract).

That was the last time I made that mistake. Since then I have followed an inviolable policy: inform the CEO and other top executives when I intend to finish the engagement well in advance of actually completing the work.

Q. With a phone call?
A. No. With a hand-delivered, written memo.

Q. Why the CEO and other top executives?
A. Because in many companies the CEO is not the prime decision-maker for the functional areas in which I work. If there is any disagreement about activities included in the scope contract at this stage, the odds are high that it will emanate from one or more of the company's executives or managers, not the CEO. Of course, in smaller companies where the CEO makes all decisions, the situation is different.

Q. How far in advance do you notify these executives?
A. That depends on the nature of the engagement.

Ending an extended-term engagement can be very tricky. On the other hand, for a project engagement, with a definitive end that everyone can see, such as the joint venture example, I like to set the stage for the finale about two-thirds of the way through the job. This gives me time to adjust my schedule if the client wants to extend the scope, which usually happens.

ENDING AN EXTENDED-TERM ENGAGEMENT

Q. When would you give advance notice on an extended-term engagement?

A. Ending an extended-term engagement gracefully can be extremely difficult. By extended-term, of course, I am referring to jobs involving substitute management, indefinite monthly retainers for general advice, long-term international market/customer work, and so on.

As we discussed earlier, the tendency in long-term (or extended-term) engagements is for both the consultant and client management to become so accustomed to working together that the consultant is treated as an employee, even if he only works one or two days a week. We have seen how deadly the results can be. Instead of providing independent advice, we become workhorses, actually performing activities that client personnel should handle.

When we eventually decide we have had enough and tell the client we are through, all hell breaks loose. "You can't leave now. Who will do the work?" or "You agreed to see us through this problem and it hasn't been solved yet." Once we exit, company executives call us in the middle of the night and on weekends asking for advice to solve minute operating problems they have become dependent on us to resolve.

Q. How do you suggest getting out of these nightmares?

A. If you have an open-ended scope agreement, and that is usually the case for this type of engagement, the decision to stop is entirely up to you. Once you set a date, the more advance notice you give the client, the easier it will be to disengage.

An extended engagement is equivalent to a novel that never seems to end. The beginning was there all right. But we get so bogged down in details and descriptive dialogue in the middle that we lose track of the story. We never reach the ending because we continually backtrack to reread ambiguous sections or chapters.

With long-term engagements, we begin all right, but then get swamped with the day-to-day routine of managing a function or department. We lose our independence; we can't see the forest for the trees. When we get that feeling, it's time to head toward the exit. Regardless of any unfinished work for next week, next month, or next year, we have to draw the line someplace. When we begin to feel more like employees than independent consultants, the only logical conclusion is to draw that line.

A good friend of mine concentrates on consulting to troubled companies. He likes to call his specialty "crisis management." Nearly all of his assignments are extended-term. He usually ends up managing one or several functions for the client—marketing, finance, warehousing, production, and so on.

Having been caught once or twice in a never-ending assignment, he now makes sure that an end date is specified in the original scope contract. Regardless of developments in the company, he adheres to this date or negotiates a new scope contract with a new date. In either case, about one month before the end date, he writes a short note to the CEO reminding him that the end is thirty days away. Although most CEOs extend the due date two, three, or four times, the end is always out there. The thirty-day notice allows the client time to find someone else for the job, or to renegotiate.

CONFLICT RESOLUTION

Q. How does conflict resolution become part of the closing process?
A. Those of us with big egos—and what management consultant doesn't have one—like to believe that we are always right, and that our recommendations are always the best course to improve a client's operations. Unfortunately, we are not infallible, and our recommendations are not always the best, or even among the best.

On some jobs we miss the boat completely and come up with totally wrong answers.

If our errors are pointed out during the course of the engagement we can learn and make adjustments. If they surface near the end of a job, we're in trouble. Goodbye graceful exit!

This is one reason interim reports are so essential. If we begin heading toward erroneous conclusions, hopefully someone will catch our misdirection from the interim report and set us straight.

When we make recommendations toward or at the end of an engagement and client personnel disprove their validity, only one step remains. We must correct our erroneous analyses and come up with appropriate recommendations. That inevitably means lost hours, but if we hope to keep the client, or at a minimum get a reference, I don't know of any alternative.

On the plus side, by resolving client disputes prior to wrapping up a job, we should be able to salvage at least a modestly graceful exit.

Q. What if I run into serious problems during an engagement that I can't resolve? Should I break it off?

A. If necessary, yes. But first we have to define "necessary". Nearly all conflicts that evolve between consultant and client personnel can be resolved with a little diplomacy and a lot of effort.

These four conflicts seem to arise more frequently with smaller clients than any other. Occasionally they also appear in large companies:

- Personality conflicts
- Nepotism conflicts
- Conflicts of interest
- Financial conflicts

I would be very surprised if you don't run into a personality conflict with at least one key employee on every engagement. There are always one or two who don't want your help, who regard your presence as an intrusion on their empire.

Whether the engagement should be ended or not depends on the seriousness of the conflict and the position of the employee. If the personality conflict is with a lower-echelon employee, chances are good that it won't make much difference in the outcome of the engagement. If it gets too bad, the boss will have to arbitrate. I have never heard of a personality conflict at this level causing a job to end.

A personality conflict with the CEO or a close advisor is another matter. Hopefully, role playing gets us out of most hot water. Being in the business for a while, consultants usually learn how to deal with practically any tough customer they might run across.

On the other hand, I have seen occasions when the fireworks between CEO and consultant are so hot that no amount of diplomacy can extinguish the flame. If the problem can't be resolved, the only way out is to withdraw from the engagement as diplomatically as possible. Mustering all the tact at your disposal might at least save a reference. It will probably involve losing unbilled hours, but that's the way it goes.

Q. Suppose I have a situation with a client where nepotism creates very real conflicts: The owner-manager has his daughter working as sales manager, a nephew as controller, and a son-in-law as warehouse manager. The internal politics are terrible. What should I do?

A. I do not have a solution to nepotism conflicts. I can provide a couple of examples of my responses with the problem, however. Although neither completely resolved the conflict, they might stir some ideas to use in your own case.

Contrary to sound management practices, nepotism exists in companies of virtually any size. Fortunately, in the larger ones, relatives are usually assigned to separate departments. I have never had a large corporate client where the CEO employs close relatives in vice president positions. Usually they appear lower in the organization. That doesn't mean it can't happen. I just haven't seen nepotism in top management roles, except in family-held companies.

I find nepotism one of the most difficult obstacles to overcome, mainly because nepotism breeds family loyalty, which no outsider can penetrate. The worst case arises when husband and wife are joint owners and managers of the company.

Several years ago, I took on an engagement involving the design and installation of a computer-based accounting system for a small investment banking firm. A husband-and-wife team were the general partners in this limited partnership firm. He was the dealmaker: she was vice president of finance. Although she knew next to nothing about either accounting or computers, she thought she was expert in both.

She objected to every recommendation I came up with: every hardware and software configuration I suggested, every change to the existing accounting system, every idea for reorganizing the accounting department to make it more efficient. The situation was unbearable; I was at wit's end.

To make matters worse, her husband was never around. He was always out of the office making deals. I knew I could never finish this assignment, yet I wanted to salvage a reference at least. Since the husband wasn't available for a meeting, I wrote him a letter, explaining as tactfully as possible why I had to withdraw from the engagement. I also suggested the names of two other consulting firms qualified to do the work and offered to review the status of my work with either one he chose.

That was as graceful an exit as I could muster, but it must have worked. I have used this company as a reference twice, and still get an annual Christmas card.

Q. Can you ever resolve a nepotism problem on an assignment?

A. The only reason I took the job with the investment banking firm was that a short time previously a nepotism conflict had worked out well.

The company managed several international construction projects. My job was twofold: arranging financing for a project in Egypt and setting up cash management controls at all foreign job sites.

I was setting up controls for a site in the Caribbean. The owner gave his college-age son the job as site controller. He wouldn't take directions from me and continually undermined my recommendations. I told his father, the company owner, in a calm, gentle manner, that either the boy or I had to get off the site. The son returned home: I finished my assignment on the site.

That is the only positive suggestion I can offer for coping with nepotism conflicts. If the top executive sides with relatives and won't take action on your request, get out of the job as tactfully as possible. But do get out.

Q. You also mention conflicts of interest. What do you mean by that?

A. We frequently run into situations that call for bringing in outside expertise: legal, tax, insurance, estate planning, and so on. If the client doesn't know experts in the specific field, we suggest a friend or associate, or a firm that we have worked with on prior engagements. An analogous situation occurs when we recommend a doctor or dentist to a friend.

If the suggestion is accepted and the outsider's advice satisfies the client, everyone benefits. Occasionally, however, the client is not satisfied. In the judgment of either the CEO or a key employee, the outside expert's advice is less than adequate. Charges of incompetence are leveled. The next thing we know the CEO accuses us of playing favorites, or suggests that our recommendation was made with some ulterior motive in mind and that we have violated the client's confidentiality.

Such claims are deadly. Nothing will destroy a reputation faster than unsubstantiated conflict-of-interest accusations or rumors. Even if you are innocent, such charges can damage a consultant's reputation practically beyond repair.

Let's assume that while working a job you recommend hiring an insurance professional to review and modify the company's group health policies. The client engages the firm and implements its recommendations. The client then learns that the same coverage could have been obtained from a different underwriter at a much lesser cost. The CEO accuses you of recommending the insurance person to get a kickback from them or to get a referral to another client. If the charge is true, that's a conflict of interest.

A second situation can arise when you have two clients in the same industry competing with one another. Since without a reputation for confidentiality few management consultants would ever get work, an accusation that you divulged a client's secrets to a competitor can be extremely damaging. The truth or falsehood of the accusation is irrelevant. You are guilty until proven innocent. Your reputation may never fully recover.

Q. If I can't clear my name, how to I close the engagement gracefully?

A. In the first instance, the only safeguard is to put suggestions for hiring outside experts either in a letter to the CEO or in an interim report. But get it in writing. Offer two or three names, not just one. Insert a sentence stating that it is irrelevant to you whether the client hire one of your choices or someone else. If the client elects to go with one of your suggested firms, write a letter to the CEO disclaiming any responsibility for the results of this outsider and include a hold harmless clause. (Your attorney can help you draft one.) If you can, get the CEO's signature accepting the letter.

These steps will not eliminate conflict of interest rumors, but they do help to forestall overt claims.

The second case is more difficult to handle. Unless a client has concrete proof that the only way a competitor could obtain secret information was through an insider such as yourself, accusations of complicity remain rumors. A hold harmless clause in the scope contract restricts legal claims. There is no protection against rumors except a stalwart reputation built up over many years, and even that is not fail-safe.

Q. How do I exit gracefully when financial conflicts arise?

A. By financial conflicts I presume you mean situations where either the client cannot or will not pay your invoices or the client doesn't have the resources to implement your recommendations.

Let's take the first case first. When we discussed collections techniques earlier, we examined how to handle a client's reticence to pay invoices. Only in rare situations can a client claim lack of cash. As long as the business continues to operate—even in chapter 11—cash is available to pay our invoices. If a client won't pay and insinuations or threats of stopping work don't change the decision, we can either continue, finishing the job without getting paid, or try to negotiate one of the alternate compensation schemes we discussed. The latter is obviously preferable, and allows an exit without rancor.

The second case, when a client doesn't have the resources to implement our recommendations, creates a real dilemma. Short of a financial emergency, however, this case should not arise. If it does, perhaps you have not done sufficient analysis prior to making your recommendations.

A consultant I'll call Mary Jo and I had a close working arrangement, assisting each other on small business engagements. I picked up a new client that needed help deciding whether to add a fleet of delivery trucks or to continue contracting with a common carrier. I was tied up full time with a bankruptcy client before the engagement started and turned the new job over to Mary Jo.

Six weeks later I received an angry call claiming that Mary Jo's recommendation for purchasing a fleet of seven trucks was completely off the wall, that there wasn't enough cash in the till to make the investment. In defense of Mary Jo, I pointed out that when the engagement began, adequate credit was available from the client's bank. Mary Jo did not realize that a commitment to purchase three large pieces of equipment had been made in the interim. We resolved the issue by placing our client with a national truck leasing company that was more than eager to do the deal.

It seems self-evident that recommending actions beyond the client's financial means represents a failure to fulfill our obligation to give expert advice. Occasionally we all slip, however, and give impractical advice. When it happens, the only solution is to back off, admit our mistake, and come up with alternatives within the client's means. If we do that, previous errors will be dismissed and a graceful exit can be assured.

USING THE FINAL REPORT TO EXIT

Q. Once the engagement concludes, do you have any final report recommendations that will close the door gracefully?

A. As I mentioned earlier, a final report can be a very effective client relations tool for soliciting new assignments. I will never understand why some consultants ignore the advantages of putting their conclusions in writing, but they do.

Written and presented properly, a final report serves as an excellent vehicle for exiting. We have already covered these topics briefly, but the importance of the report deserves a few additional comments.

In addition to reiterating recommendations and summarizing our interpretation of the results of the engagement, the final report provides an opportunity to praise the efforts and abilities of key personnel and top executives. If at all possible, I prefer to end the report with such gracious language as:

"The success of this engagement is directly attributable to the outstanding cooperation of many, extremely capable people at XYZ Corp. I take this opportunity to personally thank John Doe, Susie Que, and Marcie Mole for their assistance. Please let me know when either myself or our firm can help XYZ Corp. or anyone in the organization again. We look forward to serving you in another assignment."

Q. What do you think about letting company personnel help write the report?

A. This is an excellent idea that accomplishes two objectives. First, client personnel will verify your recommendations as practical and needed. You are alerted to potential conflicts that might arise either in the acceptance of the report by the CEO or in the implementation of the recommendations.

Second, it brings key employees into the mainstream of your work. By actually helping to write the recommendations, employees have the opportunity to clarify any misunderstood or confusing points which in turn makes implementing or sustaining the changes you have already made more likely.

On most of my engagements I like to follow these steps when writing the final report:

1. Review my findings, recommendations, and any serious problems I have encountered with the CEO before I write the report. Pre-acceptance preempts surprises.
2. With approval from the CEO, circulate an outline of my comments to key personnel. If I have missed something, this flushes it out.
3. Actually write the report with the functional manager most affected by the project. Include comments from other managers.
4. Obtain the signature of this co-author on the report as evidence of acceptance.
5. Review the report personally with the CEO. The co-author may be present at the CEO's discretion.

I have followed this process for many years. It has always paved the way for a graceful exit, and more times than not, has been a major factor in landing additional assignments.

Q. But some engagements don't warrant a report. How do you exit under that condition?

A. I presume you are referring to isolated contingency-fee engagements such as an acquisition or a divestiture. I can't think of any other engagement that doesn't benefit from a final report.

Even contingency-fee engagements provide the opportunity to utilize a co-authored final report. Except for my first acquisition engagement, I have always co-authored a final report with a key executive (below the CEO). In addition to the previously shown client relations language, the report can be used to solicit additional work during the transition period. Nearly all key employees welcome this help, and with their co-authorship the final report serves as a good door opener.

Q. How would you handle the situation where the CEO doesn't like the way you have handled the engagement or doesn't agree with your conclusions?

A. You should learn about this long before final report time. We have already discussed several options for coping with recalcitrant CEOs.

In the unlikely event that we don't learn about the CEO's displeasure until the final bell, co-authoring the report with a company executive goes a long way to smooth the feathers of the boss. No CEO wants to look foolish in front of key employees. To remain ornery after a valued executive agrees with you would certainly put the CEO in a compromising position. I have never seen one reject suggestions as long as a key employee supports and co-authors the report. In the final analysis, however, it is your job to make sure there are no "ticking bombs" in your final report.

EXITING BEFORE IMPLEMENTATION

Q. Do you have any tips about what to do when it becomes necessary to end an engagement while top management is still happy with your work, but before all recommendations are implemented?

A. This frequently happens, especially on long-term engagements. As a practical matter, continuing engagements never end—they just fade away.

This is another high-voltage danger point for consultants who specialize in long-term, management-type work.

We face a real dilemma in knowing precisely when to call a halt. The jobs do not have a beginning, middle, and end. Specific results are not easily measured. Once we win the client's confidence, this type of work can go on indefinitely, if we let it.

Q. If a job goes on forever, why call a halt?

A. Because the longer you are on the assignment, the less value the client places on your assistance. Top management begins taking your presence and advice for granted. Eventually, if the assignment lasts long enough, you cease being an independent consultant and become, for all practical purposes an employee, as we discussed earlier.

Q. But how do I know when to call a halt to the assignment?
A. If we don't get emotionally involved with a client and can put our egos aside, our intuition lets us know when it's time to say goodbye. Most of us have a difficult time cutting off long-term engagements because we get so caught up in a client's affairs that we forget our passive roles as consultants. We begin playing the role of the boss. In many cases, we are allowed to make management decisions. This kills our objectivity.

Except for M&A work and, occasionally, international assignments, I try to follow a general rule that the most successful consultant I have ever known once related to me: On a continuing assignment, never spend more than three days per week at the client's facilities and never allow an engagement to drag on for more than six months.

Q. What if the work I have contracted to do isn't finished? Assume I contract to develop a strategic planning process with client personnel. During the engagement two other projects arise: to recruit three key managers and to arrange refinancing for the company. What then?
A. The scope contract should call for a strategic plan engagement only. New contracts should be executed for the recruiting assignment and the refinancing—one for each, with estimated time periods.

Q. Let's change the assumptions. The scope contract calls for helping a business owner turn his troubled company around and refinancing current debt. The turnaround involves firing the marketing vice president; I assume his position temporarily. I am unable to find a bank to do the refinancing. The engagement is now in its ninth month with no sign of completion. What do I do?

A. This is actually a very common situation in turnaround work. At the fourth month I would tell the owner that the length of this engagement has already exceeded original estimates and continuing to manage the marketing function, which should be a full-time job, deprives me of servicing other clients. I would tell the owner that other commitments make it necessary for me to finish the engagement in two more months.

During that time, I will recruit my replacement for the marketing function and attempt to arrange refinancing through non-bank sources. I can't guarantee the results, but will expend my best efforts. In any case, two months from now I *must* withdraw, unless I can negotiate a new scope contract that limits my involvement.

Q. Won't that create ill will from the client?
A. That possibility always exists. But it's not as if I abandoned the company. I am more than willing to continue work on either the refinancing or any other assignment, but I must have a new scope contract that defines more precisely the part I will play. Very few reasonable business owners or CEOs object to that scenario. They know you have your own business to run. And reminding them that you must honor commitments to other clients should elevate your stature in their eyes.

I have used this tactic several times, always with favorable results. Without exception, the engagements have continued, but on my terms, not the client's. The exit from one scope contract and the entrance to another permits me to continue earning fees without assuming the role of an employee.

Q. Let's take one final case. This time the scope contact involves evaluating the market demand and competition for a proposed new product line. The company wants my advice before proceeding with their R & D program. I do the work and write a final report with several recommended action steps, none of which are even started by the time I leave. How do I leave gracefully when my recommendations haven't been implemented?

A. In these cases we must remember that we have not contracted for the *implementation* of our suggestions, only for advice. We are careful to disclaim responsibility for the results of implementation. There are no guarantees.

If the scope contract reads like that, you shouldn't have any difficulty extricating yourself before the action steps are taken. On the contrary, this type of engagement encourages further work to assist with the implementation steps. But that's a separate engagement calling for a new scope contract.

If, on the other hand, we contract to assist in implementing our recommendations and then withdraw prior to doing so, we have not fulfilled our contract. This happens frequently when the client needs a time gap between our work leading to recommendations and marshaling the resources to implement them. In that case, we are merely withdrawing temporarily until the client is ready for further assistance. The job hasn't ended and no exit protocol is involved.

Before we leave the subject of graceful exits, I'd like to comment briefly on the difference between exiting at the completion of a job, or, with the client's concurrence, before the end is reached, and withdrawing from a job for personal reasons.

The longer I am in the management consulting business the more frequently I run into situations in which I feel compelled to exit for personal reasons before the job is completed. I won't list all the personal reasons I have encountered, but such matters as health problems and family concerns are the most obvious.

Although I have worked for several companies with CEOs or owners whom I can only classify as less than stellar when it came to human relations, I have never seen, nor heard from other consultants, of a case where the client objected to a consultant withdrawing, or postponing completion, for personal reasons.

Perhaps I'm just lucky, but I like to think it has something to do with human nature. Even the most obstreperous CEO seems to feel compassion for human illness or tragedy. At any rate, I would never hesitate to tell a client I must withdraw for personal reasons, even if it was immediately and without referring the client to another consultant. But I would be very careful to be certain that the personal reason was serious enough to warrant the action.

Chapter 15

HANGING IT UP
How to Sell Your Business When its Time to Retire

Q. Well, I guess we have come to the end of the line. Starting a business, getting new clients, performing jobs, handling administration, and making a graceful exit. That takes care of succeeding in consulting, right?

A. Wrong! We still have to deal with disposing of the business when it's time to retire. I realize that that time is probably long into the future and the last thing you want to worry about now. But sound strategic planning dictates planning a getting-out position as soon as possible after starting a business. We preach that to clients, and we should practice it ourselves.

Q. I can't imagine my business will ever be worth anything to a buyer. I'll probably just walk away from it. Wouldn't you?

A. Your business does have a value. You can't just walk away. And no, I wouldn't.

Q. My business is selling personal services. How can it have a marketable value?

A. Every business that generates income has value. I've been buying and selling businesses all my life and have never found one in any industry that couldn't be sold to someone. Although it may not be readily apparent, consulting businesses are no different from other service businesses.

Regardless of the market niches, a consulting business consists of three types of valuable assets:

1. Current and prior clients
2. Referral contacts
3. Office furniture and equipment

In some cases the business name also has value. This is usually true with multi-partner firms rather than sole practitioners. Under the right circumstances, however, even a sole practitioner's company name has brand recognition, and therefore value, regardless of how many people it includes.

Let's take a brief look at the how, when, and where of selling a consulting business. Six broad issues need to be addressed:

- Making the liquidation versus selling decision
- Managing clients and ex-clients
- Identifying tax implications
- Structuring a sale
- Writing the buy/sell agreement
- Managing the transition period

Q. Why not just sell my office equipment?
A. You could. There is usually a good market for used office furniture and equipment, although you shouldn't expect to recover anything close to your original investment. On the other hand, by including these assets with the sale of your entire business, you will increase their value.

IS IT SALABLE?

Q. I can understand how you can sell a business that has repeat clients—such as a public accounting tax practice where clients come back every year. But a great many consulting businesses don't have that luxury. How would you differentiate those that are salable from those that can only be liquidated?

A. Some consulting businesses are not salable simply because they do not generate repeat business. Without repeat business, goes the conventional wisdom, there is no value to a buyer. Or is there?

As I have mentioned several times, we all know that consultants build a business on reputation more than anything else: a reputation for confidentiality, honesty, and all the other ethical characteristics; a reputation for technical competence; a reputation for delivering a specific service better than competitors.

It's entirely possible that even without repeat business a consulting firm's reputation establishes it as a market contender. In that case, the firm's reputation equates to goodwill, which is always a salable commodity.

A good analogy can be made to a law firm that specializes in bankruptcy law. It is highly unlikely that once a client files for bankruptcy, it will need the services of such a specialist again. Yet most bankruptcy law firms maintain reputations as experts in this highly specialized field. New clients are attracted, not because they have done business with the firm before, but because of its expert reputation.

Q. What consulting specialty would be comparable?
A. Take a consulting firm that specializes in advising clients about how to clean up hazardous waste to meet EPA requirements, or one that handles divestitures or liquidations. It is unlikely that these specialties will ever generate repeat business from the same client. Yet these jobs require highly specialized skills, and consultants who specialize in them get new clients primarily on reputation.

Q. How do you go about transferring reputation to a buyer?
A. The only way that I know to solve this problem is to form a partnership far enough in advance of retirement to train a successor in your specialty. Assuming this can be accomplished, the firm's name should be left unchanged when you leave. The expert public image rests in the firm's name, not yours. If a successor can perform with the same expertise, and maintains the same firm name and address, new clients should be attracted to the firm's reputation as readily after you leave as before.

THE PRICE

Q. If I do decide to sell the entire business, how do I set a value on it?

A. Buyers look at two aspects when valuing any business, especially a service business: (1) how much it would cost to replace the hard assets in kind, with the same models and age, if the business were started from scratch, and (2) how much cash the business will generate and how fast cash will be generated in the future.

To determine the potential for cash flow in the future, a buyer must consider repeat engagements from existing and prior clients, the amount of new business that can be originated from existing referral contacts, and the market impact of the firm's expert reputation. In buy/sell parlance, referral lists, client files, and reputation all have value. Accountants call it goodwill, and that is as good a label as any.

The valuation question then relates to the value of hard assets and the value of goodwill.

Q. Can you tell me more about goodwill?

A. The most widely used measure of goodwill is annual gross billings for the current year. Not infrequently, sellers try to negotiate a two- or three-year historical average, on the theory that engagements extend over a year-end, or that this time spread is a more reasonable measure of repeat business. Buyers tend to discount billings from prior years on the theory that some lost business will occur simply because the seller leaves. They typically argue that current year's billings is more than generous.

Both sides have merit. It just depends on how bad the buyer wants to buy and how bad the seller wants to sell. The one with the higher motivation usually acquiesces to get the deal closed.

Q. Why not look at profits, as in a normal acquisition or divestiture, rather than gross billings?

A. Mainly because after the closing, a buyer will structure the business differently, incurring substantially different costs than the seller. Office expenses, payroll, automobiles, and so on, are totally under the control of the owner. Historical expenses bear little relevance to goodwill. Buyers might like to know how much rent, utilities, and taxes apply to the current location, but for information purposes only.

The price should be based on two factors: annual gross billings (goodwill) and the value of hard assets included in the sale, whether recorded on the books or not. In addition to furniture and equipment, hard assets include office supplies, reference libraries, automobiles, and real estate. Usually, but not always, the seller retains any open accounts receivable and automobiles.

Although negotiations determine the ultimate value of gross billings, typically annual billings are multiplied by a factor of one to one-and-one-half times as a starting point. I've never heard of consulting goodwill valued at more than 1.5 times annual billings nor at less than three-fourths, although I'm sure both have happened in special situations.

The price for furniture and equipment should be no less than depreciated book value and no more than original cost. Supplies, reference libraries, and other hard assets are normally priced at cost.

Once a value is negotiated for each segment, the total, of course, represents the selling price.

Q. I can understand the logic of that when selling to a stranger, but what if I sell to a partner?
A. That's a different story. I don't know of a commonly used valuation technique when selling to a partner. But I can offer a few possibilities that I have heard about.

The main concern for any buyer is whether the current and prior clients will generate additional business after the seller leaves. The best way to assure this happening is to bring in a partner a year or two before you decide to leave. This provides an opportunity to introduce the partner to clients and referral contacts. A partner can also work with you on assignments to ensure that the transition of current engagements is trouble-free. Few clients object to a consultant leaving once they build up confidence in the consultant's partner.

Lawyers, physicians, dentists, public accountants, and other professionals have used this technique for years.

Q. What about valuation?

A. As we covered during our discussion about raising capital, a partner will (you hope) kick in with a capital contribution. The amount contributed is typically determined by how much benefit the new partner gets from the existing client base (i.e., goodwill). This establishes a value for goodwill at that time and is a good starting point for negotiating a selling price.

Another, more straightforward method establishes a buyout price in the buyout agreement. Such a price serves as one factor for determining how much capital a new partner contributes.

If you intend the partner to be your successor, establish a getting-out date when executing the buyout agreement. The buyout price is then calculated at that date on a prearranged formula. It may be based on book value multiplied by a factor, current year's gross billings, annual profits times a multiplier, or any other formula that makes sense.

A third method utilizes an outside business appraiser to value the business at the date of sale. When choosing this route, it's a good idea to name the appraiser in the buyout agreement to avoid future disputes.

THE TAX IMPACT

Q. So much for valuations. How about the tax impact when I sell?

A. Let me repeat that I am not a tax expert. I leave that to the CPAs and tax attorneys. Therefore, I recommend that you check with competent tax experts before taking any action on the suggestions I make.

The type and the amount of tax liability depends to a large extent on who is selling what and on how much of the purchase price gets assigned to each asset category.

Issuing stock from a corporation is simple. There is no gain and therefore no tax. If the corporation buys the stock back, the gain is taxable to the corporation. With an S corporation, the gain passes through to the remaining shareholders.

Selling an interest in a partnership gets extremely complicated—far too complex to examine in full detail here.

Q. I understand from a friend who is a CPA that selling assets could result in lower taxes. Is this true?
A. Very possibly. With an asset sale, the buy/sell agreement specifies how much of the selling price gets allocated to each category of assets: equipment, furniture, accounts receivable, supplies, goodwill, and perhaps a noncompete covenant.

The selling price in excess of the book value of equipment and furniture is taxed as a capital gain (except for recaptured depreciation, which is ordinary income). No gain should be realized on receivables. The sell price allocated to supplies is ordinary income. That assigned to a non-compete covenant is also ordinary income. Goodwill is ordinary income to you, but a non-depreciable capital asset to the buyer.

Smart buyers insist that the entire price be allocated to assets other than goodwill. They cannot take a deduction for goodwill either in the year of the transaction or through write-offs in subsequent years.

Q. Can I get a tax break by taking deferred payments?
A. Deferred payments are classified as an installment sale by the IRS. The general rule states that to use the installment method, cash basis taxpayers, which categorizes most management consulting businesses, report taxable income in the year they receive the payments. Gain is calculated as the total gross sales price less the asset cost basis, multiplied by the fractional cash received each year.

But all is not as it appears with the IRS. With an asset sale, all forms of gain normally taxable as ordinary income—such as the sale of receivables, supplies, or a noncompete covenant—are taxed in the year the asset is sold, not when cash is received for it. However, the proportionate allocation of gain based on cash received still applies to gains realized on the sale of furniture and equipment, as well as the total gain on the sale of common stock. (This assumes that your own shares are sold.)

If part of the sale price is to be paid on an earn-out contract or other form of contingency payment out of the profits of the company, it will always be treated as ordinary income. Without fixed minimum amounts, contingency payments are not part of the sale price of the business. Therefore, contingency payments cannot be used in the calculation of installment sale income.

Consultants suffer as much as public accountants, lawyers, and other professionals under this provision. In nearly every case that I have seen, payment terms are at least partially structured on a two- or three-year payout based on a percentage of payments received from the seller's clients.

To take advantage of installment sale provisions, use a separate agreement to cover the sale of hard assets. Obviously, this agreement also must specify how much of the selling price gets applied to these assets.

Again, consult a qualified tax specialist for advice on the specifics of your situation.

MANAGING CLIENTS

Q. **If clients don't stay, and ex-clients don't want additional work, my business wouldn't seem to be worth much. Do you have any ideas about keeping clients satisfied with a new owner?**

A. Yes, I do. But the task is not easy and don't expect everyone to remain.

Client relations requires a different approach now than when trying to build a business. Efforts must be divided into two segments: steps to take when the sale is announced, and steps to take during the transition period.

While it is certainly true that clients have contracted with you, not your successor, you have a right to manage your own business as profitably as possible. You have a right, and perhaps even an ethical obligation, to do what is best for yourself and your family. If these rights and obligations converge on a decision to get out, then the ethical issue becomes one of deciding on the best way to avoid damaging your clients.

There will always be hurt feelings and sour grapes; but as long as you make an honest effort to avoid damaging the client's business your ethical obligation is fulfilled.

What I'm suggesting is that you concentrate on creating a minimal impact on your clients' businesses, rather than on trying to satisfy the egos of CEOs or other managers. We can't keep everyone happy all the time. And we have our own lives to live. Ethically, our obligation is to the client business, not client personnel. This doesn't mean ignoring the personal relationship side; it merely means that the business takes precedence.

Q. So what actual steps should I take to minimize the damage?

A. The first order of business is to announce the sale as diplomatically as possible. This can be most easily accomplished if the client has already met and developed a level of confidence in your successor.

One way to manage this step is to sell to a member of your consortium or network, or to a consultant with whom you have an informal partnership. As part of the planning process, you should intentionally bring this person (or firm) into an engagement. Let the CEO see that this associate has the skills to handle the same type of work you do and hold to the same ethical standards. Since the subsequent takeover will be by a known entity, clients should have little complaint when your retirement is announced.

An even better way is to form a partnership well in advance of the sale. This makes it easy to convince clients that the job will not be interrupted and work standards will not be altered. The transition will be so smooth that clients will hardly notice your departure.

Selling to an outsider is a bit stickier because the client does not know who will be taking over. I would avoid this condition as much as possible, even if it means bringing the outsider along on engagements for a period of time before the sale closes.

Q. What reason should I give clients for selling?

A. That's the key question.

We have already discussed the situation calling for withdrawal from an engagement for reasons of health, family, and so on. Few clients chastise a consultant for postponing an engagement or withdrawing completely for personal reasons, provided the reason is serious.

The same holds true when selling, as long as three rules are followed:

1. Make every effort to take care of the client.
2. Transfer job responsibilities to a reliable party.
3. Offer a very good reason for getting out.

Chances are very high that by following these simple rules, clients will stick around long enough to give the successor a chance.

An ex-consultant who was once in our consortium violated the third rule and all hell broke loose. Rick was about 47 years old and had run his consulting business for nine years. Always ambitious and impatient, Rick decided he had been in consulting long enough. He decided to try his hand at running a small resort in Jamaica.

He located a young man trying to get started in consulting and negotiated a three-month phase-in. Rick sent a memo to all his clients and ex-clients announcing the new partnership and that he would be retiring in three months. The reason he gave was the truth: that he was tired of consulting and had decided to move to Jamaica. The three clients he was currently working for quietly contracted with different consultants to finish the jobs, never giving Rick's successor a chance.

Does the reason for getting out make a difference? You can count on it.

Q. What do you consider justifiable reasons for retiring?
A. Failing personal health. Failing health of a family member. Family catastrophe. Those are the only three I have ever seen clients readily accept.

THE TRANSITION

Q. You mentioned techniques for managing clients during the transition period. Can you comment on that?

A. Managing the transition period is nearly as touchy as announcing retirement. When selling a business with contingency payment terms, you must do everything possible to retain the goodwill and reputation you have built up over the years. Everything can be lost if you blow the transition. This is precisely what happened to my cousin John, who ran a consulting business in Minnesota.

John's wife contracted a lung disease that forced the couple to move to Arizona. John brought in a successor partner six months before announcing his retirement. He took the partner on several in-process engagements and every one of this clients gave their approval. John did everything right—until the final transition step.

John left town two days after the closing. As it turned out, John should have remained long enough to make sure his successor finished the jobs properly. Although a talented young man, his successor was still rough around the edges. During the first week he managed to alienate two of the three CEOs on the engagements that he was trying to finish. Word spread fast. It didn't take long before the firm's reputation, the reputation John had nurtured so laboriously, vanished in the wind. After three years, John received only ten percent of the contingency fee he had counted on to start a new business in Arizona.

Q. How do you recommend managing a transition period?

A. Two steps must be taken. First, stay long enough to be certain that a successor has the skills to finish in-process jobs, and that clients accept the new person as a satisfactory replacement.

Second, after the jobs end, follow up with both the successor and client management to ensure that everyone is satisfied with the transition. This might mean returning to the business for a brief period, perhaps accompanying your successor on follow-up calls or attending a luncheon or a concert with client personnel. Perhaps phone calls will suffice. The main idea is to stick around long enough to make sure the transition has been smooth and your investment is protected.

Q. How should I handle a transition with referral contacts or with prospects I have already called on?

A. Both can be handled the same way. Tactful introductions and follow-up should convince referral contacts as well as prospective clients that your successor can and will be as talented and skillful as yourself.

One last comment before we leave this topic. Over the years, several friends and associates of mine have sold their consulting businesses. Some have had excellent results, others were disasters. The difference seems to be the careful attention paid to a smooth transition. Those who have walked away too soon, lost. Those who took the time to gradually phase out did much better. Referral contacts can be the lifeblood of a consulting business. In many respects it's more important to treat these people with TLC than existing clients.

Handling the transition with prospects isn't quite as important, since they are not part of the business yet and, consequently, if they drop out, no monetary loss occurs. Ethically, however, it only seems right to make an effort to bring them into the fold with an introduction to your successor.

MECHANICS OF A SALE

Q. Could we go back over a few of the major points I should consider when structuring a sale? Can we begin with the preparatory steps?

A. I strongly recommend that long before bringing in a successor partner, any loose ends in your business be cleaned up, such as collecting overdue accounts, paying off equipment loans, negotiating lease transfers (if applicable), developing a plan to minimize taxes on the sale, and making provisions to move from your home office (if applicable).

The question of office location often becomes a major stumbling block. A lease on an external office can easily be transferred to a new owner. Shifting a home office to a partner can be a nightmare.

A new address requires new letterhead and business cards. A new telephone number needs to be transmitted to clients, ex-clients, referral contacts, and prospects already marketed. Office furniture and equipment must be physically moved. Files have to be updated and organized.

These tasks are difficult enough on their own. To make a move in the middle of engagements with the telephone ringing, reports to be written, follow-up calls to be made, records to be maintained, and so on, is usually a challenge for even the most organized mind.

I don't have an easy solution. I have heard of consultants renting an office outside their home in anticipation of a sale. When I thought of selling my practice, I brought my successor partner into my home office. Although I did not sell the practice at this time, we continued to work together for two years.

Q. Do you have any tips for structuring a buy/sell agreement?

A. Most consultants, as well as lawyers, doctors, and other personal service business owners, prefer to sell to a successor partner over a period of time. The time frame coincides with the training and introduction period and helps make the transition period smoother.

A typical arrangement might be:

1. Seller A and successor partner B negotiate a three-year buyout period and a total price of $200,000 (including office furniture and equipment).
2. B makes a down payment of $40,000 in exchange for a 20% share of the business.
3. If at the end of the first year, either partner believes that the arrangement will not work, B gets 50% of the $40,000 back, but no share of that year's profits—and the partners separate.
4. If, at the end of one year, both partners agree that the partnership/succession should go forward, the following takeover schedule becomes effective.

    (a) At the end of that first year, B purchases another 15% of the business for $30,000.

(b) At the end of the second year, B buys another 15% for $30,000, assuming the annual gross billings remain at least constant. If total annual billings from a combination of their clients exceeds the base year, the increment is priced at an amount equal to 15% of 50% of the incremental billings.

(c) At the end of the third year, B purchases the balance of the business for $100,000 plus 50% of 50% the incremental billings for that year (25%).

Assuming the business continues to grow, these calculations might follow:

A. Down Payment in exchange for a 20% interest $40,000

B. At the End of First Year
Cash profit from the business was $144,000
of which B is entitled to 20% or $28,800

A takes B's promissory note for $1,200
at 10% interest, payable in 2 years

C. At the End of Second Year
Cash profits on base year billings are
$140,000 of which B is entitled to 35%
or $49,000. B keeps $30,000 for his own
draw and pays A the difference: $19,000

Billings increased by a $50,000 increment
of which B is entitled to 35% or $17,500.
B uses part of this as the excess payment
$50,000 x 50% x 15%: $3,750

B uses another $11,500 of this incremental
income to pay the balance of the 15% due: $11,000

TOTAL PAID IN YEAR TWO: $33,750

D. At the End of Third Year

Cash profits on base year billings are $152,000 of which B is entitled to 50% or $76,000. B keeps $40,000 for his own draw and pays A the balance:	$36,000
Billings increased by another $60,000 this year, of which B is entitled to 50% or $30,000. B uses part of this as the excess payment of $60,000 x 1/2 x 50%:	$15,000
The balance is used to pay against the base price	$15,000
B uses his share of the incremental billings from the second year ($50,000 x 35%) to pay against the note from the first year (plus interest):	$1,440
For the balance due against the base price, A takes another note at 10% interest payable in two years, secured by B's entire interest in the business:	
	$49,000
TOTAL PAID IN YEAR THREE:	$116,440

Now the business belongs to successor partner B, although B still owes A $49,000 on a note.

Although similar arrangements are widely followed, this is only one example of many different ways a succession partnership buy-out can be structured. In the end, the agreement must creatively meet the needs of both parties. You should definitely consult with your attorney on matters of this nature.

Q. How about key clauses in a buy/sell agreement? Are there any I should be particularly concerned about?

A. Five special clauses protect sellers from nearly any unfavorable eventuality. Although some consultants disagree with me, my experience has been that these clauses are essential to avoid difficulties during the partnership period and subsequent to the final sale.

1. *Escape Clause:* Leave the door open to dissolve the partnership if, for any reason, you become dissatisfied with the arrangement.
2. *Price:* Establish a fixed price for the business as it exists at the time of executing the succession partnership agreement. In addition, a price should be established for additional business that each partner brings in up to the time of complete takeover.
3. *Time*: Fix specific dates for the sale of incremental ownership interests as well as for the final buyout.
4. *Early Buyout:* Specify the price and terms in an early buyout clause in the event you should die or become disabled prior to completing the full takeover.
5. *Responsibility:* Define specific responsibilities for each partner. This clause should cover additions or changes in overhead costs and marketing and production judgments relative to prospects and clients. In other words, who will decide the outcome of a dispute? What voice will each party have in decisions affecting clients each brings in?

Q. If I structure a buy/sell agreement with deferred payment terms, such as contingency payments, how can I be sure I'll collect? Is there any recourse once I turn over the entire business?

A. This presents a problem unique to personal services businesses, whether consulting or any other. When you sell a retail or manufacturing business on deferred payment terms and the buyer defaults, the seller can always foreclose and take back the company. This is nearly impossible with personal service businesses. And the longer you stay away from the business, the harder it is to retain clients upon foreclosure.

I have never heard of a foreclosure working with a consulting business. This certainly constitutes a strong argument against agreeing to deferred payments. Unfortunately, some type of deferred payment is nearly always required as a practical matter.

The best solution is to insist that the buyer collateralize deferred payments. The security must be external to the business, however. In effect, you become a banker lending the buyer the amount of the deferred payments. As such, it makes sense to follow the same collateralization rules we discussed earlier when we looked at financing options.

At that time we talked about banks insisting on personal guarantees. To be worth anything, guarantees must be secured by assets convertible to cash in the event of default.

Since the tables are now turned and you need the security rather than a bank, it's only good business to insist that a buyer provide such a guarantee. Then you can file a lien against the buyer's personal assets. Although the precise amount of the deferred payment will not be known (as with a contingency payout), an approximation can be made. Clearly, the buyer must furnish adequate collateral to cover at least a significant part of it.

Although collecting against a personal guarantee is at best difficult and at worst nearly impossible, it does provide a significant psychological deterrent to missing payments.

LIQUIDATING

Q. I'd like to wrap up this discussion by going over the pros and cons of liquidating my business rather than selling it. I can certainly conceive of situations where I can't find a buyer or don't have time to phase out gradually—if I get seriously ill, for instance. Do you have any ideas that will help with a liquidation?

A. Any number of circumstances could arise that make it impossible to sell a business in its entirety. If the decision has been made to leave, only two alternatives remain open: give the business away or liquidate it.

When the final bell rings for me, I intend to give my business to another consultant. I don't want to go through the agony of finding partners and gradually phasing out. Furthermore, I would rather give the business to a capable colleague than leave my clients high and dry. I should be able to get a few dollars for my office equipment, but that's as far as I intend to go.

In my case, I don't intend to hang it up until I am physically unable to continue. You may have a different objective.

Q. I want to get something for my business, even if I can't sell it intact. How about some liquidation tips?
A. Let's tackle the easy items first. Nearly all office furniture and equipment has a value in the secondhand market. Used equipment dealers are always eager to pick up anything that still works. They won't pay much for it, but anything is better than nothing. Time permitting, you should try to sell each piece separately with newspaper ads or any other approach that makes sense. This will probably bring more than selling *en masse* to a dealer. (If all else fails, however, a used equipment dealer is certainly one option.)

As I see it, the biggest problem with a liquidation is making a graceful exit from client engagements. It is not ethical to leave them in the lurch with half-finished jobs, unless you have no other alternative. Most of us do have alternatives, however. We can transfer the work to other consultants within our consortium. Without a consortium, we can recommend other consulting firms that handle our specialty and then phase them into the job. It's possible that a non-consulting firm in a network might be able to finish up if skills are available.

Aside from ethical considerations, it's vitally important to take care of our clients if for no other reason than to collect outstanding receivables. Walking away will surely eliminate the likelihood of further collections.

Once arrangements have been made for someone to look after clients, it's a simple matter to dispose of furnishings and equipment. We've already discussed the option of advertising. Not infrequently, another consultant will purchase some or all of the pieces. If you're still having trouble selling things off, you might try local public accounting firms. They generally utilize the same equipment consultants do. If the equipment is relatively new, perhaps a local office supply store or a quick print shop would be interested.

In the case of a serious illness, there isn't much to be done either for the transfer of clients or for the disposal of hard assets. This is precisely why a getting-out plan should be set up early in the game.

For example, I decided long ago that I wasn't willing to risk serious illness or death and leave my wife holding the bag with my business. As part of my estate planning, I have arranged for a competent estate attorney to be the executor and administrator of my estate, with specific instructions about how to liquidate my business. It may not prove to be a fail-safe method, but it's better than nothing.

I would like to make one last point before we end this discussion. We all like to think we are invincible, that we can go on forever, that accidents happen to other people, not ourselves.

But as experts in business matters of all kinds, we advise clients to act prudently. We argue that it just makes good sense to manage a company's affairs using sound business principles. What could be more prudent than providing a getting-out position while we still have our health? And could there be any more sound business practice than to make sure our family as well as our clients do not suffer unnecessarily when we are not here? If I haven't learned anything else during over 30 years in the business world, it is that planning a worst-case scenario always makes reality hurt less.